PETER BRAZAITIS is an internationally known authority on crocodilians—their conservation, management, and care. He began his career as a reptile keeper at the New York Zoological Society's Bronx Zoo in 1954, and rose to become superintendent of reptiles. He later served as curator of animals at the Central Park Zoo until his retirement in 1998. A forensic expert on species identification of crocodilians, their hides, and manufactured products, he works as a consultant to the U.S. Fish and Wildlife Service and other wildlife law enforcement agencies. Peter holds a bachelor's degree in science, specializing in forensic herpetology, from Empire State College SUNY, and a master's degree in cell biology from Long Island University. He and his wife, Myrna, have authored two books on snakes and a comprehensive book on wildlife entitled *The Fight for Survival*.

YOU BELONG IN A ZOO!

TALES FROM A LIFETIME SPENT WITH COBRAS, CROCS, AND OTHER EXTRAORDINARY CREATURES

VILLARD NEW YORK

YOU BELONG IN A ZOO!

PETER BRAZAITIS

2004 Villard Trade Paperback Edition

Library of Congress Cataloging-in-Publication Data

Brazaitis, Peter
You belong in a zoo!: tales from a lifetime spent with cobras, crocs, and
other extraordinary creatures / Peter Brazaitis.
p.   cm.
ISBN 0-8129-6790-9
1. Zoo animals—New York (State)—New York—Anecdotes.   2. Zookeepers—
New York (State)—New York—Anecdotes.   3. New York Zoological Park.
4. Brazaitis, Peter.   I. Title.
QL77.5.B72 2003
636.088'9'092—dc21 [B]   2003047997

Villard Books website address: www.villard.com

Printed in the United States of America

246897531

Book design by Carole Lowenstein

To my son, Peter;
my daughters Wendy and Bonnie;
and my grandchildren.
The world is what they make of it,
and I hope they do a darn good job.

ACKNOWLEDGMENTS

To thank everyone in my life who contributed to the events leading to this book would fill a volume larger than the book itself. I especially thank my late father, Peter, and my late mother, Jeannette, who shaped my character and provided me with the genes that have served me so well throughout my lifetime, and Rose, my late stepmother, who endured my growing-up pains and unknowingly provided me with the title of this book so many years ago. I thank my esteemed colleague and dear friend, Itzchak Gilboa, and my first wife, Winnie Bulriss, who shared with and supported me through some of the most difficult and exciting years at the zoo. I owe them all a great deal.

Special thanks and my gratitude must go to my wife, Myrna Watanabe, and my agent, Kris Dahl, whose prodding and support got me to put words on paper; to Dr. Herndon G. Dowling, who I don't think ever forgave himself for telling Myrna she had to meet me; to my colleagues and close friends, Bruce Foster and Joel Dobbin, who helped create and often to share my many adventures; to John Soto, Bob Brandner, Kathy Fitzgerald Gerety, Bill Holmstrom, Tom Probst, and Joe Martinez, who knew how outrageous I was, but helped me measure crocodiles and chase snakes anyway; to Anthony Brownie; and to John Behler, who became one of my dearest friends. Special Agents William Donato and John Meehan of the United States Fish and Wildlife Service provided the spice and intrigue in my career, for which I am ever grateful. My gratitude would not be complete without a special note of thanks to the Wildlife Conservation Society, Dr. William Conway, and Richard Lattis, who made my zoological career a possibility.

I also wish to thank Valerie Carr, Phyllis Edelman, and Tanja Schub, who helped edit or comment on the early manuscript, and especially thank my editors Bruce Tracy and Katie Zug at Random House for all their suggestions, comments, hard work, and support.

INTRODUCTION

While this story may appear to be about zoos and reptiles, it is really the story of a city kid who found determination and strength and realized that being different was just fine. These are the stories that unfolded along the way, from catching alligators in the reservoirs of New York and capturing giant frogs in West Africa to finding mummified human heads in a Bronx apartment, eels on a bus, cobras on the loose, and crocodiles that make change. My path to success and accomplishments was not easy; it was strewn with obstacles, both real and imagined. And throughout, I had a great many adventures.

I was born in 1936 in a fourth-floor apartment in an eight-family tenement building in Brooklyn, New York, to ordinary working-class parents who had very little money. Our railroad-flat apartment derived its name from the arrangement of the four rooms, one after another in a series: a kitchen and the bathroom at the back of the building, two bedrooms, and a "parlor" at the front. There was no central heat, only the kerosene stove in the kitchen and a gas heater in the parlor. The latter was closed off with sliding pocket doors during the winter and left unheated except for Christmas week, when the white sheets that covered the sofa and velveteen chairs would be taken off. Then the room would come alive with the arrival of the Christmas tree, lights, and presents. Otherwise, the frigid parlor became a natural refrigerator throughout the winter, and smelled wonderful from the hanging homemade sausages and hams we stored there.

My father was a warm and sensitive man. He came from Pennsylvania and, having dropped out of grade school to work in the local coal mines, had never had the opportunity to finish his education. Dad was a truck driver, and he loved animals. Mother was a tiny dark-haired woman with a down-turned Roman nose that advertised her Italian ancestry but did not detract from her simple beauty. She was a special person, having tutored her brother through college and graduate school, although she herself had little education. Sometimes she would take a violin from the closet and softly play it in the semidarkness of the bedroom I shared with my grandfather. She'd play only a piece or two, then put it away for another fleeting time.

Mom died from cancer when I was twelve years old, but not before she and my father gave me a treasure—their caring and compassion for animals and a curious interest in everything that moved, particularly if it had scales and everyone else was afraid of it. It was during her long illness that Mom encouraged me to take a correspondence course in taxidermy, hoping to give me some diversion from the troubles ahead. The ten-dollar tuition was a lot of money, but the path it set me on would give me a direction from which I would rarely deviate: a love and respect for animals. I write this while one of our cats walks across the keyboard, generating her own editorial comments.

Catholic grade school ended poorly for me, and public high school was worse, punctuated with failing grades and capped by a minimal general diploma. I was a hostile, rebellious, unconventional teenager. By ordinary standards, my future looked bleak. I, however, was not ordinary. When I began high school, my adviser, a well-meaning English teacher who hadn't a clue as to who or what I was, told me to forget any future as a veterinarian, which was the only career anyone had suggested for me. I seemed to march to the beat of a different drummer. The teacher's problem was that she could only hear the band the "system" played. I liked animals; worse, I liked snakes and everything about them. To her way of thinking, if you liked animals and you wanted to amount to anything, your only future was as a veterinarian. Any interest in snakes was viewed as a repulsive childhood waste of time, a childish expression of rebellion and hostility, indulged in by a teenager. In fact, given my poor grades, she was most likely thinking I had no future at all. Today, I probably would have been considered to have a learning disability. Back then, you either would make it in the system or you wouldn't. I wouldn't.

My introduction to reptiles and animals came early. Our family traveled to an upstate New York resort each year for a week in the country, as the guests of my affluent aunt and uncle, and I was sure to return each year with an assortment of turtles and frogs to keep as pets. I never knew life without a dog. Every stray pigeon and abandoned hamster found its way to our home. There were trips to the Bronx Zoo, the Central Park Zoo, the Prospect Park Zoo, the New York Aquarium (then at Battery Park in lower Manhattan), and the American Museum of Natural History. I didn't know it then, but I would look at these places as second homes for the rest of my life.

My first paying job, at the age of eleven, was after school, carrying fruit and vegetable crates for a fruit stand across the street from home. I held that job until the owner's son hit him in the eye with a potato, giving him a shiner, over an argument about the old man never coming home. I never saw the old man's wife. The store soon closed permanently. I guess he finally went home.

My father remarried two years after my mother died. He was afraid that a young boy left to his own devices throughout the day could soon come to no good end. Dad was right, as my failing grades had begun to tell. Rose, my stepmother, could not replace my mother. And I obnoxiously grew to know everything about everything—all anyone had to do was just ask me. Before my dad remarried, I'd been pretty much on my own. Soon, a young brother came along to occupy Rose's time. We moved to a larger house of our own, and I claimed the basement as mine. It became a workshop and private haven for me and a handful of equally reclusive friends. I even cleverly created a false bookcase down there, which hid a tank holding a baby American alligator I had purchased at a local pet shop. I was surprised one day to learn that my father had not only found out my secret but was surreptitiously feeding the alligator pieces of bologna in my absence.

Throughout high school, while other kids were going to proms and dating, I worked. I got a job after school and on Saturdays with a commercial taxidermist by the name of M. J. Hoffmann Co. It was an interesting and bizarre place. I soon found that a taxidermist could not practice his skills without one important ingredient: dead bodies. When I needed birds, I would go through the garbage cans of local pigeon fanciers and racing-bird shops looking for dead pigeons. Some shops magnanimously charged me twenty-five cents each for "fresh" dead birds, which were preferable to the "aged" dead birds that had to be dug out of the bottom of the shop's trash cans. When I needed fish to practice on, the local fish market sold whole fish. It was useless to try to explain why I wanted the fish uncleaned. Mammals were more difficult; other than an occasional road-killed fox, raccoon, or opossum, none were available.

I recall my parents' distress when an inspector from the sanitation department knocked on the door and asked if we were killing dogs. They had come across a skinned carcass of a red fox I had disposed of in the trash that morning, and had suspected the worst. Even though Hoffmann regularly took in dead pets to mount at high prices, I loved dogs and found that aspect of the profession highly distasteful. Hoffmann usually charged the full amount in advance, knowing that after the several months it took to complete the mounting, many pet owners would not be as aggrieved as they were right after the pet died, and he might not collect the fees. I remember an exception. I was assigned to reglue the hair on a small, mounted Pomeranian that was soon to be picked up by its bereaved owner. Their grief had overwhelmed them several weeks after the dog had died and been buried, so they had dug up the dog.

Besides running a taxidermy studio, Hoffmann also operated two catalog businesses. One business filled mail orders for taxidermy supplies, such as animal glass eyes; the other imported and sold human glass eyes. The difficulty arose when clients for human eyes came to the taxidermy shop, having been led there by the same address listed for both in the telephone book.

As distasteful as the work sometimes was, I learned more vertebrate anatomy in those years, by taking dead animals apart, than I could ever have learned in a classroom. Hoffmann employed two venerable and seasoned taxidermists, who worked feverishly during the hunting season and went fishing during the "off-season." Old Man Miller was seventy-five and an artist at mounting birds of every description. Charlie did the mammals: deer heads, fox, bear, moose—and pets. They took "the dumb kid" under their tutelage and taught him everything they knew—all by hands-on experience. I skinned carcasses, prepared papier-mâché mannequins for mounting deer and elk heads, replaced faded colors on fish bodies with oil paints, made wax tongues for bear-head rugs, shaved hides to thin them, made molds of plaster to help re-create body shapes, and skinned and polished thousands of deer feet for gun racks. Every bone from every animal that came into the shop to be skinned and mounted—moose, deer, bear, dog, cat, or anything else—was buried in the yard behind the building. Every shovelful of soil I dug to bury some leg or skull only excavated some previously buried remnant of a carcass. Hoffmann was frugal to a sin and refused to pay for waste-hauling services.

An arsenic paste was painted on the inside of skins to preserve them, and this became my regular job. I knew nothing about arsenic toxicity, and apparently neither did Hoffmann. I frequently held a roast beef sandwich in one hand as I pasted with the other. I became expert at sewing linings and borders on bear, tiger, and zebra rugs—pretty skilled for a teenager.

Hoffmann would buy great horned owls from a Canadian trapper, then convert them into clever crow decoys that flapped wooden, feather-covered wings and bobbed when a chain was pulled. The owls usually came in a cardboard box of ten or fifteen carcasses.

They were apparently caught with a steel-jaw trap that had been baited with meat and placed on a tree limb. When an owl landed for the meat, it would be caught by a leg, which would often get severed from its body. On one occasion, when the birds arrived, Hoffmann reached in to pull one out to check for damage, he let out a scream. One bird was not dead, and it had seized his hand with its inch-long talons. I felt that the bird was totally justified.

I soon landed my first freelance contract with the American Museum of Natural History. The Preparation Department wanted me to mount a dove chick in a nest for a special exhibit, and they were offering a fat twenty dollars. The problem was that the fee included me providing the chick. As I walked down the off-exhibit area stairway leading from one floor to the other, on my way out of the museum, I happened to pass by an open window. There on the ledge was a dead pigeon chick, abandoned in a nest. I had my body and my twenty dollars. Later, I took on the job of mounting fifty tropical flycatchers, dried bird skins that had been collected nearly sixty years before, at ten dollars apiece. I was sure that I was on my way to becoming rich.

Little did I know then that there was a zoo in my future. I would begin my working life at the very bottom of a profession that few people can even imagine, as a broom-pushing, turtle-feeding, glass-cleaning, often terrified reptile keeper at one of the most prestigious zoos in the world, the Bronx Zoo, New York Zoological Society. I began my zoo career on Saturday, August 21, 1954, at the starting salary of $2,700 a year. I dreamed that when I broke $100 a week, I would actually be rich. Working at the zoo would hardly achieve that goal, at least not in the short term.

Dating had to be cheap to be possible. Fortunately, the zoo community had its share of fine young women who shared similar interests and lacked extravagant tastes. In those days—quite the opposite of zoo communities today—few women were hired into the animal-keeping ranks of major departments, mostly because the departments were dominated by abusive and intolerant men. Women did find part-time positions, at even lower wages, in the children's zoo, caring for the same animals men might care for at higher wages in other departments. I won't disclose the name of the young woman I asked out on a date soon after I began my career as a reptile keeper at the zoo. A couple of hours before our date was to begin, a six-foot-long American alligator died, and after a bit of begging, I was allowed to have the body to make into a skeleton. Priorities being what they were, the young lady and I, along with the dead alligator, headed by car upstate after work to find a suitable burial place for my treasure. I planned to return after several years to retrieve the alligator skeleton, which, by then, would have been rendered by nature into a fine educational artifact. At some point, we came across some open fields and a woodchuck hole. With only a little excavating, the alligator was put to rest, and we proceeded to enjoy our date without the deceased animal.

Soon after, I entered the armed services. Two years later, the day came when the alligator bones were to be retrieved. I retraced our previous route, minus the young woman, who had married by that time. Only now a new interstate highway existed where only a rural road had been before. My landmarks were gone. The alligator remains unretrieved to this day. I sometimes wonder if someday, someone digging will find my alligator and report a new northern range extension for the species. This, perhaps, may lead to a rash of publications concerning new insights into the cold-temperature tolerances of ancestral alligators. I'll never disclose the location, and I am sure the young woman will never acknowledge that date either.

The zoo became my passion. Slowly, I would rise through the ranks, first to senior keeper, then animal manager, and finally superintendent of reptiles at the Bronx Zoo.

Next came marriage and a family. I have been most fortunate in both of my marriages. My first marriage was to the zoo's switchboard operator, Winnie, a fine person and a devoted mother to our two wonderful daughters, Wendy and Bonnie. It ended in divorce after twenty years. By 1979, at age forty-three, I was a single father raising one of my two teenaged daughters in a small Bronx apartment.

My professional interests now turned to the new field of wildlife forensic sciences. National and international laws had been enacted in the early 1970s to control the commerial trade in animals, which was decimating wild populations. My specialty, crocodilians, headed the list of newly protected reptiles racing toward extinction. As I trained special agents and wildlife inspectors of the U.S. Fish and Wildlife Service, I made many new friends among wildlife law enforcement agencies. I became known as a forensic specialist who could handle any venomous snake or crocodile during inspection in a cluttered airline cargo building, be at hand when federal agents needed to enter premises where alleged smugglers might be harboring dangerous reptiles, help law enforcement agencies prosecute violators, and give testimony as a court-certified expert witness. I made some enemies as well, among members of the reptile-leather trade and even among some of my own colleagues. My career in forensic science has cost a lot of bad guys a lot of money—and a little prison time as well.

Around that time I first saw Myrna, a feisty, loving woman with a passion for science and honest living. A doctoral student interested in alligator maternal behavior, she was under the tutelage of my old curator, Herndon G. Dowling, then a professor of biology at New York University. Short, pretty, and bouncy, Myrna was a fireball of enthusiasm and activity. She was teaching as she continued her doctoral research; and, like mine, her marriage eventually disintegrated.

It wasn't until Myrna started doing fieldwork in alligator behavior that our paths crossed. Dowling urged her to discuss our mutual research interests in crocodilians, but my hard-nosed reputation had preceded me, and the terrified young woman had to be dragged to the Reptile House by a mutual friend. After that initial meeting, however, we spoke often as she worked on her thesis, observing mother alligators attending their nests and young in the swamps of Georgia and Louisiana. Periodically the phone would ring in my office and the voice at the other end would say something like "Peter, this is Myrna. Howard Hunt"—her colleague from the Atlanta Zoo—"just fell off a boat dock and broke his ribs, and I have a can full of baby water snakes you could feed to the baby king cobras. Do you want them?" "Absolutely," I would say, and she would continue to relate what her alligator mothers were doing.

Finally, one day my friend and coworker Bruce Foster urged, "Peter, why don't you get together with that little alligator lady and take her out?" It was a brilliant suggestion and I did, but there were times when it seemed that our relationship could hardly hold together, as we both led our own exciting lives. At one point, I went off to Cameroon, West Africa, on an expedition to hunt giant Goliath frogs as her flight took her to China for three months on a Fulbright Scholarship to study Chinese alligators. But we were well suited for each other, and we were married in 1984, by a judge in his chambers, on his and our lunch breaks.

My professional reputation grew with each new publication in scientific journals, magazines, and books. My secret, however, was that I was barely educated. Although my work on crocodilians and reptile husbandry was referenced in scientific publications around the world, I did not have a college degree. Myrna now used her new powers of wifely persuasion and an army of close friends. At age forty-five, I found myself back in school, at Empire State College (a branch of the State University of New York), pursuing a bachelor's degree in biology and forensic science under the mentorship of a tiny, wonderful African-American professor, Dr. Dorothy Burnham. Compared to the rest of the student body, I felt old—and terrified—but I was trapped. Next came a master's program in cell biology, at Long Island University. The department chairperson, Dr. Dennis Curley, and Myrna, who had taught there as an adjunct professor, had me boxed in; I would be educated, despite my protestations. I had dozens of publications to my credit. I had again been most fortunate.

After years of painstaking and often frustrating lab work, I finally finished my degree. Graduation day seemed to excite everyone except me. Our young son, Peter; Myrna; and her dad, Sheldon, insisted that I attend graduation exercises. I protested, but to no avail. I was the oldest graduating student among several thousand, and I would stick out like a sore thumb. *Give me the diploma and let me go in peace!* I cried. *No!* they answered—my son deserved to see his father graduate from graduate school and be proud. I relented, against my better judgment.

Graduation day went badly. We were late, and I ran to catch up with the procession of young, smiling people marching up the steps of the Brooklyn Academy of Music, a concert hall in downtown Brooklyn. A sea of black robes and caps with golden tassels flashed as thousands of parents captured their offsprings' crowning moment on film. As I caught up to my unknown partner in line, a pretty young woman just out of her teens, I wanted to die. Donning my black robe, I pulled my graduation cap from its protective plastic bag and jammed it on as we entered the doorway. "Excuse me, sir," the young woman said, looking up at my head. "Why is your hat light blue when everyone else's is black?"

Death had struck. My hat was blue in a sea of thousands of black hats, for everyone to see. "I am old, and blue is the color for old people," I replied. "Oh," she said acceptingly. I don't know why, in the luck of the draw, I had gotten a blue cap, but it's typical for me to be different, whether I like it or not. The robe company had probably sent my black cap to some graduate who should have been wearing blue. I was now sure that the dean would stop the proceedings in mid-graduation and ask from the podium, "Sir, why is your hat blue?" I closed my eyes and told myself it was not blue; it was black. Several thousand polite and generous people in the audience that day took pity on a terrified old man and said nothing.

One day in 1988, I received a call from the new curator who was overseeing the reconstruction of the Central Park Zoo in Manhattan. The New York Zoological Society (later to become the Wildlife Conservation Society) had recently taken over the management and operation of all three of the badly run city zoos and was rebuilding them one by one. Ten years later, I would retire as curator of animals of the Central Park Wildlife Center; hold an appointment as research associate, Science Resource Center, Wildlife Conservation Society; and enjoy a professional reputation as an author, forensic scientist, and expert in my field.

My travels have taken me from the deep forests of West Africa in search of giant frogs, to Amazonian forests and the endless grasslands of the Mato Grosso of Brazil, to the mangrove swamps and giant crocodiles of the western Pacific islands. This book is a chronicle of my experiences, trials, and tribulations. I would not trade a single one of them away, for never have any two days in my life been the same, or boring or mundane. I have worked with thousands of people and animals throughout my career. In certain places in this book, I have changed the names of some people to preserve their privacy. It is less important what their names are than what and who they are, what they did, and what took place. Besides, animals never need to be apologetic or evasive about who and what they are or what they do.

The stories told here are true. Many of the incidents involve animal escapes, or at least animals forgoing the confines of their captivity. These episodes are rare indeed, and certainly not a normal occurrence in a professionally operated institution. They are often best recalled as the source of much amusement—and sometimes a great deal of curatorial anxiety.

While other people may remember the stories presented here in different detail, they are my stories, and I reserve the right to relate them according to my own recollections. To my colleagues and me, they are not necessarily unusual encounters or unique experiences. Then again, I am not the best judge of what is amusing or exciting to most people, and my peers are undoubtedly of the same square-peg stock as I am. Nothing I say in this work should be construed to give instruction, particularly where dangerous animals or venomous snakes are concerned.

I do hope that a youngster or two, somewhere, laboring over his studies and beaten down by the careless words "You will never be able to . . ." will manage to find some determination and trust in themselves, and perhaps a few laughs and a little excitement in these pages. All things are possible.

YOU BELONG IN A ZOO!

1

YOU BELONG
IN A ZOO

My stepmother finally reached her limit of endurance and declared, "You are an animal, and you belong in a zoo!" I immediately took her at her words, more out of spite than anything else. But where? I had visited the Bronx Zoo many times as a child, being bitterly disappointed when I found the Reptile House interminably closed for renovations, over what seemed to be years. The Bronx Zoo was more than just a place named in a book; it was real. Wouldn't it serve her right, I thought, for me to get a real job and get paid for working with snakes, the very thing that had marked my animal-keeping interests as "childish and immature"? Did I dare?

But I speculated that my chances were nil. I was just eighteen years old and had no real experience with taking care of reptiles, other than the pets I had kept through childhood. I had read volumes on reptiles, written by the late Raymond L. Ditmars, the first curator of reptiles at the Bronx Zoo. It was 1954, and his last books had been written in the 1940s. He was dead, but who had replaced him? I immediately addressed a letter to the Curator of Reptiles, Reptile Department, the New York Zoological Society, whomever he might be.

I extolled my live animal-keeping accomplishments, which really were very meager compared to my experience with dead animals and my great interest in reptiles. I asked for a job.

To my surprise, and my stepmother's, I promptly received a reply from Dr. James A. Oliver asking me to come to his office at the Bronx Zoo for an immediate interview. A few days later, I found myself at the Administration Building, a grand edifice with a lounge for members of the New York Zoological Society that was replete with working fireplaces, plush sofas, potted palm trees, and oil paintings of flamingos and cranes. Oaken shelves filled with books about animals and scientific journals lined the hallway outside Dr. Oliver's office. Even the smell of lemon-oil furniture polish made it seem like an important, serious place, and a respectful hush filled the air. Oil paintings of scholarly looking people hung from the walls and over the fireplace: Madison Grant, William T. Hornaday, and Henry Fairfield Osborn. All the men wore a suit jacket, a white shirt, and a tie. A tall, gray-haired man in a brown plaid suit, smoking a distinguished-looking down-curved pipe, was leaving the building. Another venerable-looking balding man, with silver hair and a silver mustache, sat reading from a leather-bound book about birds. Neatly dressed women in businesslike dresses, wearing elegant but unobtrusive earrings and necklaces, spoke in whispers as they carried sheaves of white papers from office to office. This was all very intimidating to a kid from Brooklyn who had barely made it through high school. My experiences with white-shirted intellectuals had largely been with teachers, the insurance salesman, and the family doctor. These must be scientists, I thought. I was glad I had worn my Sunday clothes rather than my black leather motorcycle boots and denim jacket.

Dr. Oliver was an imposing figure, tall, heavily built, with a wonderfully clear speaking voice. Oliver was a respected herpetologist and an academician, and in the coming years, I would never see him wearing anything other than a white shirt and tie. I was terrified—not of the illusory prospect of possibly having to catch and restrain a large, dangerously venomous snake as a possible test of my nonexistent credentials, but because I thought I knew something I was sure

Oliver did not know: I was a fraud. In fact, Oliver understood exactly who I was: a young, interested kid looking for his first real job.

Oliver's secretary, a pretty, young, dark-haired woman in a simple but elegant blue dress, ushered me into his office, then returned to her typewriter and proceeded to spit out a string of tapping sounds. Oliver greeted me from behind his oak desk, surrounded by books, files, and piles of papers. On top of his desk sat a small glass aquarium, warming under a gooseneck lamp. There was no water in the tank, only sand and a rock cave from which the spiny, thick tail of a lizard protruded. I would later learn that this was Oliver's special lizard, a spiny-tailed Indian dabb lizard from the deserts of North Africa and Asia, belonging to the genus *Uromastix.* This species derives all of the fluids it needs from the foods it eats. Each Saturday and Sunday, for the next several years, I would dutifully turn its light on at 8:30 A.M., off at 4:00 P.M., and place exactly three leaves of lettuce in its tank for food. As I never really saw the entire animal, for all I knew I may have been feeding a rock with a spiny tail. Oliver took care of it himself the rest of the week.

The interview proceeded quickly and was not nearly as painful as I had expected, largely due to Oliver's kindly manner. He could have been anyone's father and teacher. "Tell me about your experience keeping reptiles and amphibians," Oliver said. "What animals have you had and how long have you been successful in keeping them alive?"

I recounted having had a dog all of my life, a small white-haired mutt called Bessie that had been given to me by my aunt Roberta for my first birthday. Bessie still lived—albeit barely, given her advanced years. I related how we took family vacations at a resort in Yulan, New York, each year and brought home an assortment of turtles and green frogs we had caught in the local lake. The following year we would take any survivors back to the lake. There was always a turtle or two to return, if that counted. I once had caught and unsuccessfully tried to choke and drown a water snake near my grandparents' house in Pennsylvania. "Why did you do that?" Oliver asked. I wanted the snake's skin, I explained. He appeared to be neither impressed nor amused. I continued: "I took a correspondence course in taxidermy from the Northwestern School of Taxidermy, in Omaha, Nebraska, when I was eleven. Throughout high school I worked part-time for a commercial taxidermist, the M. J. Hoffmann Company in Brooklyn." I was quite expert at taking animals apart and replacing their unneeded bodies with artificial components. I said that I had also purchased a blue racer snake from the Quivera Specialties Company, a mail-order animal dealer. I was secretly glad there really was such a snake; all too often, animal dealers make up common names that have no relationship to officially recognized species. I did not tell Oliver that in fact I had ordered a Mexican imperial boa constrictor, but instead they had sent me a bag of about ten snakes that had immediately escaped—most of them down a drain—when I had unpacked them in my father's rented garage. One of the snakes was indeed blue—at least I had glimpsed the color blue as its tail disappeared into a crack in the garage wall leading to the garden behind.

I had also purchased a king snake from a pet shop, I said, and had kept it for several months. It was a poor feeder, I added. In reality, I had found it shriveled and dehydrated one day about a month after I got it. Feeling sorry for the snake, which I thought was suffering from an agonizing disease, I had killed it with a shot from my .22-caliber rifle. I later learned that the snake was simply in the process of shedding its skin, and the old skin, being deprived of sufficient moisture, had dried on its body. Had I known better, I could have soaked the snake in warm water and taken off the old skin harmlessly.

"How about other live amphibians, like toads," he asked. "Did you keep any of those?"

"Of course," I lied; I was feeling bolder. "I have kept a toad for more than ten years."

Oliver smiled, knowing better than to believe me. "Have you read books on reptiles?"

Here, I could answer truthfully. I had, indeed, devoured every book on snakes and reptiles I could get my hands on, especially those written by Raymond L. Ditmars, the first curator of reptiles at the Bronx Zoo.

At this point, Oliver said, "Let's give you a chance. The job starts right away as a probationary keeper at the Reptile House. The work is dirty, and the supervisor is hard. You have to work forty-two hours a week and pay half the costs of your uniform and medical plan. You get one and a half days off a week, not necessarily together. The pay is twenty-seven hundred a year—plus or minus. Report to the supervisor of the Reptile House on Saturday," he concluded. (Thirty-four years later, I would have another such interview, prior to becoming a curator in charge of the world-famous Central Park Zoo.) My career had begun.

As the lurching cars of the Lexington Avenue express carried me back home to Brooklyn from the Bronx, my mind was filled with expectations and fears, and I couldn't wait to flaunt my success to my stepmother, Rose. As usual, she had dinner ready for me, and I was hardly seated before I blurted out, "I did it!" I was now working at the zoo! She smiled in disbelief, not only at my signs of ambition but also at the zoo's willingness to hire me, whose shortcomings she knew only too well.

To my surprise, she, too, could not wait. As my father came in the door after work, Rose said, "Guess what your son did today?" Without waiting for an answer, she announced, "He got himself a job at the Bronx Zoo." For the first time, there was pride in her voice.

2

WALKING
INTO HISTORY

It would be difficult to set the scene for where I would spend the major portion of my working life without first describing something of the origins and evolution of the place and the people who created it. The zoo had a character of its own, and anyone who became part of the zoo community was expected to share and project some of that character. Moreover, it is the world I would become an integral part of and that would mold my character and define who and what I was to become.

The zoo's curatorial staff was the elite, and the trustees were rich socialites and influential businesspeople. To be sure, I never felt I was—or could be, or wanted to be—a member of the inner circle, or "upper class," of the institution. I first entered the zoo's world almost sixty years after its founding. During that time, the fundamental organization had not changed a great deal. Men dominated all job levels and positions except for those as lavatory matrons, restaurant and gift-shop workers, and secretarial and administrative assistants. At that time, there were no women among the wild-animal-keeper ranks other than at the children's zoo, which was devoted mostly to

*Crocodile and alligator pools in the Reptile House
at the Bronx Zoo as they appeared in 1900.*

domestic animals. "Working with bears is a tough man's job," one weather-beaten supervisor said. Today, women perform outstandingly at all levels of the zoological community. I can only recall one African-American at the zoo, "Old Joe" the carpenter, as he was called. Unfortunately, this has not significantly changed, and there continues to be a dearth of African-Americans among upper zoo management.

Much of the society's history is chronicled in the news bulletins and annual reports that were the society's original publications. In fact, the *News Bulletin of the Zoological Society* was born as plans came into place for the building of the new zoo in the Bronx. In his book, *Gathering of Animals: An Unconventional History of the New York Zoological Society,* William Bridges, by then retiring curator of publications, gives perhaps the most incisive accounts of the society's origins.

Ironically, the New York Zoological Society, as it was called upon its creation in 1895, had its origins in the Boone and Crockett Club, which was founded in late 1887 by Theodore Roosevelt and ten guests at a dinner party. Membership was highly selective and included only a hundred prominent, influential, and wealthy men, including Roosevelt as club president. Roosevelt fit in well with the elite group, a collection of men who, above all else, shared a love of the sport of big-game hunting and a quest for bigger and record-sized trophy heads and horns.

The club members, to their credit, were extraordinary activists. They soon expressed great concern that the world's big game animals were being squandered by useless killing, and they predicted that the repeating rifle and disease would put an end to many African species. The sport was in danger of being lost; they might not have big game to kill in the future.

A closer immediate focus was the uncontrolled hunting of deer with dogs in New York's Adirondack Mountains. A committee within the Boone and Crockett Club was conceived in 1894, when Madison Grant, a young Columbia University–educated lawyer who virtually lived for the sport of big-game hunting, urged Roosevelt to act. Roosevelt did, brashly and literally without club authorization. He created a committee to establish a zoological society and build a zoo and installed Grant as its chairman.

Madison Grant and his politically prominent brother, De Forest Grant, propelled themselves into the effort. These powerful men had been instrumental in ousting the corrupt Tammany Hall political machine that had dominated New York City, and now they resolved to introduce legislation both to stop New York State's exploitive deer killing and abusive commercial hunting practices and to create a zoological society with powers to establish a zoological park in the City of New York, dedicated to the conservation and propagation of big game. They hoped that from the zoo animals' offspring, a future stock for trophy hunting would be supplied. Around 1888, the City of New York had acquired lands for public parks; thus, the timing for establishing a zoological park was perfect. Other cities had already established or were in the process of creating their own zoological parks: the National Zoological Park in Washington, D.C., in 1889; the Zoological Society of Philadelphia thirty-six years earlier; and the Zoological Society of Cincinnati. Why not a zoo in New York City?

On April 26, 1895, by an "Act to incorporate the New York Zoological Society and to provide for the establishment of a zoological garden in the city of New York," the New York State legislature mandated the creation of the New York Zoological Park. Two years later, on March 24, 1897, the City of New York accepted the society's proposals for a new zoo. The city granted the society a "tract of wilderness" that would become an oasis, a jewel in the heart of urban development.

For every supporter for the building of the new zoo, there was someone in opposition, particularly among New York pet dealers and traders, who feared that the new, moneyed zoological society would compete with them in selling domestic animals that might be bred at the zoo. Troublesome, too, was the small collection of animals, known as "the Central Park Menagerie," held under decrepit conditions behind the Arsenal Building at the southern end of Central Park. It was considered the "poor man's zoo" for the many New

Yorkers who had little money to spend on entertainment, and who could view the animals at Central Park for free; the wealthy upper class who lived along Fifth Avenue deemed the collection an eyesore and a nuisance. It was reasonable to assume that the "big" zoo in the Bronx, run by the rich and powerful, might consume the smaller menagerie. The society's founding fathers actually had no such intention, being, indeed, rich snobs, disdainful of the lower classes, and desirous of preserving their lofty goals and social status in the new zoological society. Even in recent years it was rumored that one concern of the founders was that opening the original membership of the society to the general public would "mongrelize" the society. In the first *News Bulletin of the Zoological Society,* number 1, June 1, 1897, membership in the New York Zoological Society called for "no initiation fee." However, with individual annual membership dues of $10, a life membership of $200, a patron's fee of $1,000, an associate founder's fee of $2,500, and a founder's fee of $5,000—all considerable amounts for the times—there was no danger of the lower-class masses of New York joining.

This division of social classes was perfect fodder for the Lower East Side politicians who thrived on the popular vote of the masses. The land upon which the new zoo would be built had to be provided to the incorporated New York Zoological Society, under legal agreement and legislation by the City of New York and the Commission of Public Parks. Control of the infant zoological park was almost wrested from the Boone and Crockett Club when it was found that Andrew H. Green, a popular New York political figure, had already introduced a bill in the New York State legislature to create an alternative zoological society and build a zoological park in New York City. He had no intention of allowing such a political plum or the mass voter appeal of the Central Park Menagerie to fall into the hands of the rich. Some quick creative stacking of the board of incorporators for this second zoo with Boone and Crockett Club members and their relatives avoided the takeover. A clause requiring the New York City Parks Department to turn over the Central Park Menagerie animals to the New York Zoological Society was changed to indicate that if the Parks Department elected to dispose of any animals, the society had first preference in acquiring them.

Little did I ever dream that nearly a century later, in 1988, I would find myself as curator of animals at the Central Park Zoo (now called the Central Park Wildlife Center), the site of the original Central Park Menagerie, dealing with the same political animosities and rules of engagement set down in those earlier years. The concerns and predictions of the Lower East Side politicos and pet traders had come true. By 1985, the New York Zoological Society had grown into a global conservation organization known for its world-class institutions, the Bronx Zoo and the New York Aquarium. It had thousands of members from all economic levels and all walks of life. Meanwhile, each of New York's boroughs had developed pitiful "menageries" at the whim of their individual elected local politicians. These small zoos were always understaffed and underfunded, and their animals languished under substandard conditions, in cramped, barred cages.

The society did, indeed, consume the city park zoos, but not by design. After a series of tragic and fatal mishaps involving zoo animals and humans, and in response to the concerns of animal-rights organizations, New York City turned over the administration of all city zoos to the New York Zoological Society. These were reluctantly accepted, torn down one by one, and rebuilt to modern standards. To be sure, the zoological society's executive board continues to be made up of the social elite and wealthy. But today, these are men and women who are genuinely concerned with the future of wildlife for the sake of wildlife as a treasured living heritage and who are deeply involved with the zoo's administration. Rather than promoting big-game hunting, board members use their political forces, influence, and drive to change the face of conservation policy and wildlife science around the world.

The big-game sport-hunting motivations of the Boone and Crockett Club are long gone, having been replaced with a strategic intent to further wildlife conservation, education, and research. The Boone and Crockett Club's Heads and Horns Museum of trophy big-game heads, horns, and antlers still stands as it was built in the early days, on Baird Court in the heart of the Bronx Zoo. However, it now houses not the trophy records of sports hunters but the administrative offices of various society departments.

I knew the Heads and Horns Museum well. As a young keeper, I had to service a herd of giant Galápagos tortoises that we regularly overwintered in the warm basement of the Heads and Horns building. Once the animals were fed their rations of fresh fruits and vegetables, I would wander into the darkened recesses of the basement. Stone rooms the size of some New York apartments were filled from floor to ceiling with skulls and horns of African and Asian antelope, sheep, elephants, and rhinos, moldering trophies whose misplaced value had been in their size as seen through a hunter's gun sights. Every so often, I would catch a small glint of light, reflected from an eye, and momentarily be startled in the semidarkness, only to remember that the lifeless eyes were made of glass and the animal had lived long ago. I would walk along the length of one immense horn extending from the skull of an Asian water buffalo and stabilized by the stack of skulls and other horns buried beneath it. At the end of the horn I could reach between the mildewed heads and pull free the dainty spiraled horns of a gazelle, or the tusk of a wild pig. It was a sad place. One day, these relics too, would be gone, allowed to decay in the dampness of the basement, like the bodies of the wild animals they came from, and then ingloriously buried in a Bronx garbage dump.

The first major renovation of the Reptile House had just been completed prior to my arrival in 1954. Remnants of the people who had come before me, as well as their work and accomplishments, could still be found in those portions of the building that had either escaped the architect's imagination or had not escaped the red pencil of budgetary constraints. Brass coat hooks from 1898 still held winter coats and hats on the inside of the office door. The head keeper's desk, still painted official forest green, with the metal identification tag of the Department of Parks, showed the scars, chips, and wood splits of decades of service and a million bruises from rolling office

*Renovated crocodile and alligator pools
as they appeared on the author's arrival in 1954.*

chairs being drawn in as thousands of daily reports were completed. The concrete heads of turtles, frogs, and alligators, building cornices removed during construction, lay piled in a heap of broken cement in the Reptile House's basement. I recall the difficulty in sweeping away the water that collected on the floor of the main exhibit passage because of the gouges and irregular depressions worn into the concrete by fifty years of footsteps as dozens of keepers before me had cleaned the cages of thousands of snakes.

Although the original 1898 outside of the building was not changed, and still included its original architecture of red and yellow firebrick walls, concrete entrance columns, great wooden entrance doors, and cornice figures of alligator, crocodile, toad, and turtle heads, the inside public display halls and exhibits had demanded a drastic modernization. A leaky roof, cold weather, and an insufficient coal-fired heating system had, over the years, cost the lives of many warmth-loving reptiles. Basically, the interior of the Reptile House had been gutted of its main exhibits. The building was so cavernous as to allow a second floor to be installed midway between the first floor and the roof. Yet the office, storage room, and kitchen at the north side of the building had been left to the ages, as had the lobby entranceway and basement, although a completely new oil-fired heating system had been installed.

The new second floor held a treasure. Two inconspicuous cardboard boxes lay against a wall, as though awaiting the final verdict in a trial that would determine what should stay and what should be erased from future memory. Besides the dust and crushed cement debris of construction, the boxes contained all that remained of the correspondence of Dr. Raymond Lee Ditmars, the first curator of reptiles. To generations of kids fascinated with reptiles, Raymond L. Ditmars is an icon. Born in Newark, New Jersey, in 1876, Ditmars had no advanced education and received only an honorary doctorate in 1930, after many years of scientific accomplishments. In many ways, I would follow in his footsteps.

In his early years, Ditmars's position as a journalist for *The New York Times* served him well. In 1899, his editor assigned him to write an amusing story about an amusing character, himself, as an unusual lover of snakes. Instead, he decided to interview Dr. William T. Hornaday, the director of the new zoo then being completed in the Bronx. Ditmars walked out of the interview not only with a side note to his own story but with a new job as curator of reptiles and, much to his parents' relief, a new home for his private collection of snakes.

Over the decades, he succeeded in taking the science of herpetology and the study of reptiles from the dead, musty world of museums and European universities to the exciting world of public interest. His books and articles chronicling his discoveries and adventures over his many years at the Bronx Zoo are long out of print. But even today, copies—no matter how used, tattered, or worn—remain for only a short time on bookstore shelves before they are purchased for the delight of reptile enthusiasts throughout the world.

Ditmars pioneered the captive care of reptiles, took thousands of photographs to describe them and record their habits, made people aware of the reptile and amphibian species that lived throughout the northeastern United States, and brought new and exciting tropical species to New York, to be exhibited for the first time to a curious public. He worked throughout his life to dispel the public's many myths and fears about reptiles and other strange animals and focused on exhibiting such creatures as vampire bats, poisonous snakes, spiders, and scorpions. His special interest was the possible use of snake venoms in the treatment of disease. When a keeper at the Bronx Zoo was bitten by a venomous snake, Ditmars was one of the first to use a new serum, manufactured from the venom of South American pit vipers, as an antivenom. Ditmars died in 1942, after retiring due to illness. His obituary in *The New York Times* featured a most appropriate heading: "Enthusiasm Unconquerable."

I had come on the scene as a new keeper just in time to be part of what might be called a shakedown period. Truly, the new building was a huge departure from the traditional way in which reptiles and amphibians had historically been exhibited. It was modern in design, and not only were new environmental systems incorporated to help ensure the well-being of the animals but the well-being and mental health of the visiting public were also considered. At the time, it was a psychological given that reptiles and amphibians, particularly snakes, were disgusting, reprehensible, and certain to initiate nightmares in even the most insensitive visitor. I can still recall when a young mother came into the Reptile House with a four- or five-year-old child in tow. On entering the main exhibit hall, she wrapped a sweater over and around the child's head, then proceeded to race through the building, all the while describing the hideous and revolting things that the child was being spared from seeing. I wondered what nightmares that kid was going to have from this parentally induced experience, having only been able to imagine what sinister evil creatures had surrounded them outside the darkness of the sweater.

Because of such fears, concern for the continued mental health of the visitor had figured in the design of the newly renovated building. The inside was a marvel of its time. The floor of the public space was of institutional green, gray, and black terrazzo, and an aluminum railing swept the perimeter of the exhibit hall. The railing was intended to offer some slight feeling of safety by enforcing a secure arm's-length distance between a timid visitor and any "disgusting" snake on the other side of the glass, yet bring the visitor as close as possible for a view of the animal. It might also have been intended to act as an impediment to would-be animal tormentors. The railing never accomplished either purpose, but it did provide seating for small children who had become a burden to the parents who had carried them about the zoo all day.

The second floor had been designed with a balcony opening at each end; one was a sweeping oval in shape, the other a square bordered with planters from which artificial plants and flowers hung down into the public space. Huge beige canopies, unfortunately, prevented the public from looking up through the openings to see the beautiful original ironwork that supported the roof.

The building's new floor plan promoted a leisurely stroll from exhibit to exhibit. The visitor entered through the original wooden doors into a lobby that faced a large display, and was drawn immediately to the awesomeness of two twenty-foot-long, huge-bodied reticulated pythons from Southeast Asia, coiled high in the center of the exhibit. From there, the visitor walked in a horseshoe direction, around an "island" devoted to giant snakes, poisonous lizards, and snakebite; past open pools of piled-high turtles; and along gracefully curving low walls holding gothic stone planters, behind which four giant twelve- to fourteen-foot-long, eight-hundred-pound alligators basked. Three open pools for crocodilians had been added at the west end of the building in a glassed-in greenhouse conservatory setting complete with broad-leafed tropical plants, scarlet-flowering Bolivian shrubs, and hanging beards of Spanish moss on dead cypress tree skeletons, with tropical vines growing everywhere. Eventually, the visitor exited at the side of the building, but not before passing three large aquaria containing a mammoth alligator snapping turtle, sea turtles, and water snakes.

The building as a whole was designed to provide the visitor with an exciting experience that put them in a naturalistic setting of tropical plants and exotic animals while still maintaining an institutional feeling, which meant safety and security from the "loathsome," dangerous creatures within the exhibits; it was no little philosophical contradiction. Because of this feeling of protection, people were being brought closer to snakes to learn more about them and to thereby assuage their fears, rather than being simply kept far away from them. In the 1950s, most people were preoccupied with looking to the scientific marvels of the future; so why shouldn't a reptile house have the same futuristic look?

The Reptile House's exhibits would set the trend for all future zoological exhibits. They were, indeed, far advanced for their time and new in exhibit concept. Mrs. Helen Tee-Van, the wife of the zoo's director, had great artistic perception and was a major influence on how the building looked and felt. (Mind you, she had no great love for snakes either.) Exhibit techniques had not yet advanced beyond the traditional presentation of having one exhibit after another, like so many paintings hung side by side in an art gallery. It was only a generation before, under the direction of Raymond L. Ditmars, that collections of living reptiles had been considered to have scientific merit. Husbandry and the environmental needs of animals were barely known. Herpetology was still light-years behind ornithology or mammalogy as a scientific discipline. Ditmars, by trial and error, had developed techniques for keeping reptiles alive in captivity. Now it was Jim Oliver, a member of a new generation of scientist-herpetologists, who would take keeping reptiles in cages to a higher level of captive husbandry and research—and I was there.

Instead of presenting a series of snakes or lizards lying on bare concrete floors with only a crockery bowl for drinking water, the designers made every attempt to create an artistic display of each and every exhibit. We still called them "cages," although in the 1970s the word *cage* was replaced by *enclosure,* and still later by the more sanitized *exhibit,* as zoos became more and more attuned to the criticisms of the animal-rights movement. Each exhibit was painted in carefully selected hues to suggest where the animal found its home. Pinks and reds indicated desert regions, greens were used for tropical forest homes, and yellow or beige suggested a wide range of habitats.

Each exhibit also included a pool large enough for the animals to soak in, with a drain and individual plumbing, and running water kept at eighty-five degrees Fahrenheit. It was the reptile equivalent of the first private home to be fitted with indoor plumbing and a toilet, replacing a bucket of cold water and an outhouse. Instead of bare concrete, the exhibit floors were covered with different grades, sizes, and colors of gravel or pebbles, selected to not only enhance that individual exhibit but to complement the exhibits to either side and those in that gallery as a whole.

Imbedded in the pool and concrete floor were rocks and minerals obtained from the American Museum of Natural History geological collections. Green copper ore gave color to one exhibit, while white crystalline stalactites from a western cave garnished another; silvery mica sheets and white, clear, and pink quartz crystals dazzled in others. Artfully contorted driftwood, brown cypress knees, cactus skeletons, cork bark, and plant mulches offered decoration and limited the places where the animals could hide, out of visitors' view. A hot-water heating coil, imbedded in the floor immediately in front of the glass, ensured that any snake or lizard that wished to bask and warm itself had to come into the visitors' view to do so. Each exhibit was fitted above with theatrical lighting that ranged from intense colored spotlighting (achieved with a combination of glass and gel filters), to infrared lamps and ultraviolet lights to promote healthy growth to inmates that were otherwise deprived of natural sunlight.

Each and every one of the ninety-odd exhibits that made up the visitor experience was planned, executed, and documented down to the position of each stone and branch and each nuance of illumination and color, so that no part of the exhibit would be subject to unplanned change. Last but not least, the visitor would be continually lulled by the sound of specially chosen, soothing classical music, played over a hidden public address system. I hated it. As the new keeper, I was assigned to replace and reset the six or seven 33 1/3 rpm records that were to play nonstop on the hi-fi in the Reptile House office. All too soon, the music became background white noise I no longer heard, and so I forgot to change the records when they were done. This would be my first shortcoming as a professional animal keeper: I couldn't keep the record player going.

3

FIRST DAYS

The wait for Saturday was unbearable, and when 6:00 A.M. finally came, I was already up and ready to leave. The train ride to the Bronx, the first of hundreds to come, was interminable. The few short blocks from the train station at West Farms seemed like miles. Other keepers were entering the chained gate adjacent to what had once been a boathouse and, earlier, a gristmill on the Bronx River. Around the turn of the twentieth century, West Farms had been the site of a number of breweries, which drew on wheat and barley crops grown on surrounding farms and milled right there on the river. It was all gone now, and West Farms was a hub for train and bus service into the Bronx. I reported to the Reptile House as instructed, carrying with me a can of Campbell's vegetable soup, given to me for lunch by my stepmother. Actually, I never ate the soup but kept it safely saved among my most cherished possessions for the next forty-four years, passing it on to my friend and working companion Bruce Foster on my retirement in October 1998.

When I knocked on the rear door of the Reptile House that first morning, Bob Sambuca, the department's senior keeper, greeted me. Bob was going to be my mentor as I began to learn not only about the job and reptiles in general but about the simple mechanics of how to work. I was starting from the beginning, with no discernable skills. In reality, my taxidermy job, under the frugal personality and critical eyes of Mr. Hoffmann, had taught me that I was expected to produce the equivalent value of my pay, or else. I knew how to work.

Many zookeepers had come by their jobs by way of the federal work programs that had followed the Depression years of the 1920s. Family dynasties had emerged, as each unemployed person who was placed in a zoo job—the level of their interest in animals notwithstanding—soon found a haven for scores of their equally disinterested relatives. It was good work. One long-term keeper would make believe he was deaf and dumb whenever a visitor asked him a question, so he could avoid having to interact with the public at all.

Working at the zoo would hardly provide a living: zookeepers were poorly paid, considered on a par with drunken circus part-time workers and roustabouts. Salaries were lower than low, even by 1950s standards. My two-week take-home salary, after deductions for health benefits and uniforms, usually amounted to little more than seventy-five dollars. Interestingly enough, the keepers wore a khaki uniform, which they paid one-half the cost of and were responsible for keeping clean. However, at the end of their three-month probationary period, each zoo employee was sent to the prestigious Brooks Brothers clothiers, where he was measured and fitted for a complete dress outfit of the highest quality. Each employee received a pair of green 100 percent woolen whipcord pants, a double-breasted dress jacket complete with brass buttons, an Eisenhower jacket, two dress shirts with epaulettes and zoo emblems, two khaki ties, a wide brown leather garrison belt, and a summer and winter visored dress cap. All of this amounted to a cost per person of more than $300, a great deal of money by 1954 standards. Keepers and maintenance people were mandated to wear the dress uniform, with their shirtsleeves rolled down and buttoned, whenever they were required to perform duties or patrol the public spaces. The trustees had no wish to be embarrassed by unsightly employees. We could starve, as long as we did not appear to be doing so.

To offset the poor wages, keepers often held several jobs. One keeper drove his night-job taxicab to work and ran a numbers betting business from the Ostrich House kitchen. Another operated a small electrical appliance-repair shop in the anteroom of the Zebra House. A supervisor ran a roofing-repair business, organizing schedules so that his "employee" keepers could leave the zoo in the afternoon to tar roofs. Another enterprising keeper quietly borrowed zoo animals at night, renting them out for shows and movie productions and returning them the following morning.

The maintenance departments were another matter. Large wire refuse baskets, strategically placed in the maintenance yard, always started out empty each morning. By the following morning, after a full day of extended coffee breaks and lunches by the maintenance staff and a full night of unobserved inactivity by the night firemen and watchmen, the baskets were usually filled with empty whiskey and beer bottles. Plumbing repairs frequently displayed artistic creativity in the convoluted routes and miasmic connections they made.

Bob, however, was of the next generation of keeper: young, intelligent, and interested in what he was doing. Bob was a good teacher. Tall and good-looking, he wore his black hair in a large wave above his forehead, in the style of the 1950s. He never lacked for girlfriends, despite a chipped front tooth; his smile more than made up for it. Bob was a Bronx kid, which gave him a confidence learned the hard way on the streets of New York. He eventually left the zoo to serve in the U.S. Army; he returned to the zoo later, but only for a short time. An irascible, likable, wild character, Bob had an insatiable wanderlust. Over the years, I often thought about him. Bob wasn't afraid of much, except bugs.

The first days were mind-boggling. There were unwritten rules by the score: Don't ever lean on or put your hands on the screen top of a cage; poisonous snakes can strike and bite through the mesh. Don't wear rings; if you are bitten on the hand by a venomous snake, your hand will swell tight over the ring, cut off the blood supply, and you will lose that finger to gangrene. Don't wear sneakers; wear boots or at least good leather shoes—they are more difficult for a snake to bite through. Don't open trash barrels with closed covers; we use them to soak snakes in, and there may be a dangerous snake inside. When you open a door to a room, look around, before you enter, for open cage tops or unusual items lying on the floor; the items may have been knocked over when a snake escaped its cage. Never, never, never pick up a cloth bag or what looks like a clean white rag lying on the floor or table; it may be a cloth snake bag being used to transport a venomous snake that can bite you through the bag. Always step back and open a cage door at arm's length; a snake that is lying against the inside of the door when you open it may fall out on you, rather than at your feet. Carry your snakebite kit with you at all times, even when you go to a movie. (I did, for the next thirty-four years.) Check every door you close to be sure it is locked shut. Then check it again. Then check again. Never pick up a snake you don't know. Treat every snake as though it is venomous; if you don't let yourself get bitten by harmless snakes, you probably won't get bitten by a venomous snake either. Never speak to a keeper who has a cage door open, or pass behind him; he may lose his concentration on the snake in front of him or you may frighten the snake into unexpected flight. The litany went on and on.

It seemed that any step I might take had a special *do* or *don't* associated with it. This was certainly not the place for a teenager who wanted to escape being told what to do by a parent. Despite being admonished not to open any cage door or enter any section of the Reptile House I was not yet authorized to enter, I was given a key that would unlock any cage in the building. It was not a matter of trust, I felt, but a matter of fact. I could either work there and follow the rules or not work there at all. It was that simple.

My first assignments were designed not only to test my reliability and ability to learn but also to keep me safe and out of trouble, as well as to prevent me from wasting other people's time. My superiors' efforts in teaching me would extend only as far as they perceived that their investment held the promise of future returns. If I did not demonstrate the potential for eventually working with any and all of the dangerous snakes and crocodiles in the collection, there was no point in wasting these people's time. After all, why should one keeper risk his life day in and day out for essentially the same salary that another keeper got without the risks? It was expected that I would be shielded from extreme risk well into my three-month probationary period, but the shielding would stop after that. Not that I was being exempted from getting injured, just from the possibility of being seriously injured or killed. Even the part-time summer keepers had more interesting and difficult chores to do. They had already proven themselves.

The care of some extremely dangerous animals, like the king cobras, black African mambas, and the twelve-foot-long Nile crocodile, were reserved for the experienced head keeper or, in his absence, the senior keeper, Bob Sambuca. The head keeper also reserved what he perceived as the most valuable animals in the collection for his personal care: the rare lizardlike New Zealand tuatara, and the breeding mouse and rat colony, which were used as a source of food for the animals.

My daily job began with cleaning and sweeping the floors and the front of the building. I learned that putty knives are okay for scraping up old, hardened chewing gum, but fresh gum was messy, particularly in the hot weather of August. You had to use benzene to get it off your hands. Sugar Daddies got me in trouble right off the bat. These brown candy caramel pops on a stick looked innocent enough as they lay there on the floor, undoubtedly discarded by some vicious, vindictive child. They cost only five cents at the food stands in the zoo, and they were sold by the thousands to the schoolchildren. I don't believe any child ever completely finished one.

Almost immediately, I had fifteen minutes scheduled to sweep clean an area that at home would have demanded hours of my reluctant time. The sticky brown devil lay in wait as I pushed my broom quickly down the terrazzo floor of the main exhibit hall. *Crack!* Instead of willingly being pushed along with the rest of the papers and debris, the stubborn Sugar Daddy stood its ground, firmly stuck to the floor in a grip that would have done justice to a modern space-age glue. The handle snapped from the broom head, and I came to a jarring abrupt stop. I had broken the broom. At that point in time, brooms were considered more valuable than I was. I presented the two halves of the broken tool to Bob, who shook his head in worry and quietly said, "Sugar Daddy?" I nodded. "Don't tell the head keeper or you'll be in deep shit," he counseled. "You gotta remember to hit a Sugar Daddy straight on," he added, "in the center of the push broom, not on one end or the other, or it will break your broom every time."

My lifelong career of both hating and respecting ants also began in those first weeks. Brayton Eddy, a Rhode Island entomologist, had come to the zoo as curator of reptiles and insects in 1945, and he soon transported a queen ant and the start of a colony of parasol ants from Trinidad to the Reptile House. This was established by setting a large wooden hut on legs in a large tank of water. Two ramps leading from the entrances to the hut converged on a wheel that could be rotated on its stand in the center of the tank. The ramps then continued from the opposite side of the wheel to a small concrete planter filled with soil. The object was to be able to demonstrate that by rotating the center wheel, one could disrupt the ants' pheromone trails, which they had laid down from the hut to the food planter, and the ants would be confused. It worked for several hours, but once I had confused the ants, I would invariably find a number of angry soldier ants with their giant pincers firmly imbedded in my arm or attached to an earlobe. Ants were not to be trifled with.

The whole business was completely surrounded by water to prevent the ants' escape. The ants would essentially take care of themselves; my job was to keep them happy, give them clean water, and keep them contained in the exhibit. This was easier said than done. I had to place exactly six fresh roses (delivered each day from a local florist), an orange quartered into four pieces, and a cup of fresh soil in the planter. As soon as the food was in place, the ants would begin their march from the hut, cutting the orange and roses into small pieces, which they would then carry back to the hut, holding the pieces over their heads like miniature parasols. The soil would become part of the ants' colony structure in the form of material for chambers and tunnels. The ants would use the plant material to grow fungus in an ant garden within the hut to provide themselves with food.

I soon learned that you could outsmart one ant but not the collective genetically preprogrammed motivations of thirty thousand ants. They had a built-in response to overcoming every contingency or obstacle. If I fed them too much, even one rose extra, the ants would simply work longer hours that day and rest the next day. The exhibit would have no ants to be seen, and I would be in trouble. If I did not feed them enough, they would simply use soil and other debris from the colony to build a floating bridge from the leg of the hut to the nearest wall of the exhibit. They would then spend the night foraging for more food. A long stream of ants would march through a crack under the door, down the leg of the exhibit, across the lobby floor, under the front door of the building, and outside, where they would cut down and bring in all of the ivy they could from the front of the Reptile House. Then they would take the day off, and again there would be no ants to be seen.

During my interview, Jim Oliver, almost as an afterthought, had mentioned that a major part of my new keeper job would be cleaning glass. This would prove to be an understatement. Cleaning glass immediately fell to me as a regular daily assignment. The task would become, in effect, a window on the world. Besides, I could not easily get into trouble with anything dangerous by cleaning glass.

Oliver didn't tell me that in the process of cleaning glass, I would gain a new perspective about people. There were glass-fronted exhibits; glass railings; glass on doors; glass covers on labels, portals, windows, covers, and more. There were hundreds of glass panels of one kind or another in the Reptile House, through which tens of thousands of people peered, touched, tapped on to awaken the animals, or stood on, each year. I also soon learned that there were two sides to glass: the side the curious public looked through to see the animals or watch the keepers, and the side the curious animals looked through to see or ignore the public. Over the years, I always felt that the animals had a better handle on what they were looking at than the people did. Early mornings were for cleaning glass. So were afternoons, and any time in between. The rule was "If you have time to breathe, you had better have a rag in your hand while you're doing it, and a bucket and a squeegee." Each glass panel and pane had to be wiped clean at least once each day, usually before the public began to arrive when the building doors opened at 10:00 A.M.

Every new keeper became an expert on what sticks to glass best and what removes it. There were greasy fingerprints from the thousands of touching, tapping children who streamed past the exhibits in an endless flow, from 10:00 A.M. to 2:00 P.M. each school day. I soon figured out that the prescribed period of time was dictated not by any educational formula but by the labor union contracts of the school or charter bus drivers who brought the students and teachers to the zoo. I could not imagine what educational benefit was derived by forty or fifty high-decibel children, sometimes tethered together with ribbon, racing past the exhibits without explanation, from one building to another.

Left behind were "nose runnings" from kids pressing their snouts close against the glass to get an eye-to-eye view of the creature on the other side. Winter was the best time for a keeper to observe nose runnings. Then there were the great gobs of slimy goo, left from hair pomade, when teenaged males sporting fashionable hairstyles accidentally pressed their heads against the glass to gain a better look. Sometimes the goo was green.

Monday, the day after a crowded Sunday, was the best day for semen, left behind by perverted visitors who managed to ejaculate over the sight of snakes, or were secretly rubbing themselves against other visitors in the crowded, darkened hall. The World of Darkness Building also suffered from the same visitations. I hated cleaning glass on Monday morning. Dried semen requires tough cleaning agents, which themselves leave the glass streaked and dirty. Once we had to put in a call for advice from an expert, a sales representative from a company that sold specialized cleaning agents. As he sat in my office that hot August afternoon, he complained bitterly about how one of his most difficult clients was an operator of a Forty-second Street peep show, with several dozen private viewing booths.

While the public dirtied the glass on the outside, the glass also had to be cleaned on the inside. What Oliver didn't tell me that first day was how I might be expected to accomplish this task. I would have to work that puzzle out for myself, if I were to preserve my body intact.

Clean glass is the essence of a successful visitor experience. The illusion of glimpsing a wild creature in its natural setting is dispelled by streaks on dirty glass. One might think that the keeper would simply remove the animal and clean the window. No; if the keeper were to remove every animal from its exhibit before cleaning the glass, the keeper would never get done. Instead, you must work with the animal in the exhibit with you. Think about standing in a cage with a sleeping twenty-foot-long reticulated python, covered only with a tarpaulin over its head to keep it from noticing that your intentions are merely to clean its glass. While you hope the snake will remain calm, the "helpful" public always seems to think you are unaware of the 150 pounds of python lying just next to you. People pound furiously on the glass in an effort to get your attention. Usually it's the snake whose angry attention they get, which then ends up focused on you, the keeper.

In my first introduction to cleaning glass on the inside, I was told never to allow fish oil or scum to build up on the glass along a water line. This is difficult, especially when the inhabitant of the exhibit is a two-hundred-pound alligator snapping turtle that eats fish and defecates as it wishes. In those days, keeping such a large turtle, with a shell fully three feet long and two feet wide, in a tank four feet long and as wide, was considered perfectly acceptable. Its shell filled the floor of the tank nearly to capacity, and the poor beast could barely turn around. It had to stand on its rear legs and extend its neck to the limit to reach the surface to breathe.

Alligator snapping turtles feed underwater by holding open their immense jaws to expose their tongue, which has a light-colored wormlike appendage at its tip. The appendage is wriggled, like an erratic drowning succulent worm, in the dark cavern of the algae-covered jaws. Sooner or later a fish swims by, sees the "worm," approaches curiously—and in an instant the jaws snap shut. So strong and sharp are the razor-edged jaws that anything caught up is neatly cleaved in two. A human hand, arm, or foot would not pose any obstacle. And so, dutifully, each Monday, Wednesday, and Friday after feeding, I would drain the tank with the turtle in it, then climb down and stand on top of the turtle's shell to scrub the oil slick from the glass around it. I always felt that the turtle, capable as it was of removing any of my own appendages whenever it wished, also knew that the glass had to be cleaned. Perhaps dirty glass ruined its natural view of the public?

Dirty glass would, out of habit, become a lifelong obsession of mine. Recently, when my son and I visited the newly renovated planetarium at the American Museum of Natural History, we marveled at the futuristic exhibits. Here were dozens of glass viewing portals, windows into time and space, images of swirling galactic dust clouds and glimpses into the vastness of the universe. Hundreds of thousands of dollars had been spent to create the illusions of space. But the glass was dirty, left streaked and muddy by a careless workman with a greasy rag. How can you believe you are looking into the vastness of the universe when your window is dirty?

Forty years after my first day with a squeegee, as curator of animals at the Central Park Wildlife Center, I would continue to be plagued to the point of madness by obsessions with dirty glass. I can still hear my equally afflicted boss calling me on the two-way radio to complain that the tufted puffins were again splashing water on the glass of their exhibit as they bathed, leaving grease-stained droplets behind. How shameful that by "glass" standards, I could be considered a curatorial failure.

Working side by side with Bob, I learned what to do and how to do it. By watching his example, I also learned what not to do. Sometimes I was too dumb to know the difference, and there were other things Bob had learned badly himself. To this day, Bob credits me with saving his life, although I must admit that I don't recall the incident being anything more than hilariously funny at the time.

Bob was teaching me how to handle a large constricting snake. Grasping a six-foot-long juvenile African rock python by the base of the head to keep it from biting him, Bob demonstrated its strength by allowing it to coil around his arm and begin to constrict it. Boas and pythons have an incredible ability to compress their body muscles around prey. This is how they kill a small animal for food or a predator bent on killing them. Contrary to what most people think, the prey is not crushed during the process. Rather, the snake coils around the animal's rib cage and takes up the slack every time the animal exhales, preventing it from expanding its lungs to draw another breath. The animal quickly dies from asphyxiation and compression of the rib cage on its heart. Even a small python can kill a large animal if it manages to coil around the animal's throat or chest.

Bob explained that the way to remove a coiled python from around your arm was by unwrapping it tail first, not from the head end. This technique took advantage of the way the snake's muscles worked most efficiently. "There is no need for a snake to have special strength to uncoil its body, only to kill its prey," he explained. It made sense to me. The snake began to shift its coils from Bob's arm upward, in search of a more successful hold. Bob continued to lecture. At one point, Bob's hand, still grasping the snake behind the head, became tired, and he now tried to exchange handholds. Sensing a loosening of Bob's grip, the snake shifted too. This time, the snake's tail searched up around Bob's neck, followed by a coil, and then another, with its tail tucked deeply inside the coils. The snake tightened its new hold. I barely noticed the labored tone that entered Bob's voice. He started turning pink, then a little red, then bright scarlet. His lips took on a blue hue. Bob sank to the floor, still trying to tell me how to handle a python. With short, breathless words, he plucked in vain for the snake's tail.

I began to giggle, then laugh at the prospect of having to explain how my mentor had been choked to death by a relatively tiny python as he was explaining how not to be choked to death by a relatively tiny python. I was glad Bob had first relayed the information about how the only way to unwind a constrictor snake was tail first. The technique worked amazingly well, and I simply unwound the snake's coils from Bob's neck, starting with the tail. Poor Bob. Just as he sometimes sported a black-and-blue hickey from the amorous activities of a girlfriend, he now sported a circle of black-and-blue snake-scale impressions around his throat. I often wondered how he explained them.

Bob had a mean streak. Knowing I was not yet permitted to enter a cage containing a venomous snake, Bob soon found that he could frustrate me by putting my bag of lunch in a cage with a rattlesnake or cobra just before the noon meal break. I was usually broke, so buying lunch was not an option. It didn't take me long, however, to notice Bob's bug weakness and figure out how to use it. The Reptile House was infested with two-inch-long flying American cockroaches. They were harmless enough, but not very pleasant. If one landed on you, the sharp hairlike spines on its legs pricked your skin as it walked. Or it might quickly try to hide by running down into your shirt collar. When one landed on Bob, he would panic, lose all composure, tear his clothes off, and shower in the kitchen. Armed with this knowledge, I plotted and waited for the next time Bob took my lunch.

Insecticides were not often used in the Reptile House because reptiles and amphibians are particularly sensitive to poisons, so we continually trapped roaches to keep their considerable population from getting out of hand. As I was the most junior keeper, this task instantly became my domain. Trapping roaches was a science. Widemouth gallon jars that had once contained mustard or mayonnaise were purloined from the zoo cafeteria. These would be placed against corners and walls where roaches abounded. A crumpled piece of paper towel was used to bridge the gap between the wall and the edge of the jar's mouth. A few slices of fresh banana made an irresistible roach bait, while a fingerful of petroleum jelly wiped around the inside of the jar's mouth would prevent any roaches that toppled in from climbing back out. One correctly prepared trap could yield several hundred roaches overnight. I recall how the head keeper regularly patrolled the roach traps to be sure that I was dutifully performing my task. Bob taught me to always make sure my traps had some roaches in them for him to see, even if it meant transferring roaches from productive traps to nonproductive traps for his inspection.

Sure enough, the day came. Bob found my lunch and locked it in a snake cage. I was ready with a jar full of freshly captured roaches. To Bob's horror, I reached into the jar and picked up a handful of roaches, while another dozen or so, quickly sensing the escape route I offered, scurried up my arm and over my shirt. I approached Bob with revenge in my eyes and roaches in my hair. He shrank, screamed, and ran. I gave chase, and we soon found ourselves at a dead end in the keepers' passageway. Bob sank to his knees and begged. I got my lunch, never to be taken again.

I learned a lot from Bob, and later on, as a supervisor myself, I could immediately recognize a new keeper who might have reams of academic credentials and knowledge about specific animals but no actual work skills. There really is a way to hold a broom and dustpan that allows you to collect all of the dirt on a floor. There is a way to rinse a mop to get rid of the dirt it has already absorbed, so that you don't simply spread it back on the floor with each successive sweep. There is a method for unpacking live frogs from a cardboard shipping box so that they can't leap out en masse in every direction as soon as you lift the first flap. There is also a way to open a cage door behind which lurks a dangerously venomous snake or, at best, a flighty lizard looking to escape. I needed to learn it all, from using a mop to developing the safe habits and methods that might keep me alive, or at least keep my fingers and other body parts intact. I give Bob credit for teaching me most of what I learned and have since taught to dozens of others.

In contrast to Bob, Head Keeper Spencook was in absolute charge of the Reptile House and dictated every aspect of how it operated, but he taught nothing. His philosophy was that the more an underling knew, the poorer he himself appeared, and every new keeper was a threat to his position. He had ascended to the position by default; his predecessor, who suffered from advanced diabetes, had been absent from the department on a disability leave for many years. The head keeper had a reputation throughout the zoological community as a very difficult man, and most keepers who worked under him at the Reptile House for any length of time eventually left for positions in other institutions.

I soon found that Spencook was cunningly stupid, and engaged in dictatorial minutiae to cement his position. Yet with a little help, he would often fall victim to his own edicts, infuriating him. A memorandum dictated that whoever broke a light pull cord when turning on the lights in the morning had to replace it immediately. We promptly soaked all of the light cords in strong bleach. The next morning, we orchestrated our arrivals so that he would be the first to turn on the lights, causing all of the cords to break. Another document mandated replacing the toilet paper when the dispenser was empty. The keepers countered this by ensuring that only one sheet would remain for the head keeper's visit to the lavatory each morning. But Jim Oliver, never being directly involved in Reptile House operations, and being a staunch believer in adhering to a chain of command at any cost, felt that the head keeper was the best there was.

Spencook, a man of German descent, had come to the Reptile House as a keeper during the early 1940s, when most able-bodied men were being drafted into military service. Rumor had it that he had previously been a factory foreman and when the factory became involved in war production, he had espoused Nazi sentiments and had been beaten by his colleagues. I disliked him as a person. He openly professed everything I had been taught was wrong: racism, anti-Semitism, and bigotry. He idolized the wisdom of Adolf Hitler.

Even people in other departments had no liking for Spencook. One day, Larry the plumber was called to fix a finicky drain valve for the Nile crocodile pool. As Larry toiled in the oppressive heat and humidity, Spencook stood over him, taunting him without reason. Larry ignored it at first, but his patience had a limit. Finally, Larry stood up with a large wrench in his hand and a sinister look in his eye and faced Spencook. Spencook, inherently a coward, knew what the look in Larry's eye meant, and immediately bolted up the stairs to the second floor.

Thinking to outsmart Larry and take a circuitous route back to the safety of his office, Spencook then ran to a second circular stairway on the second floor and took a shortcut back down to the main floor, sure that Larry was still in hot pursuit. Larry wasn't. He knew the building as well as Spencook did, having worked on the maze of plumbing many times since the renovatation. Larry had already doubled back, and sure enough, Spencook arrived in the hallway just as Larry had anticipated. Aghast at finding Larry there, Spencook sprinted for his office and attempted to slam the door behind him. But it was too late, and Larry was on him. Grabbing Spencook by the throat with his powerful, greasy hands, Larry threw Spencook onto his own desk and began to shake and throttle him. Spencook's eyes bulged, and his lips took on a bluish cast.

Standing quietly in one corner of the office, barely noticed, was Lloyd Sandford, the society's staff artist, who was sketching a lizard in an aquarium for a new exhibit label. Lloyd was a quiet, impeccable man who always dressed in a spotless white shirt and neat bow tie. He liked everyone, we thought, and they liked him. This time, he watched amusedly as Spencook was now on his way to losing his life. Several of the keepers, me among them, rushed in, the whole episode having taken only a few minutes, and pulled Larry from Spencook's throat. Red and blue hemorrhages showed where Larry's fingers had found their mark. Spencook lived in the zoo directly behind the Reptile House, so, coughing and holding a cold wet cloth to his aching throat, he left for home. "Lloyd," we asked, "why didn't you try to stop it?" Lloyd responded with a sly grin. "Well, Larry didn't look like he needed help, and I would never think of helping Spencook." The matter was eventually settled, albeit grudgingly, with cursory handshakes and apologies. I was truly getting an education.

I was eighteen and yet shocked at the entourage of women who visited the behind-the-scenes areas of the Reptile House on Sunday afternoons: fat, ugly women and young, giggling girls. I was usually ordered to patrol the public area and not disturb Spencook in his office. One such visitor we nicknamed the Alligator Lady, because she frequently came to the Reptile House carrying a four-foot-long alligator wrapped in a baby blanket. Spencook had given her the alligator as a gift, purportedly stolen right out of the animal collection. I would be left to care for the alligator while she and he locked themselves in the office. Her visits ended when she told us that her hus-

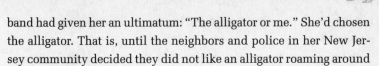

band had given her an ultimatum: "The alligator or me." She'd chosen the alligator. That is, until the neighbors and police in her New Jersey community decided they did not like an alligator roaming around in her front yard.

The Caiman Lady was another such individual, having purportedly acquired her animal the same way as her counterpart. We hated her visits. She would come to the building with her four-foot-long caiman wrapped similarly in a blanket to protect it from the cold. Although caiman are closely related to alligators, they are not at all tolerant of cool temperatures and poor nutrition. Unlike alligators, which tend to be placid in nature, caiman are vicious and ill-tempered. This poor beast showed all of the signs of being kept under barely minimal conditions. Its teeth protruded from their sockets in abnormal directions. Its feet and toes were twisted and malformed as a result of poor bone mineralization, from lack of calcium and sunlight. Its tail sported a permanent kink, indicating a spinal deformity. The Caiman Lady, who called herself its "mother," would kiss it on the snout repeatedly. Eventually, the animal would be left under our care, on the floor of the office, as she and the head keeper wandered off to their own devices. As soon as she left the room, the animal became enraged, snapping and leaping at anyone who came near. The moment she returned to the room, the creature calmed for its kisses and hugs.

One of my first assignments was to care for Mack, the scarlet macaw. The new design of the Reptile House endeavored to give the visitor a glimpse of life in a tropical forest. The three crocodile pools—one large pool flanked by a smaller pool on each side, with a backdrop of tropical plants—offered the perfect opportunity to incorporate some nonreptilian tropical species into the scene. To this end, a scarlet macaw and a gold-and-blue macaw were each perched on a branch, set upright in a pipe, stemming from the center of a green steel flanged drum designed to discourage the bird from climbing down to the crocodile pool. The perches were set behind each of the entrance gates to the smaller pools. Plantings on the rear wall of the exhibit hid the stands from view, so all that the visitor was able to see were the macaws, on natural branches, seemingly perching in a forest of leaves.

Both species, the scarlet macaw and the gold-and-blue macaw, range through portions of Central America and South America. Macaws are the largest, most spectacular, and most brilliantly colored of the Psittaciformes, a group of about 315 species that also includes the parrots and parakeets, conures, lories and lorikeets, cockatoos and cockatiels, and budgerigars. At the time, people were familiar with macaws from the many popular jungle films Hollywood produced. A macaw sitting on a branch as the great white hunter and the beautiful client's wife picked their way through the tropical scene, accompanied by peacock calls in the background, immediately told the mesmerized popcorn eater that this was a real "jungle."

By habit, macaws are considered good "liberty" birds. That is, if given a comfortable perch and sufficient food and water in a location where some activity will keep the birds amused, they will simply stay put. This quality plus Hollywood's influence inadvertently created a public demand for macaws that nearly drove the birds to extinction, and the danger still persists today. By the 1950s, macaws were freely being sold on the pet market for a few hundred dollars each. The species was still abundant, but populations in the wild were declining because of overcollecting for the pet trade and birds being killed for their feathers. Nearly all birds sold as pets were taken directly from wild populations. Wild-caught birds were cheap—too cheap to make it worthwhile to spend the time and money to breed the species in captivity. Today, these birds cost in the tens of thousands of dollars, and all legal birds are from captive-bred sources. It took international and national restrictions and prohibitions on commercial trade in the 1930s, 1970s, and 1980s to block supplies of live wild birds and drive up prices to the point where it became very profitable, and legally less problematic, to supply the pet market with birds from private aviculture colonies.

Until then, zoos were often inundated with offers of free macaws from people who had succumbed to the lure of having a macaw on a perch in their living room, just like in the jungle movies. The prob-

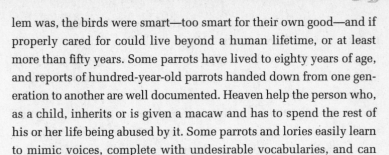

lem was, the birds were smart—too smart for their own good—and if properly cared for could live beyond a human lifetime, or at least more than fifty years. Some parrots have lived to eighty years of age, and reports of hundred-year-old parrots handed down from one generation to another are well documented. Heaven help the person who, as a child, inherits or is given a macaw and has to spend the rest of his or her life being abused by it. Some parrots and lories easily learn to mimic voices, complete with undesirable vocabularies, and can even learn the grating noises made by power tools.

At best, macaws are raucous; their earsplitting screeches and screams may cause insanity in their owners, and thoughts of homicide in neighbors and friends. If left without attention, macaws may scream from dawn to dark—or until they're beheaded. Some friends of ours who lived in a brownstone apartment in Brooklyn kept a Moluccan cockatoo for a number of years. As soon as they left for work in the morning, the bird would begin screaming; the moment it heard its owners put their key in the door lock downstairs, it would fall silent. It wasn't until our friends overheard the neighbors talking about hunting down and assassinating whoever owned the screeching bird in the neighborhood that they decided it was time to move to a private house.

Macaws have incredibly strong beaks, capable of splitting the toughest Brazil nut or hardest wood, and they must put their beaks to constant use to keep them worn down and trimmed sharp. One couple who donated a pair of macaws to the zoo had come home to find their heirloom oak dining room table destroyed. The birds had walked along the edge of the table, methodically tearing off huge splinters of wood as they went.

This abundance of free donated macaws, coupled with a desire to create a familiar "jungle" scene for the public to experience, had led to the inclusion of the two macaws as backdrops for the new crocodile pools. Mack and his cohort became a daily part of my keeper life. Each week, I would have to go off into the forested areas of the zoo grounds and find just the right size and shape of one of the hardest woods in the Northeast, the American hornbeam—also known as the ironwood tree—to use as a comfortable perch for Mack. It had to be just right, for if the side branches were left too long and reached too far out, Mack would hang by his feet and destroy every tropical plant within reach in a neatly clipped circle around his perch. Then, satisfied that he had ruined hundreds of dollars in plantings, he would turn his attention to his perch and reduce it to an ugly splintered skeleton in a matter of a day or two. Of course, I was responsible for Mack and the exhibit, as the head keeper was quick to remind me—each and every week.

I decided almost immediately to make friends with Mack. But he was evil, and my wish was delusional. Mack seemed friendly and acted interested in what I was doing when he saw me delivering a pan of fish to the turtle tank nearby. As I had to prepare fish in the kitchen, I decided I would pick Mack up on my arm, as I had seen Mike Dagnon the gardener do, and carry him to the kitchen. Perching him on the back of a chair, I talked to him and gave him tiny offerings of fruit and fish, which he ate while holding them with one foot. He murmured quietly to me, in the friendliest way. But he was just setting me up.

One morning, like any other, I went down behind the crocodile pools and Mack came over to greet me. He climbed willingly on my arm and murmured as we walked back to the kitchen, talking. But when we got to the chair, things changed. Mack struck. He tightened his grip on my arm and the hackles went up on the back of his head. One by one he severed the buttons on my shirt and its pockets with quick snips of his wickedly curved beak. He laughed an insidious *he, he, he* call as he then began to shred my shirt, with me in it. I shook my arm, but Mack would not let go! I could envision his curved beak sinking into my arm just as easily as it went through the tough hulls of Brazil nuts. Grabbing a long-handled brush with the other hand, I managed to force Mack off my arm and onto the chair. Mack was enraged. I was ashen. The battle lines had been drawn. Mack and I were at war.

Each morning, feeding Mack was a challenge and a nightmare. I would barely get my uniform shirt out of my locker at 8:00 A.M. before Mack would hear me and start screaming to be fed. The head keeper would then begin looking for me, demanding to know why Mack had not gotten his food. It was a no-win situation, because even if I fed Mack before starting work, he still screamed at the appointed time.

Mack had a cup for water at one end of his horizontal perch and a cup for food at the other. As I approached with the container of water in one hand and a container of sunflower seeds and peanuts in the other, Mack would plan his strategy of attack. If I reached up to fill the water cup first, he would race to that end of the perch and try to bite the hand holding the cup. I would try to feint, then quickly fill the food cup first. But Mack was faster, and could turn and race for my hand at the other end of the perch before I could pour the seed. Sometimes his cunning was sinister. He would hold one wing in front of him like a cape, peeking over the edge, as he advanced to bite, hoping the ruse would get him closer to my hand before I noticed him. If I succeeded in pouring seed into his cup, Mack would scoop it out on the floor as I walked away and begin screaming in defiance. He knew that unless I repeated the feeding until he was satisfied and let the bowl be filled, he could scream and alert the head keeper, who would promptly want to know what was wrong. Mack also figured out that if he hung by his feet and reached out as far out as he could, he might be able to bite me as I backed out of the entry gate after feeding the juvenile crocodiles in the adjoining pool. He was indeed cunning as well as smart.

Mack soon learned to mimic the sound of the head keeper calling "Bob," the name of another new keeper, in the head keeper's voice, complete with a German accent. Needless to say, when the head keeper called, you had better drop what you were doing and run. Poor Bob. Throughout the day, Mack would periodically call out a perfect reproduction of Spencook's "Bob!" Bob would race to wherever the head keeper was and ask what was wanted of him, only to be told "Nothing. Don't you have work to do?" The tragedy was that even knowing what Mack was up to did no good, because Bob couldn't risk failing to respond in case the call was genuine. Bob would sometimes be run ragged.

Mack also learned that if he mimicked the closing procedure at the end of the day, he would be fed a few minutes early. It was not beyond Mack to call out, "Closing up, everybody out!" from his hidden position. More than once, a keeper, hearing the cue, fed Mack and started sweeping and closing the building, only to be chastised for closing to the public too early.

Throughout all of this, Mack seemed to have an unexplained romance with Mike. The gardener could scratch Mack's head, ruffle his feathers, feed him, and treat him with impunity. I did not understand. Finally, I could take it no more and asked Mike, "How do you do it?" In his best Irish brogue Mike said, "Come along, and I'll show you." He proceeded to get a cup of water, and we approached Mack on his perch. Mike talked soothingly to Mack as he began to fill Mack's water bowl. Mack gestured with his open beak—just a little gesture, nothing more. Whereupon Mike smashed Mack in the head with the cup, sending the bird squawking off his perch. I was astonished. Shocked. Mack recovered his balance almost immediately and began making friendly murmurs again. Mike said, "See, you got to show the damn bird who's boss right off. He's a good bird, but you got to show him who's boss!" Although I never had to use the cup technique, after that, Mack and I had a healthy respect for each other because he always anticipated I might well smack him. Mack had taught me an important lesson in animal appreciation.

Then Mack made a fateful error. I came in one morning as usual to feed him, but his perch was vacant. A few brilliant red, yellow, and blue feathers floated in the crocodile pool. The idea of using macaws on perches to enhance the crocodile pools had run its course.

Food preparation took up most of the rest of the early day. Fish had to be thawed and cut for the afternoon crocodile feeding, along with a dozen or so frozen white rats and several fresh horses' hearts, cut into strips or large chunks. Frozen rats were nasty business, as it was easy to impale a hand on the end of a frozen pointed tail tip, get a claw imbedded in a finger, or receive lacerations from protruding teeth. Chopped horsemeat made up many diets, heavily laced with cod-liver oil and powdered bone meal. Eventually, we would learn that all of these diets were detrimental to the health of most of the animals that ate them. They were the cause of many deaths, or resulted in poor or no reproduction.

Turtles, lizards, baby crocodilians, and a few snakes fell under my immediate care. In the afternoon, I would eventually get the opportunity to clean a row of snake cages on the second floor. These were animals no one cared about. They included water snakes, garter snakes, and a rat or chicken snake or two. They could do me no harm, and it didn't seem to matter if I killed them with my ignorance. How times have changed; today, every animal death is accounted for, and no amount of money is spared in the treatment of every disease and nutritional problem.

By the end of the day, I would be back to cleaning and preparing for the closing of the building. I understood why few people remained at careers in the reptile department, but I was determined to be an exception. At 9:10 A.M., on Sunday, the second day of my first real job, the head keeper dressed me down for some incomprehensible reason, and I cried.

4

CALL ME CHICKEN!

Peter, my good man, how long have you worked here now?" Dr. Oliver called. I had just entered the behind-the-scenes area, a narrow corridor behind the exhibit cages called the north passage, carrying an assortment of empty stainless steel food pans laden with the remains of chopped fish, horsemeat, and sticky earthworms. "Just about three months now, Dr. Oliver," I replied. "Good," he said. "It's time you learned to 'pin' a poisonous snake." Until now, it had been forbidden for me, as a new and inexperienced keeper, to even open the door to any cage or exhibit that held a venomous snake.

Dr. Oliver inserted his key into the lock on one of the twenty-three thick aluminum doors that gave the keepers access to the exhibit cages that displayed some of the most dangerous venomous snakes. Each waist-high door was emblazoned in red with THINK BEFORE YOU OPEN, as a last-minute reminder that once the door was unlocked, it would be too late to begin to focus on what you were doing. I was focused, and the memory of the moment is still vivid.

Dr. Oliver pulled back the sliding plate, which covered the glass over a small viewing portal on the back of the door. "Always look first," he said, "so you know where the snake is before you open the door." The cage was one of several "shift" cages located between major exhibit cages. Each shift cage had at least two doors, one of which accessed the adjoining exhibit. The idea was that for the most dangerous animals, the shift door could be opened and closed by the keeper from the rear passage via a steel cable, allowing the snake to enter the shift cage and be isolated while the keeper then safely serviced the exhibit. The only problem was that there was usually no reason for the snake to cooperatively exit the safety and security of its exhibit home. The alternative was to poke and prod the snake into leaving, not to mention possibly arousing its anger and eliciting a wild flight out of its cage and into the passage with the keeper. Thus, it was usually safer to let the snake alone and work quietly around it. Dr. Oliver peered into the cage through the viewing port for a moment, then unlocked the door, opened it slowly, and stepped back. Should the snake rush the open door and fall out onto the floor, Dr. Oliver was positioned well out of immediate danger.

Inside the cage lay a six-foot-long bushmaster, the largest and one of the most dangerous venomous snakes of the Latin American rain forests. I was terrified. The snake seemed unaware of what was to come, its slender forked tongue periodically flicking out of its mouth to test the air and provide it with some information about the intruders—us. Dr. Oliver demonstrated with a homemade "pinning stick," a wooden stick about three feet long fitted at one end with a short wooden crossbar padded with soft rubber. "Quietly, but very firmly, place the crossbar across the base of the snake's head and force its head down against the concrete floor," he instructed. "Not too hard, but not too gently. You do not want the snake to suddenly pull its head out from under the stick just as you are about to grasp the snake. The snake is not feeding, and we need to take it out and carefully examine it. Once you have the head firmly pinned to the floor, holding the stick with one hand reach down with the other and place your index finger on the base of the skull and your thumb and middle finger under the base of the jaws, compressing the skull between your fingers. That way you will be safe, out of reach of the fangs. Just be sure you hold on in case the snake thrashes, or we surely will be bitten."

I trembled; my heart raced and my lips were dry. The only thing I knew about bushmasters was the story I had heard on the radio as a boy, of a cargo ship sailing home from South America. Crew members had mysteriously begun turning up dead, one by one. Finally, the ship's mascot, a dog, sensed a danger in the galley. A giant bushmaster, which had stowed away at some tropical port of call, emerged to attack. It had prowled the ship each night, inflicting its fatal bite on any unsuspecting crew member it encountered. As it came from behind the stove to defend itself against the barking dog, the hero, one of the last remaining officers, quickly dispatched it with a shotgun blast.

I carefully followed Dr. Oliver's instructions, pinning down the snake's head before it realized what was going to happen. As I grasped the snake's head between my fingers, it began to twist against my grip. Its two-inch-long fangs reached forward, searching to embed themselves in whatever attacker was involved. Amber droplets of venom literally flowed from the tips of its fangs and dribbled down my hand and arm. The snake's body felt like a rasp, as each scale was coarsely raised in a hard keel.

I began to lose my grasp. Dr. Oliver began to lose his nerve, as well, watching me struggle to keep control of the snake, but he was helpless to intervene. When I switched the snake's head from one hand to another without getting bitten, it was almost more than he could bear. Finally, I returned the snake to its cage and turned it loose.

Dr. Oliver told me I had done well for my first time. I doubted that, but I had survived the ordeal. The implication that my future would hold more of such activities was ominous. The experience suggested that the career of reptile keeper had a self-limiting component designed to continually make room for new personnel.

It did not take long for me to learn what my real worth as a new keeper was. The revelation came when Nina Lean, a noted wildlife photographer, needed a fearsome picture of an angry king cobra for a forthcoming publication. There is nothing that can strike fear into the heart of even the bravest person as a ten- or fifteen-foot-long venomous snake that rises up fully half of its body length, stands its ground, faces you eye to eye, and all but says, "I am going to make you dead." King cobras are noted for their fear-nothing, aggressive attitude, and ours were no exception.

Our two females, ten-foot-long banded individuals from Malaysia, were intractable. Any disturbance to their cage would instantly cause the animals to raise the front halves of their bodies, stand straight upward, and spread a threatening hood that started at the head and tapered gradually to where the body touched the ground. In this upright position, with mouth partly open and tongue rapidly flicking in and out, the snakes would face an intruder, ready to rush forward to deliver a bite at the end of a growling strike. My job that day was simple: I would be the bait used to entice the cobra to attack me, while the head keeper held it by the tail just out of camera range. Nina would shoot a close-up of the snake with its mouth wide open, at the apex of its strike, using her telephoto lens.

The head keeper took one of the female cobras from its cage and secured it in a large, covered, galvanized trash can. To gain a natural setting for the shot, the whole operation would be done on the grassy lawn behind the Reptile House. This was madness, I thought. Any mishap, or a bite to a keeper—me—could result in the snake escaping into the nearby bushes, or even into the zoo itself, with all of the visiting public nearby.

Finally, the stage was set. As the head keeper removed the lid of the trash can, the snake lunged and raised its body upward. Resting on the edge of the can, it towered above me, looking down. The head keeper had seized it by the tail while, as planned, it was distracted by seeing me. I dutifully waved a burlap bag, as instructed, and the snake lunged, sinking its fangs into the bag. Nina snapped away behind me. Had the head keeper lost his hold on the tail, the snake would have turned both Nina and me into purple dying bodies.

Nina had no inkling of the possible consequences of what we were doing. "Just a moment," she said, as she went to her camera bag; she had used up her film and had to reload. To me, it was an eternity, as I maneuvered in front of the snake, just out of range of its strike, trying to keep its attention from the head keeper at its tail. Again and again we repeated the process, until Nina's film stores were exhausted. The snake, too, was exhausted, and frustrated at not having bitten anyone, or at least driven them away. Finally, it allowed itself to be lowered back into the darkened recess of the trash barrel. The head keeper was rewarded for his bravery with the gift of a new thirty-five-millimeter camera and lenses. I got to clean my uniform of a number of new deposits, mostly my own body fluids.

Venomous snakes fall into several basic types, relative to the threat they pose to the people who must work with them. Regardless of the toxicity of the venom, just how dangerous a snake can be depends on its size, whether it has fangs large enough to inject venom if it does bite, its aggressiveness, and its disposition. Coral snakes have highly toxic and potentially lethal venom, but the fangs of many coral snakes are too short to penetrate clothing or even skin, and some species have to actually be picked up before they will bite. Many bites are inflicted on small children who pick up the brightly colored animals.

Some species of sea snakes have all of the components to make them potentially very dangerous animals, except that they refuse to bite, even when tormented. Rattlesnakes and vipers have everything going for them except aggressiveness. A person standing six feet away from a four-foot-long viper is about as safe as if they were forty feet away. The snake may defend itself with a strike if the intruder comes too close, but it will usually make no effort to advance on the intruder and attack. Cobras and a number of other related species are extremely agile, very fast, highly irritable, and aggressive; they will even press an attack on an intruder that may be several feet away. Of these, the king cobra is one of the most notorious and intelligent of the snakes. Its large size—up to eighteen feet long—combined with its half-inch-long fangs and copious quantities of extremely toxic venom make it one of the most dangerous snakes in the world.

Our own Junior was huge, fully thirteen feet long, and was the first king cobra to be bred and born in captivity in a North American zoo. Junior had literally been raised by hand and was familiar with people. Each morning when the exhibit glass was being cleaned, Junior would move to the front of his cage and, pressing his head against the glass, try to catch sight of the keeper as he washed the glass of the adjoining cages, until he was finally at Junior's cage. Junior would then watch attentively, calmly, but with great interest until the keeper moved on to the next exhibit.

King cobras are exclusively cannibalistic, feeding only on other snakes. At that time, it was common practice to purchase a hundred pounds of live harmless snakes and western diamondback rattlesnakes from dealers in Texas. It was interesting to watch Junior distinguish between the two types of food snakes: one venomous and potentially a danger to him, the other of no real consequence. King cobras are immune to the neurotoxic (nerve-damaging) venom of cobras and other related species from the regions of Southeast Asia where king cobras are found. But they can be killed by snakes that possess largely hemolytic-type venom, which destroys blood cells and other tissue cells.

When a harmless food snake was introduced into Junior's cage, Junior would immediately approach it and seize it anywhere on the body. The snake would die immediately from Junior's toxic venom, and would be swallowed down. Rattlesnakes, however, were a different story. Junior would approach the snake, then stop, frozen, as though instantly recognizing the danger. Arching his body high above the rattlesnake and far out of reach, Junior would then lunge downward and seize the rattlesnake safely behind the head. Soon it too would be dead and swallowed. Once an accidental bite from a rattlesnake almost cost Junior his life, until we injected the king cobra with anti-snakebite serum designed to counteract rattlesnake venom. In an irony of sorts, we treated a venomous snake for snakebite.

Junior's danger lay in his voracious appetite. He would wildly rush out and seize anything that he perceived as possible food, whether it was or not. Thus, Junior might well think a shovel handle, a hose, or a keeper that moved was food, attack it, and try to eat it. Once he had just begun to chew his jaws along the body of a dead food snake, in an attempt to reach the head and swallow it headfirst, when the body of the snake passed under Junior's own body. As Junior reached his own body, he mistakenly transferred his jaws to his own coils and proceeded to chew down his own back. At feeling the pricks of his own teeth, he jumped and twitched. Junior then thought the "food" (himself) was alive and bit down harder to kill it (himself), whereupon he twitched and jumped more from the pain, and bit harder. We had to break up the confrontation.

I felt as if Junior and I would share posterity together. I would have to catch Junior regularly, grasping him firmly behind the head to avoid being bitten. It was always a very dangerous operation. I would then remove his dried eye caps—skin left over after shedding, covering the eyes—with a pair of tweezers. On one occasion, I had just gotten Junior safely in hand when he began to struggle. His thirteen-foot-long body was muscular and strong. Before the other keepers could assist me by grabbing hold of Junior's body, Junior coiled around my shoulders and neck. As he searched with his tail for some hold, his tail snaked around my head, whereupon he defecated directly into my ear—huge gobs of vile-smelling, yellow-and-white viscous fluids, complete with undigested scale epidermis from a previous meal. The other keepers laughed so hard they cried. Junior would gain fame as the only king cobra in the world to defecate into a keeper's ear, while I would gain the lesser fame of being the only keeper in the world who had had his ear defecated in by an adult king cobra and had lived to tell about it.

Over the years, I had many unsettling episodes with cobras. Always active and alert to every opportunity, cobras continually test the confines of their cages, taking advantage of any means of escape. On one occasion, a king cobra lunged out through its cage door and onto the floor of the narrow keeper passage, literally at my feet. According to the keepers, I jumped into the air to avoid the snake, but on coming down I found the snake directly beneath me. They said I immediately ascended once again, without ever touching the ground. Somehow, I do not believe one word of their version of the story.

I do, however, recall standing in one of our rather small animal holding rooms with a group of four or five keepers and the veterinarian, attempting to identify the tattoo number on the underside of an Asiatic cobra's tail. I held the front part of the snake, loosely draped on the end of a three-foot-long snake hook, while I raised the snake's tail with my other hand. At that moment, as we were crowded together with this relatively docile but extremely dangerous snake dangling loose between us, the lights went out, plunging everything into darkness. There had been a time change from eastern standard time to daylight saving time, and no one had reset the time clocks that controlled the room light. I knew I held the snake's tail in my hand, but where the head was could have been anyone's guess. I think everyone in that room stopped breathing until someone managed to find the timing mechanism in the dark and switch the lights back on.

These are the kinds of simple, unexpected happenings that make keeping venomous snakes anywhere but in a scientific, professional setting sheer stupidity. To my eternal amazement, amateur herpetologists still feel they have to prove their masculinity by keeping such dangerous animals in their private home collections. As for me, call me chicken where venomous snakes are concerned.

5

SEXING CROCODILIANS AND OTHER CHALLENGES

An animal keeper in a zoological institution certified by the American Zoo and Aquarium Association (AZA) is a caring professional, taking part in sophisticated programs that utilize the resources of a multitude of sciences. Today's animal-care worker, even as a junior member of a department staff, can become a member of a professional society, help develop interzoo captive-breeding programs that may be a critical part of saving an endangered species from extinction, take part in wildlife programs in foreign countries, and publish articles and reports in scientific and educational journals. A keeper today uses the scientific names of animals as casually as his or her own name, identifying animals by family, genus, and species. Keepers are familiar with genetics, population management, behavior, species reproduction, and how to implement veterinary treatments. They do infinitely more than just scooping up poop. The AZA conducts vocational workshops and formal education courses in conjunction with university programs for college credit. Many keepers pursue graduate degrees or specialize in some aspect of animal management. This is serious stuff. I only wish I could have had these resources available to me during the early part of my career.

As a new junior keeper, I listened to my supervisor dribbling continual words of wisdom to me, about how if I followed his advice and experience, my animals would "live forever." It was a baseless statement. One look around the collection or at the numbers of deaths logged in the daily report could not possibly support it. At least, he professed, any animals new to my care would live longer than those I had inherited would. At that time, in the mid-1950s, the job of animal keeping was just rising above being a rather crude occupation, a mere step above that of the roustabouts who were picked up for a few hours of work when the circus came to town. In fact, the head keeper of mammals would still send word to the local bar when he was looking for some extra men to do a few hours of work moving animals. Animal keeping had scarcely advanced from the primitive practices of the previous decades.

While the ornithological sciences already enjoyed a well-established history of breeding and keeping birds in captivity, the same was not true for reptiles. Most crocodilians at the Reptile House died young, rarely reaching adult breeding size. Even when they did survive, we did not know how to distinguish males from females. It was not unusual for two animals housed together to continually fight with each other, until they were termed "hopelessly incompatible" for their entire lifetimes, when the simple problem was that they were both males being forced to share a single insignificantly sized territory.

When the Reptile House reopened in 1954 after its first major renovation, the main crocodilian pool was one of several principal exhibits and, as such, had to exhibit something special to wow the public. Four monster alligators were procured from a Florida dealer. The beasts were twelve to fourteen feet long and weighed upward of eight hundred pounds. The moment they were put together, they began to fight, each clamping its great jaws on the other's tail and both of them rolling their bodies in an iron grip. Their thrashing and rolling sent great waves of water across the pool and over the exhibit wall into the public space, drenching anyone who might be standing at the railing. Everyone thought they were males from the deep bellowing roars that shook the building from time to time, but no one knew for sure.

Finally, someone decided to give them hormone injections to see if it would make them more placid. It did. In fact, they stopped eating altogether and spent all of their time languishing motionless in the pool. They were thus relatively safe for a young keeper like me to be assigned to care for, as there was nothing to be done with them except change their water each week. They didn't eat, so they didn't defecate, and they wouldn't bite, because they didn't move. I would prepare fresh mackerel for them at feeding time, enter the pool, and feel rather foolish as I smacked the edge of the water with the dead fish in an effort to entice the alligators. I would then turn and leave without the alligators having given me so much as an interested glance. I felt bad for the alligators, for at this rate, the only end they were headed for was death.

Unwilling to stand by and see that happen, I decided to do something to get them stimulated. Perhaps some exercise would get their blood circulating and spark some movement, I thought. At night after work, I went to the alligator pool, took off my trousers and shirt, and waded into the shallow pool with the alligators. Stepping over and onto the back of the biggest alligator, I began to push him around the pool with my feet and a broom. It was like paddling a giant living log. On one after the other, I repeated the process for a few minutes each. Several nights a week, I would push my alligators around the pool. Finally, after several weeks, the hormone treatments began to wear off and the alligators began to move on their own. At that point, riding alligators no longer seemed to be the thing to do. Eventually, the alligators went back to fighting and were sent to another zoo in England.

As a keeper assigned to care for the crocodilian collections, I could not imagine having an animal that could reach fifteen feet in length, in a lifetime of fifty or more years, and not even know if it was a male or female. There was almost no literature on crocodilian behavior, and the most comprehensive information came from a book about the American alligator by E. A. McIlhenney, who lived on Avery Island, off the coast of Louisiana, and simply liked to watch alligators. (Besides insights into how alligators live, the McIlhenney family also brought us McIlhenney's Tabasco sauce.) One day in

1967, after reading an article describing how to sex alligators by the size of the scales surrounding their cloaca, the common opening through which crocodilians both breed and pass bodily wastes, I could hold my curiosity no longer.

Commandeering some of the other keepers on duty that day, I selected five four- to six-foot-long alligators from the exhibit pools, and we brought them to the Reptile House plant conservatory. There, despite the alligators' protestations, we rolled each on its back and, using an age-old technique for soothing alligators and putting them into a trancelike stupor, rubbed their bellies until they relaxed and lay quietly. Now that they lay side by side, I carefully examined the size of the scales I had read about. I could see no sexual differences. Yet I could not believe that among the five animals, both sexes were not represented.

Then one of the animals moved. A white cartilaginous shaft emerged from the animal's cloaca and was immediately retracted back through the opening. We were ecstatic. We had just seen a crocodilian's penis. This sighting may not seem momentous to many other people, but to me it was a major find. I plunged my index finger into the animal's cloaca after the white object, hoping my digit would be long enough to reach whatever might be there but not really knowing what I might find. The alligator, firmly held by its jaws by one of the keepers, slept on. Feeling something hard lying just inside the opening, I hooked it with my finger and pulled it back through the cloaca. This had to be a male, I thought.

The next animal had nothing inside its cloacal vent to compare to the size and firmness of the organ found inside the previous animal; it had to be a female. Moving down the line of animals, I found males and females now as distinguishable as day and night. I could hardly contain my excitement. I had the keepers repeat the process to see if they could detect the same differences as I could. Indeed, they could—although somewhat hesitantly, embarrassed by the act they were committing.

This simple but basic finding meant that it was no longer necessary to hold animals for years, hoping they would breed. We could now specifically select certain alligators with desirable traits and pair them for breeding, just as we would pair any domestic animal. Excited, we captured several other species of crocodilians and repeated the process to see if other crocodilians could be sexed as easily as an alligator. It worked on every species we tried.

By the late 1960s, most of the world's crocodilians were facing extinction. This simple technique would make it possible to plan captive-breeding programs for endangered species, as well as to understand behavioral patterns that might be displayed by males or females.

The next morning, when the curator, Dr. Herndon Dowling, arrived, I could hardly contain myself, so excited was I by my discovery. I described what I had done and invited him to stick his finger into the cloaca of the alligator I was holding. He looked at me as though I had gone off the deep end. But he was a scientist. With some trepidation and a bit of fanfare, he mentally prepared his pinky finger, anticipating the forthcoming excursion into the unknown; then with a gentle sidewise twisting motion, he stuffed the tip of his finger into the alligator's cloaca. He smiled. The alligator did not. Dowling responded in his southern twang, "I'll be go to hell." It worked.

It would be another two years before I would put aside my frustration at the failure to receive official permission to publish my discovery. It seems that publicly reporting that I had stuck a finger into an alligator's rear end to determine its sex was a little too risqué for the times, at least for the staid zoological society. I would, however, push ahead and publish a scientific paper on sexing crocodilians in a prestigious British scientific journal. In the meantime, other herpetologists would share the same curiosity and stick their fingers in other alligators' rear ends. Today, sexing crocodilians is the basis for all captive breeding and conservation programs around the world, and I consider this discovery my most important professional achievement. To commemorate the event, the keeper staff awarded me a glove with one finger removed. Many years later, my wife-to-be would learn of me and the "Brazaitis method" of sexing crocodilians through her professor, the same Herndon Dowling, as she began her career in the study of crocodilian behavior. How lucky could I get? I would secure both fame and a wife as the result of one inquisitive act.

Today, we speak in terms of F1, F2, and F3 generations—the first offspring, the next generation, and the third generation of offspring. We talk of founder stock and of managing the genetic diversity of a group of animals to ensure genetic survival for two hundred years or more. The majority of animals in most zoos today are born in captivity in a zoo, perhaps to parents and grandparents that were born in captivity as well. There are no unimportant animals in a zoological collection today, and the cause of death for even the smallest frog is a matter of medical investigation and accountability. In those early days of my career, dead animals were simply tossed in the garbage.

The animals I was assigned to care for were often those that were ill, were unimportant because they were "common" species, or were species that had a history of not doing well in captivity. Many species did not do well in captivity. Most Australian reptiles died within months after their arrival because they held no immunity to the diseases carried by cagemates from other parts of the world. The list of species that were continually replaced as their predecessors died could fill pages. Animal-keeping records were a joke. Animals received an inventory number when they arrived, whether by donation, purchase, or birth. When they died, their number was vacated, but only until the next animal of the same species arrived. It then assumed the previous owner's number. The result was that dozens of animals, such as common garter snakes, could arrive and die in succession, but the records would indicate that a single animal had lived for decades.

Snakes at the Reptile House seemed to die from unknown reasons, mostly as babies, and from a host of parasitic, bacterial, and viral infections. Most wild-caught snakes and lizards died soon after arrival, not only from the parasites they harbored but also from the medical treatments they received and from cross infection from other diseased species they were forced to live with. All reptiles were thrust into the general environment rather than a specific environment that answered their biological needs. Simply put, every zoo reptile collection at that time held a few hardy animals that lived a very long time, while most of the rest of the collection (with the exception of turtles) died every year or two. Turtles would live regardless of how badly they were kept. However, the diseases they harbored seemed to kill everything kept around them.

Texas horned toads had, for years, fallen into the category of common pet-market species. Millions were captured, sold, and died. Despite their name, horned toads are not toads or amphibians at all. They are lizards. A number of species inhabit the hot desert regions of the southwestern United States, where sand temperatures can soar above 120 degrees Fahrenheit and there may not be any appreciable rainfall for months. The animals have evolved to do very nicely in the wild, living under these harsh conditions. They feed mostly on ants and other small insects, which they hunt and eat in great quantities. At such high temperatures, their metabolism races in high gear during the day, then slows dramatically at night as desert temperatures plummet. Their bodies are flat, as though a wandering prospector had stepped on them. Their heads and backs are covered with sharp, pointed scales, like tiny horns. Each species displays its own unique horn size and arrangement. To escape the hot blazing sun, the little animals, only three to four inches long, bury themselves in the sand, leaving only their head, horns, and eyes at the surface to watch for passing insects. Since their coloration is brown with dark spots, once they are buried, the animals are all but invisible.

Because horned toads are so strange looking and never bite, they were captured by the tens of thousands for the pet trade, and were often sold in pet shops and circuses for as little as a dollar apiece. The problem was that the animal could not survive in captivity because it lacked proper food and the variation and extremes of temperature its physiology demanded. One hundred percent of the animals that entered the pet trade died, usually within six to eight weeks. It wasn't surprising, then, that we received dozens of starving and emaciated horned toads every spring, from caring visitors who had unwittingly purchased them for their home aquaria, failed to keep the toads healthy, and then thought that they might survive if they were given to the zoo. Even today, species that cannot survive long in captivity but are available in large numbers, cheap at wholesale, and highly profitable find their way into the pet trade.

These lizards were usually put in the desert cage, to which I was assigned. It was a desert cage in name and decor only, in that there was no way to duplicate the intricacies of a true desert environment, which changes from very hot to quite cold and back every twenty-four hours. The lizards died under my care just as rapidly as they would have died with the original pet owner. Each time I lost a horned toad, the head keeper would admonish me for my poor animal-keeping performance, blaming me for the death. He had kept the species for many years, healthy and well, he boasted, when he was a keeper, and had developed many care techniques, which included spraying the horned toads with water four or five times a day and capturing ants to feed them.

Now, capturing ants in a glass jar baited with sweet sugar was an opportunistic endeavor. It was impossible to capture enough ants during the summer, and absolutely impossible to find a group of ants to capture during the winter—if the horned toad lived that long. Furthermore, even when a few ants were offered, the horned toads rejected them out of hand; they were the wrong kind of ants. No matter how hard I tried, the lizards died. Strangely enough, no record of the head keeper's success could be found in the Reptile House archives.

The scene was repeated time after time: horned toads arrived, horned toads died, junior keeper was berated for presumably not following the head keeper's instructions. I finally struck on a solution. As each horned toad died, I drew on my taxidermy skills, took the body home, and mounted it in a lifelike position. A few days later, I would return the body and place it in the desert cage just as it would appear in life: buried in the sand with only the top of its head and black glass eyes showing. Each morning I would move the little guys to a new location in the cage, as though they had acted like normal horned toads during the night and had actively hunted for food, settling down at a new spot the following morning. To the head keeper,

I had finally achieved success—obviously, by following his precise instructions.

Not long into my career I became well known for my innovative way of applying my increasing knowledge and curiosity to solving those nagging little everyday workplace challenges. "Ask Peter. He can do anything" was frequently heard in the Reptile House. Necessity is often the mother of invention, and I was not handicapped with the perceptual constraints of how things had always been done in the past. After all, coming up with new ways not only could be more effective and labor saving but could also be entertaining and fun.

One day the head keeper walked by as I was feeding my charges. A pail containing several live white mice had accidentally tipped over, allowing its contents to scurry under a cage and hide among the plumbing pipes and valves, where it would be quite difficult to reach them. I appeared to be doing nothing about recapturing the elusive little morsels of food, only making entries on a pink card that was used to record the food intake of individual animals. He commented that I had better round up the mice before they got away or we would have loose mice all over the place. I replied that indeed I was recapturing the mice, and feeding my animals at the same time. Puzzled, the head keeper walked away. At that point, finished with its assignment, a cobra I had taken from its cage and sent into the plumbing maze to catch its own meal reappeared, filled to capacity with mice. By employing this acknowledged expert mouse catcher, I had saved myself the bruised elbows and muddy clothing I would have received had I crawled under the cage myself. All that was left for me to do was to make note of each mouse the snake ate and record it on the snake's food card, then pick up the snake safely with a snake hook— a long-handled wooden pole fitted with a metal hook at the end— and return the snake to its cage. (The hook is used to gently lift the snake off of the ground to transport it, as the snake hangs on to keep from falling off.)

The concept of feeding live mice to a reptile is objectionable to some people on humane grounds. Other people specifically came to the Reptile House each week to watch the snakes being fed and were disappointed to learn that, in most instances, the mice had always been humanely dispatched first. I consider it inhumane to allow any animal, including a reptile, to slowly starve to death when I know that the reptile's normal behavior and physiology have evolved for it to feed on living prey. Sometimes individual snakes, particularly those recovering from illness or new from the wild, will steadfastly refuse to eat dead mice and will starve to death unless a live mouse is offered to them. Regardless of our anthropomorphic perceptions, animals in nature prey on other living organisms and have evolved efficient ways of quickly dispatching their prey to prevent the prey's escape and avoid injury to themselves. They frequently do a better job of it than we do.

There are many challenges to the art of animal care, and dealing with these problems may be only a part of the day's work. The dictates of supervisors, administrators, and the general public all combine to tax the ingenuity of the keeper to "get the job done."

What do you do when you have a group of chuckwallas, desert lizards from the southwestern United States, that insist on eating only multicolored flowers in the dead of winter? Today, acquiring fresh flowers on a daily basis does not present any real problem. However, fifty years ago it seemed as if the lizards might well starve for lack of proper food in sufficient quantities. Pondering the question, keeper Joel Dobbin and I came up with an innovative solution. Where would be the most likely place to find a continuous, year-round supply of fresh flowers? A cemetery, of course.

We began our search at the nearby Woodlawn Cemetery. "Excuse me, sir," we asked a caretaker, "where can we find the fresh graves?" "There are none. We're full up. Haven't been any new grave sites in years" was the reply. Discouraged but not defeated, we set off in my blue Volkswagen Beetle, following the trail of cemeteries that extended northward from the zoo. The same inquiry at the next two cemeteries brought the sneering reply "We don't allow fresh flowers, only plastic ones." In desperation, I recalled that my recently deceased brother-in-law had had fresh flowers on his grave. Off we went. Not only did we fill the tiny sedan with fresh flowers, but the caretakers at the cemetery invited us back to help ourselves to as many flowers as we liked, and offered to call us at the zoo when a particularly promising funeral was scheduled to arrive. Soon our freezers were filled with bags of fresh frozen flowers for happy lizards. I knew that my brother-in-law would have approved, although I am not so sure that purple ribbon drapery and leftover funeral wreaths enhanced the Reptile House kitchen.

That was not the only time that we drew on the venerable mortuary industry to solve an animal-related problem. The zoo's carpentry shop began to complain when the reptile department started ordering the construction of sturdy wooden shipping boxes with increasing frequency. New federal shipping regulations were becoming particularly stringent in dictating precisely what was required to ensure the survival of animals during transit and against their escape, and zoos were shipping valuable and irreplaceable animals between institutions with greater frequency. Our zoo carpentry shop was not up to the task; the time consumed and the labor costs made the boxes very expensive to create. Crocodiles were a particular problem; they had to fit into a rather long box that needed to be particularly strong.

One day as I stood by at a colleague's burial, the casket was placed in a beautifully constructed outer pine box before being lowered into the grave. There was the answer. Back at the Reptile House, I pored over the telephone directory in search of a coffin manufacturer. There was one, right in the South Bronx. A woman answered, and I asked, "Do you sell those pine boxes you put coffins in?" "Yes we do," she replied. "How much are they?" I asked. "Adult or child?" she questioned. "Well, probably adult, sometimes child, I guess," I said, trying to envision the size of a coiled python, or a crocodile with its tail curled back to save space. "About twenty-five dollars, depending on the size and what kind of handles you want." "Could I have air holes drilled into the sides?" I asked. There was a pause. "You had better speak to the sales manager," she replied.

It wasn't long before the sales manager, finished with his bout of laughter at the prospect of crocodiles and pythons being shipped in his coffin boxes, saw the new opportunities for business my call represented. No, we were not interested in rayon or silk padded lining to cushion the crocodiles during transit, I insisted. No pillows either. Just plain boxes. No, the handles did not have to be made of bronze as opposed to ordinary aluminum. Yes, the inside had to be smooth to prevent abrasions. Yes, thank you, unlike the needs of your usual clients, air holes are important. Yes, the boxes would have to be delivered to the zoo.

It was a wonderfully cooperative exchange, enhanced later by the bewildered look of the truck driver and the zoo visitors as a tractor-trailer laden with coffins and boxes found its way along the public paths of the zoo to the rear of the Reptile House. One day soon after, Joel and I were at the American Airlines cargo building at La Guardia Airport shipping out a crocodile in one of our new coffin boxes. Coming in was a box containing the body of a recently deceased woman from Florida being picked up by a somberly dressed mortuary attendant. Looking at our coffin box, he seemed puzzled by the addition of air holes, as well as by the zoo emblems on our plain khaki uniforms. I kept a straight face as we exchanged comments about the high cost of shipping bodies and the inconvenience of delayed airline schedules. I never told him that our "body" probably had better teeth.

Sometimes a keeper is asked to do something that is not really possible because of the ever-changing behavioral cycles of the animals. What an animal was doing two weeks before the breeding season may not be what it's doing two weeks after the breeding season is past. Such was the case when the curator called to say that he and a special trustee were on their way to the Reptile House to hear Chinese alligators calling. Most crocodilians are quite vocal, the males calling loudly during the weeks immediately before and during the breeding season to announce their territorial rights to other males and to attract females. The time period when calling takes place is very short, often only a month or two. After that, the males may be relatively silent, calling only on occasion.

Our Chinese alligators had become the topic of great interest. The species was critically endangered in the wild in China, and our pair of animals was one of the few to be found in North American zoos. Our efforts to breed them were encouraged when, in early March, the male began producing its deep-throated call of *umph, umph, umph, umph—mmmmmmm,* which was answered by a similar, only shorter version of the call by the female. We capitalized on the occurrence for the benefit of public interest by using an electronic signal generator to replicate the call through the public address system at certain times throughout the day. It seemed to stimulate the animals to initiate courtship behavior and possibly increased the probability of the animals breeding. The only problem was that the day of the trustee's visit fell after the breeding season was over, and the alligators no longer had any interest in responding to the signal generator with their calls.

Nonetheless, the trustee was on his way, and the Chinese alligators had better call. Summoning Hugh McCrystal, one of our young keepers, to the office, I explained the dilemma. I handed him a galvanized pail and instructed him to go into the conservatory behind the crocodile pools, where he could not be seen from the public area, and wait for my signal. I would try to elicit calls from the Chinese alligators by playing low-frequency sounds from the signal generator through the public address system. If I was successful and the alligators called, fine. If the alligators did not respond, I would play three consecutive low-frequency beeps. At this signal, Hugh was to place the pail over his head, so as to produce a low-frequency hollow sound, and mimic the call of the alligator's *umph, umph, umph, umph—mmmmmmm* for the trustee and the curator to hear.

The curator and trustee arrived just as I assembled the signal generator and Hugh took his hidden place. I began my performance. The generator blared the *umph, umph, umph, umph—mmmmmmm* call, but the alligators remained impassively bored and silent. Again I repeated the process to no avail: *umph, umph, umph, umph—mmmmmmm.* There was no response. The alligators did not even move. A third time still produced nothing. In desperation, I played the three-beep signal, followed by another chorus of *umph, umph,*

umph, umph—mmmmmmm. Magically, a muffled perfect Chinese alligator roar of *umph, umph, umph, umph—mmmmmmm* returned from the area of the pool and the two alligators, although they never moved. Obviously, the alligators were practicing ventriloquism, not even moving their lips or raising their heads to call. Again I sounded three beeps, and again a perfect roar followed. "Marvelous!" the trustee shouted, barely able to contain his delight at this special treat of seeing animal behavior in action. "Just marvelous." Once again, the art of ingenuity had triumphed over failure.

Innovation also played a role in solving some of the research challenges we faced over the years. A noted radiologist and colleague who particularly liked reptiles had access to the new computerized axial tomography (CT) unit and real-time ultrasound machine at a local hospital. One evening at dinner, this colleague, a noted reptile anatomist, my wife, Myrna, and I began discussing the arrangement of the vital organs of snakes, and how CT-scan imaging and real-time ultrasound—technology just being used to diagnose human disease— might provide a good way of illustrating a comprehensive atlas of snake anatomy. The question of how well such techniques would work continued to pique our interests.

Finally, around midnight, we could stand it no longer. Gathering up a six-foot-long pet boa constrictor belonging to our radiologist friend, we proceeded to the hospital. No patients were pending, and the real-time ultrasound machine was soon humming. A broom handle from a wash closet provided a perfect snake stretcher and, with some surgical tape, the boa was immobilized in a relatively straight body line on the wooden broom handle. Slowly, the radiologist moved the probe along the snake's body, and image after image of the snake's internal organs appeared on the monitor. What a miracle of science this was. There were the heart, lung, and stomach, just as they lay within the snake's body. At each click of a button, printed images emerged from the unit. Unfortunately, our hopes for producing an anatomical atlas vaporized as our two learned colleagues degenerated into a heated argument over which side of the body the snake's single lung was being seen from, dashing all hopes of collaboration. It was nearly 2:00 A.M. when we untaped the snake and left the hospital in dismay. I did manage to sneak into the hospital the next day with a basketful of crocodile and turtle eggs. We CT-scanned the eggs between patient appointments, resulting in a fine publication showing the developing embryos within the eggs.

On another occasion, when Myrna, then not yet my wife, was teaching phlebotomy (blood-taking) techniques at a local college, we decided to do blood-chemistry studies on alligator blood and compare it to human blood—mine. Before she took a small sample of blood from a valuable alligator, I allowed her to practice on me. She did well, inserting the butterfly needle easily into a vein on the upper part of my hand. However, she misplaced the receiving vial at a critical moment, just as her boss entered the laboratory. Looking over her shoulder as my blood flowed down the leg of the table and crept across the floor, he commented that she had better do something soon if she wanted to keep me as a suitor.

Taking a fresh sample from a small alligator was going to be relatively easy, and I had just the candidate living in my bathtub at home. The next night I met Myrna at the college after work. Labeling the vials containing the reptile's blood as the patient A. BRAZAITIS (for Alligator), we sent the samples to the clinic laboratory for a complete blood chemistry and analysis. The next day when Myrna arrived at work, she received the sample report indicating that the blood was the most heavily packed with cells that the laboratory had ever seen. Undoubtedly, the patient from whom the sample had been taken was extremely ill, the report added. The analysis was incomplete because the packed cells had so clogged the machine that a technician had had to spend the rest of the night cleaning it in order to be ready for patients the following day.

How do you take blood from a reptile if you don't know where to locate the arteries or blood vessels? It was 1981 and Myrna was teaching budding podiatrists at a school for podiatric medicine. One of her colleagues had just purchased a medical device that used ultrasonic sound waves, emitted from a small, pencil-like probe, to track the movement of blood within a vessel; an audible signal increased or decreased in volume, depending on how close the probe was to the movement. The principle was based on the Doppler effect, similar to that used by radar. When sound hits a moving object, it changes frequency and bounces back at a new frequency. This device could tell a physician if a diabetic patient's foot had enough blood circulation.

Myrna and I couldn't wait to try it on reptiles. Today, ultrasound diagnosis is commonly used in medicine. But in those days, it was exciting and new. After some searching, I discovered the pioneer manufacturer of ultrasound equipment, Park Electronics, in Oregon. I dialed the number and got the office receptionist. I explained that I was a superintendent of reptiles at the Bronx Zoo and that I was interested in doing some research on how to find blood vessels on a snake. There was a long pause at the other end of the line. She then said, "I'll connect you to Mr. Park."

The man's voice on the other end was direct and simple. "What is it that you want?" he asked. I repeated that I was interested in doing some research on blood vessels in snakes and other reptiles and wanted to know how I could get access to the kind of ultrasound unit I had read about. Mr. Park simply said, "I'll send you one. You can keep it."

A few days later, a box arrived containing a small black ultrasound unit that included a speaker and a probe. I could not believe it. I rushed to call Myrna. We were ecstatic, working in the podiatry school's laboratory well into the night, locating hearts, tail and throat veins, and leg arteries on a host of small lizards, frogs, snakes, and turtles. We connected the machine to an oscilloscope and created flowcharts of blood pulsations and heart valves opening and closing, and we traced veins as they extended down through the fingers and toes of the animals and each other.

Dr. William Hodges, Myrna's division chair at the podiatry school, thought we were wonderfully insane. "Incorporate your findings into your lectures," he said. "The students will love it." Sure enough, it wasn't long before Myrna was instructing a class in human physiology, where we had the perfect opportunity to demonstrate the increased heart rate a person experiences under stress. We asked for volunteers, and Myrna brought one young man to the front of the class. Using our new Doppler ultrasound unit, we traced his pulse via the veins in his wrist. The rhythmic, stable sound of his coursing bloodflow could be heard. I then approached him from behind with a harmless king snake coiled around my hand. As I abruptly moved the snake into his line of vision, his heart rate rocketed upward, and the class howled. Myrna instantly became a favored instructor in the eyes of her students.

I, on the other hand, met with far less appreciation when I told the zoo administration of our research and discoveries. Animal keepers, even supervisors, were not encouraged to do research, especially medical-type research; the administration felt that such work should best be left to the veterinary department staff. But I was not to be so easily dissuaded from making my mark on my profession. Our resulting scientific publication in a herpetological journal was well received by both human medical and veterinary medical researchers, and this has become a standard technique for accurately picking a site to draw blood from in reptiles and amphibians. Not every challenge ends with success, but each does end in a lesson.

6

WHO'S ON THE RIGHT SIDE OF THE BARS?

In time, I became pretty fed up with the crassness of the human animal that roamed the public spaces of the zoo, and I began to feel rather intolerant toward the public in general. Were the people really on the right side of the bars?

This attitude was a pitfall that I had always tried to avoid. I intrinsically liked people. I also felt a little guilty. The shoe was on the other foot, now that I had made the transition from the ranks of the general public to the select few who actually took care of the animals. I recalled the many kindnesses by zoo and museum employees that had made my own early visits to such institutions so enjoyable. There were the keepers who had patiently answered my very important questions—explanations I now recited a thousand times over. I could tell what was coming and what my answer would be as soon as I heard the words "I have an iguana . . ." or "My turtle is . . ." I recalled the attendants at the American Museum of Natural History, who had offered me folding chairs to sit on while I sketched animals in the exhibits. As a keeper, I wondered if I could fulfill my unwritten obligation to have the same kind of positive influence on people that had brought me to the career I now loved. It would, however, take a great deal of patience and understanding, because the animals held first place in a keeper's considerations.

A number of zoos had conducted surveys on why people visited zoos. A common reply was that the individuals surveyed wished to share a nice family experience with their children, just as their own parents had shared the experience with them. Nonetheless, while every zoo employee was expected to make the visitor's experience a perfect one in every way, no one was expected to make the employee's experience a happy one. Any happiness enjoyed by the employee was usually derived from working with or watching the animals.

The public was emotionally relegated to something of an adversarial role, as intruders who invaded the quiet of the buildings and awakened the animals. To be sure, some visitors were harmless enough. Other visitors contemptibly teased or annoyed the animals. It was as though the animals prepared for and began their workday when the public arrived at 10:00 A.M. At least I got to sleep in on my day off; the animals never got a day off from the indignities that often befell them at the hands of a few thoughtless visitors.

More than once I stormed into the public area after some moron showing off to his macho friends, or for his girlfriend, aggressively pounded on the glass in an effort to make a cobra strike. Invariably, the snake would become infuriated by the annoyance and injure its snout while striking the intervening glass instead of the person. I would usually confront the individual and threaten to throw him out of the building. Sometimes, however, I would invite him to demonstrate his bravery without the benefit of the glass separating him from the snake. I would say loudly for all to hear, "If you're so brave, come with me and I'll let you tease the cobra directly, from the snake's side of the glass." No one ever took me up on the offer, but many young women who had secretly sympathized with the beleagured snake taunted their boyfriends for their sudden lack of masculinity.

Once, while feeding the crocodiles, I lost my composure—which, at the very least, was a dangerous thing to do. When a keeper entered the enclosure laden with a pail of fresh fish and dead white rats, four or five crocodiles of different sizes would race toward him. The crocodiles always knew precisely at what time their three feedings a week were due to occur and were already anticipating their meal as the keeper entered the gate. They would usually stop only feet away from the keeper to wait, with jaws open, for a rat or fish to be thrown into their mouths. Each crocodile would wait patiently, unless it felt it was going to be shortchanged on its meal or another crocodile was getting unjustified priority. There was always a second keeper, armed with a broom, ready to fend off any overly anxious crocodile or keep the crocodiles from overwhelming the person doing the feeding.

On this day, a particularly vociferous member of the public kept shouting, "Feed the one with its mouth open! Feed the one with its mouth open." The distraction had already nearly gotten my hand dangerously close to one pair of snapping jaws. Finally, as the fellow shouted once again, "Feed the one with its mouth open!" for what seemed like the hundredth time, I picked up a piece of fish in my forceps and deftly sailed it out of the pool toward the waiting open mouth of the visitor, bouncing the fish off the adjacent railing. The crowd roared with laughter as I called out, "Sorry, I missed. Shall I try another?"

My effort to feed the visitor was intentional. However, Bob, one of the other keepers, had a similar experience that was actually executed by a crocodile. He had just given a crocodile a particularly large mackerel to eat, larger than the crocodile could handle in one piece. As crocodiles do in such circumstances, it violently snapped its head from side to side, breaking the fish in two. The smaller piece remained in its mouth, while the larger piece of fish flew off into space. In this instance, the flying piece of fish sailed over the wall of the exhibit and smacked directly onto the chest of a very well-dressed woman who stood among the crowd of visitors in the public area. Bob's visions of an irate visitor filing an immediate lawsuit for dry cleaning quickly turned to astonishment. The woman, who now had fish intestines and odor added to her lovely clothing, was Bob's mother-in-law, who, unknown to Bob, was visiting the zoo with his wife.

I am sure a greater reward in the hereafter awaits anyone who can cheerfully handle the challenges of dealing with the general public, day after day, and still maintain a degree of civility and bearing. At one point in time, I was really struggling. If anything could get me fired fast, it would be rudeness toward the public—and there were many opportunities to test a keeper's endurance.

Simply closing the building at the end of the day usually brought with it such an opportunity, and a daily confrontation with humanity. The keeper began the closing process by trying to stop the flow of people entering the building through the front doors, while at the same time encouraging the people already inside the building to exit, and simultaneously cleaning and securing the building for the night, all which had to come to a conclusion at precisely the moment of closing that was posted at the entrance to the zoo. A fifteen-minute hiatus was needed, but was never built into the system. It was as though the higher administration thought that elves mysteriously swept the floors each night, checked the animals and their cages, locked all the doors, and turned off or on the thousands of lights the animals might require for their health or feeding needs.

Keepers got around the problem by having one person close the front doors as apologetically as possible, to avoid complaints, while at the same time other keepers began sweeping the floor at the receding heels of the visitors as they made their way reluctantly toward the exit. Keepers literally swept the public out of the building along with the day's debris, politely saying, "Excuse me," at each push of the broom while mentally conjuring other words. Closing the doors a minute or two earlier than the posted schedule would be sure to bring complaints from belligerent people who felt we had cheated them out of several minutes of their just due for the admission money they had paid. In reality, they had already spent hours seeing the zoo and had more than received their money's worth. Besides, if seeing the Reptile House in those waning few minutes was so important, one could question why they had not made it a priority on their list of things to see, given the posted closing times at the entrance gates. Besides, even when we permitted them a last-second look, the exhibit lights would already have been turned off and there would be nothing to see. Some people would take out a cigarette lighter and hold it to the glass for illumination. Others faced with a closing door would break into a chorus of "I pay your salary," which, of course, they didn't, as keepers were zoological society employees. Telling a keeper they had driven fifty miles to get to the zoo usually elicited little sympathy. The keepers themselves may have traveled seventy miles or spent hours on a train to get to work that day.

One day I was exiting the rear of the Reptile House when I caught a glimpse of a human figure standing half hidden at the bottom of the cement steps leading to the basement furnace room, in the restricted service area. As I approached I could see that the man, a youngish fellow, had his belt open and was holding his trousers up, half un-zipped, as he clutched his groin area. I lost my composure. I per-ceived that I had finally apprehended one of the phantom fecal depositors who elected to relieve themselves in my building instead of the nearby public bathroom. I ran down the stairs, grabbed the man by the collar, and began to shout at him in my fury. "What's the matter with you?" I yelled. "Why don't you use the bathroom over there at the end of the path? Do you crap or urinate on the floor at home? Why do you do it here? Did your mother raise a pig?"

The man paled and began to stutter, in fear, in Spanish, trying to excuse himself. I showed no mercy and continued with my tirade, shouting him down, as he fumbled frantically with his open pants. The more he tried to speak, the more I shouted, and the more he trem-bled and fumbled. Suddenly a small brown bundle of fur erupted from the waistband of his trousers and raced away. The poor man had been taking a warm afternoon nap on the soft grass when a chip-munk had chosen to enter what must have appeared to be an entic-ing entry to a new burrow, and had run up the man's trouser leg. As the irate chipmunk resisted giving up its new home, the terrified man, not wishing to undo his trousers in full public view, had dis-creetly found the basement entranceway. He had been trying to dis-lodge the chipmunk, which stubbornly clung between his private parts, when I, in a rage, had descended upon him. I apologized pro-fusely as he closed his trousers in relief and left to rejoin his family.

7

YOU MEET THE DARNEDEST PEOPLE

There are certain animals that zoo visitors place high on their "must see" list. These animals usually include the giant snakes and other reptiles, gorillas, monkeys, elephants, lions and tigers, and the host of domestic animals to be touched and petted at the children's zoo. Motives and interests vary, and the psychology behind why most people despise or at best dislike snakes yet want to see and touch them is probably unimaginably complex. Therefore, I'll leave the explanations to the psychoanalysts, who also probably want to see snakes at the zoo. The bottom line is that reptiles seem to be as much of a human attractant as they are a repellent.

The aura of mystery and fear that is associated with reptiles often attracts different types of visitors with different types of obsessions. For years, the first person to enter the Reptile House, at 10:00 A.M., each and every morning, as we cleaned the glass, was a poor fellow we nicknamed Pencils. Pencils was a rather large, balding man in his mid-thirties to early forties, usually dressed in a dark suit and a white shirt with an open collar. His shirt pocket bulged with pencils, which prompted our name for him. Pencils would stop at each exhibit in turn, peer carefully through the glass at the animal inside, and write feverishly on a small pad. We often tried to get a look at what he wrote, but there was nothing decipherable to be seen, just scribbles. Sometimes he would become agitated, begin to shout, and then leave. One day his behavior began to frighten some small children, and we had to call security. We had not seen Pencils for many months when there was a knock on the keepers' access door. It was Pencils. He began by apologizing, saying he had suffered a head wound during World War II, which was the cause of his past behavior, and had since been treated. He said he was "now fine." I shook his hand, and never saw him again.

Another Reptile House voyeur had the afternoon session. Each Monday, Wednesday, and Friday at 3:00 P.M., the crocodiles were fed for the public to watch. Each and every Monday, Wednesday, and Friday, regardless of the weather, a youngish, thin woman would appear at precisely 2:59 P.M. and stand silently in front of the glass of the crocodile exhibit. Her face was obscured with makeup; she had bright red painted lips and wore a distinctive bright blue or pink silk kerchief pinned over her head and tight to her hairline. She was truly a mystery woman. After each crocodile feeding, she would disappear until the next feeding day. She never spoke to anyone, never varied her schedule, just stood silently, watching. We began to realize that it was time to feed when the mysterious woman arrived. We never knew where she came from or left for.

One day we noticed that a man, about her age and height, had come on the scene. He, too, arrived each and every feeding day. But they stood far apart, at each corner of the exhibit, silently. The ritual continued for weeks. Slowly, on each successive feeding day, the space between them closed. The two still gazed straight ahead, looking silently through the glass, as the crocodiles were fed; then they left separately. After months, at last they stood side by side—still without speaking, as far as we could tell. That day, when the feeding ended, the two turned and, for the first time, left together. They were never seen again.

It's the wise curator who keeps on hand a few lizards, or a large, easily handled snake, usually a python, just in case a special visitor shows up with the potential for donating a large sum of money to the zoo. One such rather elderly patron would run her hands up and down the length of a ten-foot-long Burmese python, fondling each muscle and coil, as the curators in charge of development and public relations kept her from falling over. I would hold the head of the snake, just in case, although my thoughts frequently wandered to wondering about why so wealthy a person would be wearing oversized, sagging support hose.

Another patron, a rather large, elderly gentleman in a tan woolen overcoat, would literally be carried into the Reptile House, once each year or two, to see the python. I never heard him speak. The poor fellow was so hunched over that he, too, needed support, and he couldn't see anything directly in front of him, only downward. We would have to pass the snake, foot by foot, under his chin, and he would nod his head approvingly as the snake passed by. Afterward, we would wash the snake to remove any drool it had acquired in the process.

The most impressive person I ever encountered during one of these notable snake visits was the emperor of Ethiopia, Haile Selassie, accompanied by his lovely wife. Haile Selassie, born Tafari Makonnen in 1892 and later known as Ras (Prince) Tafari, could trace his biblical lineage to King Solomon. (His Rastafarian followers in Jamaica revere him as a true deity.) He was a very short man, and when I saw him, he was impeccably dressed in a dark gray suit and tie. He had a closely cropped black beard, high forehead, and tight black curly hair. He could have been taken for any Wall Street banker, doctor, or lawyer. He stood dignified, straight and strong, and virtually projected a demand for respect with an aura of spirit and power.

The emperor arrived at the main entrance of the zoo with his entourage of black limousines, aides, and bodyguards and was greeted by the zoo director and a cadre of curators and zoo administrators. The "Lion of Judea" first wished to see a lion, and he shocked the zoo staff when he suddenly reached out and petted the big cat. Next, he wished to see and touch a python. I didn't know what to expect when the call came that we were to prepare to show the emperor of Ethiopia the "pet"—readily handleable—Burmese python. The snake twisted and squirmed in our grasp as we took it from its cage. The emperor watched attentively, then stepped to the snake and first touched, then stroked it, as though assimilating its every structure and form—all without comment or expression. The task done, he thanked us politely, turned, and led the way out, as simply as if he had been behind the scenes at the Reptile House many times before. I had never met a man with such bearing and self-assurance, and I have never since then, either. He died mysteriously in prison after a military coup in 1975, and was buried secretly. His body was eventually found in 1992, ignomiously entombed under a palace toilet.

There were always unofficial visitors being brought to the Reptile House, or sometimes celebrities, who would be spotted in the public area by one of the keepers and invited to come into the keepers' seminar room to meet the staff.

Aldo, one of our former keepers and a very close friend, had a retinue of colorful and amusing friends and associates. Aldo had left his job as a keeper in the Reptile House many years before to open his own very select pet shop for a special clientele in lower Manhattan. He also did a good business providing reptiles and insects to television shows and filmmakers, and he liked to bring some of the more interesting people he knew in show business to visit us, knowing that we were a lot more conservative and reserved than he was. One day Aldo showed up for lunch accompanied by a particularly trim and brightly dressed young woman with flaming red hair. As we all chatted and ate, he introduced her as his friend from the theater who liked reptiles and insects.

After lunch, Aldo announced that his friend wanted to show us her art, and he produced a large shopping bag containing several cereal boxes. Each box had been intricately cut to open like a miniature circus tent, exposing a series of carved-sponge cages containing live Madagascan hissing cockroaches, housed like so many circus animals in a menagerie—all in miniature. Hundreds of cereal pieces had been strung together and painted to look like people in the stands, people watching the circus acts, performers, and animals. It was all marvelously creative.

Aldo then asked if she would show us her act. "Sure," she said with delight. She produced a fishnet stocking, which she pulled over her hand to create a long-necked hand puppet, then stuck a huge ostrich feather on her rear end. While her hand puppet held an imaginary conversation, she did an impersonation of a gyrating ostrich doing a mating dance. It was entertainment at its oddest—and we began to wonder, In what theater did she perform her act? As we looked at one another in disbelief, we hoped no other staff members would come by unexpectedly at that particular moment. At the end of the act, we applauded. Aldo had once again been successful in getting our attention. As she and Aldo left, she passed out her business cards, which would admit a guest to one of her performances; she was billed as "Lena, the Smallest Tits in Show Business."

The sons and daughters of notable people also have to learn how to work, or at least experience what it's like to have to function in a structured environment. The Reptile House was well known as a perfect training ground that offered seclusion and a highly organized and disciplined environment. One such young woman, who shall remain nameless, was an absolute delight. She lived in a particularly select part of Manhattan and wanted to experience "work." I was given a budget to pay her the standard salary of a summer part-time worker. I must admit, I had my reservations about having a young woman on staff who obviously came from a wealthy and privileged family and perhaps had the personality to match. I could not have been more wrong. Our lovely keeper would tackle any job, no matter how distasteful or dirty it was, from cleaning bins filled with white rats to getting on her hands and knees and scrubbing the kitchen floor.

On Fridays, she sometimes asked for permission to leave early. Her most recent boyfriend might be picking her up in his private jet for a weekend in Italy, so she might not be in on time on Monday morning. We loved it. Her world was not even in the realm of perception for any of us. Come Monday, we couldn't wait for the morning coffee break to hear her full report. Out would come a plastic scoreboard that the keepers had prepared. They would then rate her new boyfriend on a scale of one to ten for fun, innovation and creativity, attitude, personality, and how well he had impressed her.

One morning, during the peak of the 1970s energy crisis, the keepers were complaining about the high cost of gasoline and how the long lines at the fuel pumps made it hard for them to get to work on time. The complicated rationing system worked off your car's license plate number and whether it was an odd or even day. Someone turned to our young keeper—who, despite her wealth, drove a very small compact car with considerable fuel efficiency—and absentmindedly asked, "You must really be having trouble in Manhattan. How much do you have to pay down there?" She thought for a moment. A quizzical look of realization came over her face. "Why, I don't know," she said. "I never gave it any thought. I have never put gas in the car. I bring the car home and the man in the garage takes it away, and I get it back the next morning to come to work." We all loved her.

On another occasion, I received a phone call from the curator saying that I would have a new summer keeper to help out in the Reptile House. He would be someone I knew of, and special, but I should not treat him too differently, and I should make sure he did not get into trouble with anything dangerous.

He turned out to be John F. Kennedy Jr. Dressed in blue jeans and a denim shirt, the well-built teenager with the enviable crop of flowing curly hair could have been any kid who liked reptiles. Our interview was more an example of going through the motions than a process that could end in rejection. However, this kid genuinely liked snakes, and I was impressed. But not so impressed that I was going to let John Jr. do anything less than what he was there to do: work. Taking the initiative, I said, "John, I know and really don't care who you are. You're expected to follow the rules, do as you are told, and follow instructions. You have to be here on time like everyone else, promptly at eight A.M. If you're late, I expect a call." John replied, "Yes, sir."

The next morning, 8:00 A.M. came and went without any sign of John. Finally, at about 8:45, John arrived. "John," I said, "we had a conversation yesterday about being on time, and you're late the first day and didn't call. What's the story? It's really a bad way to start off," I lectured. "I know," he answered apologetically. "I set my clock and got up on time. My mother made me lunch. But the Secret Service people didn't pick me up until late." It was a great excuse, and over the years it was never topped by anyone else. There would be other times when John was late or absent from work, and he would call in like any conscientious employee. It wasn't unusual for the breathy voice on the other end of the line to announce that it was "John's mother" calling to say that she had made John lunch and he was on his way to work.

I think I went a little too far once in treating John like any other member of the department. At lunchtime, it was common practice to send someone out to Arthur Avenue, the local Italian neighborhood, where you could get the best hero sandwiches, stuffed full of Italian cold cuts, hot peppers, and cheese, or a hot meatball parmigiana sandwich oozing rich tomato sauce. "John," I called. "Go out to Arthur Avenue with one of the keepers and help him pick up the sandwiches for lunch." John had become so much a part of the crew that I never gave it a second thought. Which is particularly odd in light of who he really was. While John worked at the Reptile House, the Secret Service people would wait in the parking lot. John had lost his father to an assassin's bullet long before, and, still considered to be at great risk, he was under constant protection.

About half an hour later he returned, laden with bags of sandwiches and sodas, pastries from the Italian bakery on the corner, change for everyone, and a great hero sandwich for himself. "That was fun," he said. "I don't get to go anywhere without the Secret Service guys." It was then that I realized I had sent the son of a president of the United States out into a local Italian neighborhood, practically alone, to get take-out sandwiches. Early the next morning, I received a call from the curator. John Jr. was not to leave the building without the Secret Service people being notified—certainly not to get sandwiches for the keepers. I would have given him the best recommendation for any job he might have pursued. I will never forget him.

8

PEOPLE DON'T HAVE
ALL THE SMARTS

I have always been amazed, although I shouldn't be, at the cleverness animals display in dealing with their surroundings, one another, and people.

I recall the warm summer mornings, just before dawn, when my father and I would go fishing. Unlike country kids, who might head for the nearest stream or lake, we traveled to Sheepshead Bay in Brooklyn, where the deep-sea fishing boats would leave at 4:00 A.M. The day had to be weather perfect, for neither he nor I could swim, and Dad always had visions of having to explain to Mother what had happened to her son should the ship sink in a storm. It wasn't until years later that it occurred to me to question how Dad would relate the imagined tragedy to Mother if the ship were to sink while both of us were on board.

In any case, as we left the house, the milkman, dressed in his white work suit and accompanied by his horse-drawn wagon, would be making his deliveries for the day. Our street was lined with four-story tenement buildings without elevators. Pity the milkman who had to go from building to building, up and down the long flights of steps, carrying trays of full bottles of milk, cream, and other dairy products. These he left outside various apartment doors, filling orders according to the notes left in empty milk bottles the night before by his customers. He then carried his trays, clinking with the lighter load of empty bottles, back down the steps and to the waiting wagon. The number of footsteps the milkman took was thankfully made slightly fewer by the good graces of his horse. In fact, it was the horse that impressed me the most. As the milkman disappeared into one building, the horse would open its half-closed eyes and advance to the front of the next building that had a customer. There the horse would stop, once again lapsing into horse dream world to wait for the sweating milkman to return with the empties and pick up another tray of milk and dairy products. What was astonishing was that the horse always knew which buildings to stop at and which to skip. I often wondered if the horse got its cue from the milkman or if the milkman got his cue from the horse.

Reptiles, on the other hand, are fairly predictable, conditioning and environmental temperatures largely dictating their behaviors; few reptiles can be accused of "thinking." Crocodiles probably come closest to being the "thinkers" of the reptile world. As highly accomplished predators, they hunt their prey, sometimes in pairs, and plan their attacks to ensure success.

Anyone who has watched a crocodile in the wild stalk its prey knows exactly why they are so successful. When a bird or small mammal approaches the water's edge for a drink, a crocodile spots the movement from the bank on the other side of the river or lake. The crocodile slips artfully into the water, making barely a ripple. I have seen them do this a thousand times. There is no disturbance of the water, no splash, no noise; it's as though water is gently flowing into water. The crocodile then swims slowly toward the prey, only its eyes and the tip of its snout visible on the surface of the water, looking not much different from a harmless half-submerged piece of drifting wood. The crocodile's eyes remain fixed on its target, as though marking its position and course. Then, at some predetermined distance from the prey, the crocodile submerges. It disappears, but it is still keeping track of the prey as it continues to swim undetected toward it. Perhaps only a bubble or two of swamp gas, disturbed by the crocodile's movements as it makes its way ever closer, rises in a telltale trail from the muddy bottom to mark the crocodile's presence.

Although the crocodile knows where the prey is, the prey has no inkling that the massive jaws are only a breath away, just under the surface, out of sight. Sometimes the crocodile surfaces first, like an animated submarine coming to periscope depth before firing its torpedoes, but so silently and gently that the unsuspecting prey may never even notice the danger until it is too late. Suddenly, there is an explosion of energy as the crocodile lunges from beneath the surface. Few animals are quick-witted or responsive enough to react in time to save themselves, with the attack coming from so close by and with such fury. Fortunately, few crocodiles want to or learn to hunt people. But those that do are very successful.

I recall one particular crocodile at the Bronx Zoo that we named Sam, because he was impossible to ignore. Sam always wanted to eat you. A West African dwarf crocodile, he was stout and wide, barely five feet long, with scales as rough as the bark of an oak tree. His head, like others of his species, was massive, West African dwarf crocodiles being the "bulldogs" of the crocodile world. But at the zoo, Sam's size would never make him successful.

Sam lived in an exhibit with nearly a dozen other crocodiles, many of which were more than ten feet long. Clearly, Sam was not high up in the hierarchy of the pool, spending most of his time among the plantings and tree roots that decorated the rear of the exhibit. He entered the pool only when the other, larger crocodiles came out of the water to bask, sneaking in along the corner of the enclosure in the hope that the "bullies" would not notice him.

Overall, Sam did not have a particularly sterling disposition. Who could blame him? He lived with bigger, more powerful animals that held ownership over the best parts of the enclosure. But to the keepers, Sam was different. Sam had figured out that when I entered the exhibit each morning to clean, armed with my broom and hose, I could not watch both the larger crocodiles in the pool and him behind me under the plantings at the same time. As I began to clean, facing the water's edge and the larger crocodiles, Sam would slowly begin to creep from his retreat. Soon I would turn to see where he was. Sam would then sense that I was looking at him and freeze in mid-walk, quickly dropping down onto his belly as though he had been there all along. As I turned my attention back to the pool, Sam would once again begin his approach toward my succulent rear. Again I would turn, and again Sam would freeze in place. The game would be repeated several times; each time, Sam would get a little closer to me. Finally, when I felt Sam had gotten too close for comfort, I would shout, "Sam, what do you think you are doing?" Sam would then turn around and walk, sulking, back to his hiding place among the plants. It was a morning game Sam never tired of.

Zoo animals frequently developed their own methods for dealing with members of the public, some of whom were a source of irritation or harassment that they could not necessarily avoid. In a way, the keepers frequently colluded with the animals against a common enemy: dumb people. In their empathy for the captive plight of the animals in their care, the keepers might just delay, for a moment or two, telling a visitor that it was against the law to tease the animals, not to climb over a railing, not to spit at an animal, or not to throw food at an animal to try to make it move. Once, while visiting the zoo as a young man, I watched a man with his infant son in a stroller with a tray in front. The man kept yelling to get the attention of a large male lion that appeared to be trying to sleep. Finally the lion, tired of having his afternoon nap interrupted, stood up, turned, and sent a hot stream of pungent urine out through the bars of his cage, accurately soaking the man and his child and filling the tray as a remembrance. It was then that the smiling keeper went up to the man and politely told him, "Excuse me, sir? Please don't annoy the animals."

A huge rhinoceros in the Elephant House developed the same technique in response to being spat at. However, his urine was like whitewash and so copious that zoo personnel eventually had to place a glass partition in front of his exhibit, between the rhino and the public, lest the rhino accidentally drown one of the visitors.

One of our elephants was truly clever, if not diabolical. A stone wall encircled the old outdoor elephant yard, and the public was likewise kept at a distance by a chain-link fence and railing; the distance between the two was such that a visitor and an elephant would have to stretch nearly as far as they could to pass popcorn or other goodies between them. One elephant, however, soon figured out that if it held its trunk back a little each time a visitor offered it a snack, the visitor would stupidly reach farther to feed the elephant. This was a game of patience on the part of the elephant; while the visitor was preoccupied by the fun of feeding an elephant, the elephant had its eye all the time on the visitor's purse or camera. At just the right moment, the elephant, instead of taking the next offering of popcorn, would quickly reach out and snatch the purse or camera from the visitor's shoulder; then, to its own amusement, it would demolish the treasure. More than once, a distraught visitor rushed into the Reptile House asking that someone please call the Elephant House to have a keeper at least retrieve their driver's license, money, house or car keys, or whatever was left of their expensive camera. All we had to say when we picked up the phone was, "Hi, Ken. She just got another one."

Primates are a different story. Primates are difficult to think of as animals. Their intelligence and behaviors really make them seem like little people—or giant people, as the case might be—with affection, family bonds, communication, fears, and anxieties. It's no wonder that we, as humans, can become so close to them emotionally.

We once responded to a call that a gorilla had escaped. Grabbing the nearest carbon dioxide fire extinguisher for its "smoke and noise" effect, another keeper and I ran around the corner of the Great Apes House to come face-to-face with Oka, an adult female lowland mountain gorilla. She was placidly sitting on top of her exhibit wall, right out in the public space, with her head resting in her hands, deep in gorilla thought. She had simply uprooted a tree trunk that had been fastened into the floor of her exhibit for her climbing pleasure, dragged it over, propped it against the wall of the exhibit, and walked out. I don't think escape had even occurred to her, only a desire to see what it was that people saw from their side of the wall. Taking one look at the two of us, followed by an army of keepers armed with fire extinguishers and clanging tin garbage can lids for scare effect, she simply turned in disgust and returned home.

Our family troop of snow monkeys in the Central Park Zoo was so smart that when the lengthening days of summer came, the animals were reluctant to leave their sunny outdoor exhibit for the dark, damp, underground holding pens they were relegated to each night. Besides, the exhibit held an abundance of treats, thrown in by the public despite our admonitions not to, as well as peanuts and fruits we hid in the exhibit to allow the animals to practice foraging behavior. At the end of one summer day, the keepers went to the exhibit to open the sliding doors to allow the animals into the holding area. The doors wouldn't budge. No matter how hard they pulled on the cables, the sliding doors stayed shut. Armed with brooms to ward off any aggressive monkey, the lead keeper entered the exhibit to figure out why the doors would not lift. The reason was soon evident: the slide bolts, used to lock the animals inside for the night, had been locked closed on the outside. The monkeys had locked the keepers out so that they could continue to enjoy the warm summer air.

Primates quickly learn whom to mistrust and who poses a threat, as well as whom to trust. At the Central Park Wildlife Center, we had a lovely family group of cotton-top tamarins. These small primates, only a few pounds in weight, normally live in close family groups in dense Brazilian rain forests. A wide assortment of predators prey on them, so the colony is always on the alert. When one member of the family sights a potential predator—usually a snake, bird, or carnivore—it alerts the others with a chorus of birdcall-like chirps and whistles.

In our case, the threat was Tony, the animal supervisor. Tony was the catcher. Whenever one of the tamarins needed to be treated or vaccinated, Tony was the person who would go into the exhibit with a long-handled net, catch the animal in question, and remove it from the colony. The tamarin would be anesthetized as Tony, wearing a thick pair of leather gloves, held it for treatment; then it would be returned to the exhibit.

Over time, Tony captured all of the dozen or so tamarins. They never forgot or forgave him. Even a glimpse of Tony through the exhibit glass, walking inconspicuously through the public area outside of their cage, would be enough to send the group into an alert. The first to spot him would begin giving alarm chirps, and the others would take up the chorus, with the whole group retreating to the rearmost upper branches of the exhibit. Whether Tony was in uniform or in his street clothes, they would instantly spot him among hundreds of visitors, each and every time. Tony was bad news.

In contrast, it was not uncommon on warm Sunday afternoons to see Mickey Quinn, the great ape keeper at the Bronx Zoo, enjoying a moment of companionship with one of his charges. Mickey was a tiny man with silver-gray hair that lay in matted wisps under his keeper's hat, which he always wore. Mickey was short, thin as a rail, and probably weighed less than 120 pounds soaking wet. He and Oka, the big lowland gorilla, were as close to being in love as members of two different species could be. Oka trusted Mickey, was always willing to accept the treats he had for her, and knew the sound of his cajoling voice. On Sunday afternoon, when Oka would be let out into the yard, she would sit on one of the concrete steps in the exhibit with one hand propped against her cheek, as though pondering a deep thought. Mickey might then emerge from the doorway of her indoor exhibit and come into the yard with her. Sometimes he would have spoonfuls of canned fruit to feed her. Mickey would then sit in Oka's lap, dwarfed by her great size and huge hands. Sometimes she would preen his hair, grooming him as if he were her child or family member. In truth, he had become her family.

The old switchboard at the Bronx Zoo, with its octopus of plugs and cables that connected the many buildings of the zoo with each other and the outside world, was a natural place to locate the nerve center of the zoo's first emergency alert system. An animal escape, a snakebite at the Reptile House, a fire, or any other emergency would be signaled by pushing a button at the facility involved, which would then turn on an appropriate indicator light at the switchboard. The switchboard operator was then to call the facility, ask about the problem, and then notify whoever was needed to go to the site and coordinate the response.

The Reptile House was the closest building to the Great Apes House, so it wasn't surprising that the reptile keepers might be the first on the scene to respond to an emergency there. Late afternoon one day, just about closing time, the phone rang. It was Winnie, the switchboard operator. "Oh, Pete," she said, "the great apes building alarm just came on. I called but no one answers. Can you go over and look to see what's going on?" "Okay," I said and, commandeering another keeper, ran across the path to the great apes building, where a small group of mammal keepers were gesturing and peering down toward the basement holding area.

The building was a circular affair, with a central entrance door to the public viewing area. Inside, a round center hall was surrounded by exhibits, which corresponded to outdoor exhibits flanking the perimeter of the building. Two ramps led down to the rooms below from each side of the public entrance door and to a horseshoe-shaped passageway, which accessed the exhibit and holding cages for the gorillas, orangutans, and other primates. In other words, any animal could be let directly out of its indoor exhibit cage, through a sliding doorway, into its outdoor yard. The keeper could then access the exhibit from the rear passageway with his hose and cleaning equipment. The building was new and innovative in structure and, like most zoo exhibits of the day (and sometimes even now), had been designed and built by architects and engineers who had no inkling of the capabilities of the animals the exhibits would contain.

Two things came together this day, and were quickly seized upon as an opportunity for fun by a young adult orangutan that I'll call Andy. One was the keeper's haste to finish the day's chores and go home. The second was Andy's ability to calculate the keeper's next move. Before going home, the keeper had to call the animal to the sliding rear access door of the cage and, through the bars of the closed door, drip vitamins into its extended, willing lip. Andy, however, had quickly learned to tauntingly hold back, forcing the keeper to work to reach his lips. It had become an annoying game of wits.

I always maintain that the keepers who care for animals have to be at least as smart or smarter than the animals they are trying to take care of and keep in captivity. That is not an easy balance to strike when dealing with nonhuman primates. The primates have the edge. They have all the time in the world to figure out what the keeper's schedule is. Keepers' schedules are usually highly regimented, dictated by fixed operating routines and times. This fits nicely into a smart animal's ability to plot.

Pretty soon, the keeper learned that the chore was easier to accomplish if he opened the sliding door a few inches, having first prevented it from being pulled open all the way by placing a precut wooden block of precisely the right length in the door's track. Put the block in the track, call Andy over with a few words of encouragement, unlock the door, slide it back as far as the block would allow, dispense the vitamins, slide the door back into place, and lock it. This day, and perhaps as had been done and noticed by the animal before, the keeper absentmindedly reversed the order, unlocking the door first, then placing the block. As the lock snapped open, Andy was ready. He simply opened the door first, to face the astonished keeper "man" to man. The keeper wisely ran.

A full-grown orangutan, Andy had the ability to inflict serious injury. The keeper, reaching the end of the horseshoe passage, had the good sense to go through and lock the entrance safety gate behind him, then close and lock the gate on the opposite entrance. Andy had been hot on his heels all the time. The ends of the horseshoe were now closed, with Andy contained within the keepers' passage. However, this same passageway also held the kitchen, where the great apes' foods were prepared and all sorts of succulent fruits and vegetables were stored; the lavatory; the furnace room; the concrete and steel stairs to the upstairs area; the keepers' lunchroom; and the lockers.

As his cagemates cheered him on with a cacophony of whoops and hoots, Andy exercised his triumph over his inferior human brothers. First, to the kitchen. Bananas and oranges were bitten a few times, then thrown aside in defiance. After all, the bounty was all around. The stainless steel refrigerator would not open to expose whatever smelled so good inside, as one sniff at the door seal told him. Instead, he raised the entire refrigerator over his head and threw it to the floor. Eggs, milk, and an assortment of other goodies spilled out. Next came the lockers. Ripping open the doors, he pulled out keepers' uniforms that must have smelled exquisitely of sweat and tore them into strips. It was wonderful, wearing a shirt or trousers draped like a flag over his head.

Hearing all of us keepers, collected in front of the locked safety gate at one end of the passage, he raced to see us, not in anger or fear but in sheer fun. The great apes' keeper, seizing the opportunity that having Andy occupied at one end of the passage presented, entered the other gate to rescue his spare uniforms. Hearing these new sounds, Andy raced back toward him, while the keeper ran for it, retreating again to the gate door, the other keepers cheering him on to run faster.

Andy decided there was more booty to be had. Spotting some cases of canned evaporated milk, Andy tore open the case and, holding an armful of cans, bit into each one in turn and slurped out the sweet milk. Back in the keeper went, during Andy's distraction; there were more uniforms to save. But no. Before he got far, Andy was racing to greet him. Thinking he could not make the safety of the gate, the keeper darted into the men's lavatory and closed the door. The other keepers yelled, "No, no—he's already been in there and the lock is broken." In an instant, the keeper reevaluated his choice of a hiding spot and sprinted back out of the lavatory and through the safety gate we now held open a crack, just as the whooping Andy reached the gate.

Andy was beginning to tire of the sport and of having had too much to eat. One last chore had to be accomplished. He tore the steel stairway from its moorings and threw it at us, then proceeded to rip the plumbing from the furnace. At last the veterinarian arrived, armed with a tranquilizer gun, having been called back to the zoo after returning home. The gun was speedily loaded, and Andy's but-

sive. The snake had been born at the zoo and had grown steadily over the past several years. Mambas can reach eight feet in two years. We didn't really know how long our mamba was, because no one had ever dared to remove it from its cage. But we knew it was big.

Our veterinarian suggested that we seal off the ventilation system of the cage, a rather large enclosure six feet high and seven feet deep, then spill into it several bottles of a liquid drug that would vaporize into an anesthetizing gas. It sounded like a good idea, although we never checked with the snake to see what it thought about the plan. Three bottles of the drug, enough to anesthetize half of the animals in the zoo, were slowly poured onto a corner of the cage floor, as the snake looked on from its branch at the top of the cage. Then we waited, and waited, and waited. The snake looked fine. However, all four of us in the rear passage began to suffer from blurred vision and dizziness. The fumes were anesthetizing us rather than the snake. Scratch that idea, we thought, deciding to leave the snake alone for the rest of the day.

The next day we decided to try the straightforward method of reaching in with a long-handled snake hook and lifting the snake out of the cage and into a large plastic barrel lined with an oversized cloth bag. Once the snake was inside the bag within the barrel, we could draw the mouth of the bag closed. It sounded like a good idea; but then again, so had using the anesthesia.

I opened the cage door as the mamba looked on. Slowly, and ever so gently, I reached in with the long pole, slipped the iron hook at the end under a coil of the snake's body, and lifted. I began to believe that this could be easy. The snake, balancing at the end of my pole, seemed content to enjoy the ride as I drew it out of its cage. But the flaw in this plan soon became apparent. The snake was so long that it could keep its tail on the ground and still have half of its body draped on the hook . . . with enough of its length free that it could easily reach me with its head if it so desired. It was I who was trapped, not the snake. I could not lift the snake higher to move it either in or out of its cage, nor could I put it down. I tingled as the snake turned to look at me, its mouth slightly open, threateningly ex-

tock momentarily presented a clear target through the bars of the gate. Andy jumped in surprise at the prick of the dart as it discharged its fluids into his rear end. He quickly plucked the offending instrument out, but it was already too late. Andy's steps began to falter as drowsiness overtook him. Within twenty minutes, we were carrying the snoozing but contentedly full Andy back to his cage and a fresh new bed of straw. Andy weighed only about 125 pounds. He would have a hangover the next morning.

9

SOME ANIMALS ARE SPECIAL

There have been many animals over the years that I've remembered for one quality or another. Some I remember because they came into my life during my years as a young, impressionable keeper, just learning about animals. Unquestionably, other animals stick in my mind because of the fear they instilled in me when I had to work with them. Junior the king cobra was one such animal. He was magnificent. But it isn't the perfection of his olive-drab body that I see when I think of him. It's the feeling I got when I had to work with him in his cage. My mouth would become dry, my heartbeat would increase, and then there would be that strange weakness in my knees, a feeling universally associated with doing something inherently dangerous.

Junior, on the other hand, had absolutely no fear of me. And I knew it. Yet he was not aggressive unless he was inordinately disturbed. He would turn and look directly at me, as if to say, "Okay. Bother me one more time and I will have to deal with you in my own way." I learned from Junior that animals are to be respected and given their space, particularly dangerous ones.

Mambas always frightened the hell out of me. The mambas are related to the cobras and have some of the most potent venom. There are two green species, the green mamba of central and southern Africa and the western green mamba of West Africa. Both are at home in the green tropical foliage of treetops and bushes. A third species, the dark velvety green Jameson's mamba, occurs in central Africa and is particularly lovely. Last, there is the fearsome black mamba, also of central and southern Africa. Africans look upon all mambas with dread, and for good reason: all are deadly venomous.

Mambas are long and slender and can glide with astonishing speed over the roughest terrain or through the densest tangles of branches and underbrush. On the ground, they can reach speeds of seven miles per hour. That doesn't sound fast, but in dense brush it's a lot faster than a person can move. Large black mambas are reported to have bitten and killed several horses and riders. A colleague of mine told of seeing a large black mamba race down an embankment toward the car in which he was seated, as he waited for friends to return from a walk. The snake stopped short and reared up as it approached the vehicle. My friend suddenly found himself looking at the mamba face-to-face through the open car window. Fortunately, the mamba elected to go on its way rather than share the car with him.

The black mamba can reach fourteen feet in length. It gets its name not from its body color but from the black interior of its mouth. Mambas are nervous and sometimes aggressive. When irritated or threatened, a black mamba is like a tightly wound spring. It faces the threat with every nerve of its body tuned to one thing: striking out in a lashing fury. Its every muscle quivers with anticipation. Many bites to humans are delivered high on the body, even as high as the neck or face, and an attack may include several bites in succession. The short fangs are located so close to the front of the snout that even the slightest contact will imbed them and inject venom.

When the day came for us to remove the black mamba from its cage and place it in a cloth transporting bag so it could be shipped to a zoo that had a captive-breeding program, I was, at best, apprehen-

posing the inside of its black mouth. Its body quivered like a spring ready to be released. I was vulnerable, and the snake was in control.

The snake lunged, but not at me. It preferred to return to its cage rather than deal with our nonsense. In the blink of an eye, the huge snake left me standing bewildered and sweating, holding an empty snake hook. It slithered back to its branch at the top of its cage. It had given me a gift: I would spend the evening at home eating a warm supper. I would not be in the hospital, possibly dying from the bite of a black mamba.

Did we eventually capture the snake and send it on its way? Well, no and yes. Several weeks later, well after both the snake and I had recovered from our ordeals, I slipped the snake bag, its mouth propped open with a coat hanger, into the snake's cage one evening before we turned off the lights to leave for the night. The next morning, we found the mamba contentedly coiled, asleep, inside the bag. It was as easy as that, and I learned a valuable lesson: have patience, take advantage of an animal's natural inclinations, and let animals do what comes naturally. The snake had simply used the bag to hide in.

I will always remember Herman, a western diamondback rattlesnake. He was one of a kind. Jim Oliver had continued Raymond L. Ditmars's interest in photographing reptiles. Photographic technology, however, had advanced in the years since Ditmars's curatorship, and Oliver had embarked on a project to photograph animals in motion using new, ultra-high-speed photographic techniques. This allowed him to study exactly what was happening when animals did certain things too quickly for the human eye to see.

The first question he chose to study was how an African chameleon could extend its tongue and capture an insect so quickly. The tongue's contact with the insect had never been observed. Henry Lester, a well-known photographic researcher, was taken by this opportunity to put his new equipment to scientific use. Together, he and Oliver set up a photo table on the second floor of the Reptile House. By today's standards, the equipment was primitive. Two stands, containing dozens of large flashbulbs in a motorized revolving carousel, stood on each side of the table. The motion-picture camera would be set running and, because the action would have to be photographed in a continuous series of film frames over several seconds, the flash-bulbs would have to go off in a synchronized series at the same time. The trick was to get the animal to perform at precisely the same time that the camera was filming and the bulbs were going off.

After some good results with a chameleon, Oliver's interest turned to filming the action of a rattlesnake's strike, from start to finish. How it actually happened had never been seen before. We needed an "actor" rattlesnake that would be willing to strike on cue. Everyone knew that rattlesnakes bit people all the time, and stories of the irritable nature of western diamondback rattlesnakes were common. Besides, a rattlesnake dealer in Texas had guaranteed us that Texas rattlesnakes were the meanest, nastiest, orneriest, most ill-tempered snakes anywhere in the world.

The first shipment of twenty buzzing, rattling rattlesnakes arrived by what was then the only way to ship snakes, Railway Express. The snakes ranged in size from two feet long to more than five feet. They coiled and arched their bodies upward in an S-curved position, ready to strike at the least provocation. Twenty tongues slowly flicked in and out of twenty rattlesnake mouths, testing the air to detect what was going on. My job, as rattlesnake keeper, was not only to care for the snakes but also to threaten each snake individually with a square red sponge-rubber pad, fitted to the end of a pole, to get the snake to strike the pad while the camera and lights were in motion.

The first snake was set on the table in front of the camera, rattling and coiled. I thrust the padded pole toward its face to elicit a strike. The camera whirred and fifty flashbulbs burst into blinding light. The snake responded: it hid its head under its coils. It wouldn't strike. We replaced fifty burned-out flashbulbs and selected a second rattlesnake. The camera whirred and the bulbs flashed. The snake raced off the table and fled in fear. Again the bulbs and film were replaced. The third snake, too, hid its head and refused to strike. Twenty snakes later, Oliver still had not gotten the footage he wanted.

There was another call to the Texan, and another twenty snakes arrived. The results were the same—the rattlesnakes were cowards, and the mountain of wasted film and burned-out flashbulbs was growing rapidly. We began to wonder if our Texan dealer was selecting the wimpiest snakes to keep our orders coming.

Finally, after nearly two hundred rattling rattlesnakes had taken their turns in the limelight, Herman arrived. Herman was a fat diamondback over five feet long. Not only did he rattle incessantly at every footstep anywhere near his cage, but he struck even when there was no chance he could reach anyone. Herman was upholding the tradition of a mean Texan rattlesnake.

On the very first try, Herman gave us the first rattlesnake strike ever recorded in slow motion on film. As he reared back at the approach of the pad, he tensed his body. Then his strike began, his jaws opening, his inch-and-a-half-long fangs unfolding as his head continued toward the target. By the time Herman was three-quarters of the way to the target, his fangs aimed straight ahead. Venom began to spew from their tips an instant before the fangs, like stabbing daggers, penetrated the rubber. As the fangs plunged in, the lower jaw came up to grasp the rubber and help muscles to compress the venom glands at the base of his head to inject more venom. Then came the release, and the snake retracted back to his original striking position. It all happened in a blur, too fast for any of us to see. Herman became famous. However, he was the only snake among hundreds ill-tempered enough to bite. I wondered how many people had escaped being bitten when they'd encountered a rattlesnake in the wild because the snake was more willing to hide than to bite.

I'll never forget the biggest lizards I ever saw. Jim Oliver purchased two adult Komodo dragons, the largest species of monitor lizard in the world, from the Jakarta Zoo in Indonesia. They would be a spectacular public attraction, to say the least. The day they arrived became legend at the zoo. Each lizard was housed in a crate made from tropical hardwood trees. The ten-foot-long, two-hundred-pound male and the slightly smaller female lumbered into their new exhibit looking like prehistoric monsters. Each had a head ten inches long, with rows of flat, razor-sharp teeth that could cut through flesh. Strings of slimy, thick saliva stretched from upper to lower jaw as the animals opened their mouths to allow their twelve-inch-long, pale yellow, forked tongues to lick their own faces. Stout, muscular legs supported the body on feet with two-inch-long recurved claws, attached to thick, strong toes. The animals were so powerful that they carried the entire length of their thick, five-foot-long tails completely off the ground as they walked. Encased in a body armor of thick, beaded scales, the lizards were anyone's nightmare. But they were gentle.

We would enter their cage during the day, to the delight of visitors, and hand-feed each lizard a dozen whole chicken eggs from a soup ladle. Sometimes I would prepare the eggs in the keepers' area outside their cage door. As I did so, the lizards would sense the eggs from inside the cage, and soon two yellow forked tongues would appear through the space under the door, reach into the room, and flick this way and that in an effort to tell if the egg meal was really on its way. In many ways, they acted more like big dogs than giant lizards. Every couple of weeks, when their nails grew too long, the lizards would allow us to lift each of their feet and, toe by toe, perform a manicure.

Komodo dragons were barely studied in the wild on their native islands in Indonesia. They hunted and killed pigs, and were not fussy about eating a rotten carcass if they found one. People said that a bite from one of these animals could be as deadly as the bite of a venomous snake. The flat, serrated, curved teeth could slice flesh to ribbons, and the host of bacteria that lived in the mouths of the animals caused massive infections that were all but impossible to cure with the limited drugs of the day.

Despite their gentle nature in captivity, we soon learned that they were still capable of inflicting injury. One day, Jim Oliver asked Sam Dunton, the staff photographer, to shoot some pictures of the Komodos in their cage. As Sam stood with one foot up on a rock for balance and focused his camera on the female lizard, the curious male lizard approached him. Interested in this new human, the two-hundred-pound lizard reached up with its clawed foot, stepping onto Sam's thigh. The weight of the animal and the sharpness of its claws combined to slice Sam's thigh muscle into five ribbons of flesh, cut bone deep. Blood spurted everywhere. We tied a rag tourniquet around his thigh, and Sam survived the encounter, but only after several hundred sutures to close the wound. To the lizard, it had only been a friendly gesture.

The only time I ever encountered aggression from the lizards was the day I decided to take some pictures with my new thirty-five-millimeter camera. I had forgotten the first cardinal rule about reptiles: never smell like the things they eat. I had just prepared a lizard's meal of freshly killed chicken from the local poultry market, and the smell lingered on my clothing.

The two lizards lay placidly, as though asleep, on a wooden platform in the center of their cage. As I entered with the camera, they instantly became alert. Their tongues flicked rapidly in and out of their mouths as they caught the scent of the chicken on my clothes. In a second, they were racing toward me. I moved as quickly as they did, looking for a place to run to. Who was I kidding? We were in a cage. "They think I'm a chicken," I thought, as visions of being dismembered like a chicken came to mind. I knew I needed to divert their attention if I were to get out of the cage in one piece. Holding my new camera out at arm's length by its strap, I waded through the exhibit pool, the only escape route, leading the dragons toward the door. I got away, but not without sacrificing my camera to the indignity of being chewed to pieces by an overgrown lizard. Better the camera than me.

10

CROCODILES ARE MY FAVORITE BIRDS

As I entered the rear door of the Reptile House, something in the corner of my eye attracted my attention. Laurie, a new reptile keeper, was kneeling at an opening that separated a crocodile nesting area from the main pool. She was attempting to retrieve, out of the pool, some food that the pair of Siamese crocodiles that inhabited the exhibit had left uneaten. The act seemed harmless enough. It wasn't.

Unknowingly, she was kneeling on a slight mound of sand that had buried in it more than a dozen white-shelled crocodile eggs. She was kneeling directly on top of the crocodile's nest. I knew what was about to happen. Quietly, I looked for something that could be used to hold off an angry crocodile. There was no time; I grabbed a broomstick that stood nearby, entered the nesting area, and knelt down beside Laurie. "Don't ask, just back out of here," I whispered.

It was too late. Suddenly the head of the six-foot-long female crocodile surfaced at the edge of the door between us, mouth open, ready to attack. I yanked Laurie backward by her belt as the crocodile lunged through the opening. On my side in the sand, I held the snapping crocodile against a wall with the broomstick and scrambled to regain my footing. In an instant, it was over; I darted through the access door, and Laurie slammed it shut behind me. We both trembled a little, trying to make believe that nothing much had taken place. We had both been very lucky. The crocodiles were acting just like birds.

Crocodilians and birds share many similarities. It is easy to understand why, as both birds and crocodilians share the same archosaur ancestry, dating back to the late Triassic period, nearly 225 million years ago. The maternal behavior of crocodilians is incredibly similar to that of birds. Like birds, female crocodilians select a suitable place to lay their eggs and build a nest. Some species build a nest of mounded up twigs, mud, and aquatic vegetation or certain kinds of marsh grasses. Others dig a hole in a sandbank and lay their eggs in it, then cover it up to conceal it from predators. Like birds, the female continually attends the nest. She removes material when the nest needs to cool, piles more material on it to increase its warmth, and drips water and urine on it to keep the nesting material damp to stimulate the fermentation of the nesting material, which is where it gets its warmth. In fact, like a bird with an attitude, even an otherwise placid female crocodilian becomes a protector the moment she finishes laying her eggs. Maternal hormones are powerful in their ability to change a crocodile from an animal that kills only to eat into one that is ready to kill or be killed in the defense of her nest and young.

Laurie, by kneeling on the Siamese crocodile's nest, inadvertently became the target of the female's protective attack. People have been badly injured or killed when they innocently came upon the nest or baby of an alligator or crocodile. The male parent often remains in the vicinity as well, and may also be protective, unless he is busy courting other females in his territory.

Crocodilian eggs incubate for between two and three months, at a narrow temperature range—depending on the species, usually between eighty-five and ninety-two degrees Fahrenheit. The sex of the developing embryos depends not on sex chromosomes, as it does for us, but on the nest temperature. If the eggs are too warm, mostly males will hatch; if it's too cool, there will be more females. Once laid in the nest, the eggs are never turned by the parent. To do so would tear the embryo from its moorings inside the egg and kill it.

Birds are different. Most turn their eggs during incubation. But not all birds do. In Australia and Malaysia, a whole group of chicken-sized birds, the megapodes—also known as mound builders—do just as the crocodilians do: build a mound of sand and let natural heat incubate their eggs, piling up more sand or removing some as the nest requires.

But some crocodilians do it even better. The smooth-fronted caiman lives in the deep Amazonian rain forest, where sunlight doesn't reach the ground to warm a nest. So the caiman borrows some heat by building its nest around a termite mound, because termites use fermentation inside their nest to create heat. That's creativity.

The similarity doesn't end with nesting. Baby birds may start calling to be fed when they hatch. Once the chicks hatch, the parents protect the nest and feed the babies until they are big enough to fly away on their own. Crocodilians go birds one better here, too. When the baby crocodilians are ready to hatch, they call from inside the egg. Mother crocodilians may help break open the eggs to release the hatchlings, then carry them to the nearby water, where both the mother and the father will protect the babies for up to a year, allowing the babies to rest on their heads or backs for protection.

Myrna, my wife, spent years studying the maternal behavior of the American alligator. She found that when attacked by a predator, baby alligators produce a high-pitched distress call—just like chicken chicks do when they are being carried away by predators. Upon hearing the call, any adult alligator, whether or not it is the parent, will immediately attack the intruder to protect the babies. Myrna and I were analyzing some baby alligator distress calls one day at the Smithsonian Institution when in walked a noted bird behaviorist. Looking at the sonographic analysis of the calls, he began to explain the composition of these typical "bird alarm calls." He was astounded when we relayed that the recordings were not of birds at all, but of alligators.

Myrna and I had a relatively benign experience with an alligator mother one night. We were visiting our friends Ted Joanen and Larry McNease, managers of the Rockefeller Wildlife Refuge on the coast of Louisiana, so we could watch alligators, of course. Earlier in the day, we had gone in the bayou and had seen a mother alligator with several youngsters that had been born the year before, as well as a new clutch of recently hatched youngsters. It was in a cul-de-sac in the canal and was clearly her personal territory.

That night, we returned to the bayou with a flat-bottomed aluminum boat and powerful headlamps, to watch the alligators as they swam up and down the canal; we could see them by the light reflected by their eyes. Then, in the distance, down the canal, we caught a glimpse of a white wake in the water, headed directly toward us at high speed.

We were sure it was the mother alligator. We were between her and where she had left her babies in the shallow water when she had gone off to hunt for food. She was in full throttle. We turned the front of the boat in her direction, so that she would not attack it broadside. As she got to the boat she dove straight underneath it. The boat heaved and jostled as she slid past, her back scales scraping the bottom of the boat. We held on to the sides, hoping the boat would not capsize, dropping us into the water in the dark of night among nearly a dozen feeding adult alligators and one very ticked off mama. Just then a snapping alligator garfish, which in itself can be quite dangerous, jumped into the boat with us, landing in front of Myrna; she screamed. In the darkness, and the dim beams of our headlamps, we were sure it was the alligator coming into the boat after us. Dozens of other fish followed, leaping into the boat faster than we could throw them back into the water. As she had passed under the boat, the mother alligator had frightened them as much as she had us. In all probability, the mother alligator was only trying to get back to protect her babies.

Birds and crocodilians don't look alike, you may say. Well, yes and no. In composition, birds' feathers, beaks, and claws are made from the same type of protein, called keratin, as a crocodilian's scales. And if you have ever looked carefully at a bird's feet and legs, you will have noticed that they are covered with scales that look surprisingly like those on crocodilians. It doesn't end there, either; both crocodilians and birds have a common opening for copulation and excreting bodily wastes, called a cloaca.

One thing crocodilians can do that birds can't do is make change. Crocodilians eat hard objects, such as stones, bits of glass, and tree knots; they keep these in their stomach. People used to think that, like the grit-filled bird crop, which pulverizes the hard grains birds eat, the hard objects help the crocodile grind up its food. I found that theory hard to believe, since crocodilians eat meat and bone, and their digestive juices would dissolve the tires off a car if they could eat it. No one really had the answer. However, a scientist named Dr. Hugh Cott, who studied Nile crocodiles in Africa, found that it didn't matter if the crocodiles came from a place that had stones or not. At a certain size, all Nile crocodiles in his study had the same amount of stones: about 1 percent of their body weight. He speculated that the stones served as a kind of ballast and changed the crocodile's specific gravity in water, thus helping it dive. I did not believe that either. Crocodiles, I speculated, picked up the stones for a reason—but this reason was unknown.

When three baby Indian marsh crocodiles arrived at the Reptile House, it provided a perfect opportunity to see if they really needed to eat stones as ballast. First, we separated the crocodiles and put each into large tanks without any stones, then we X-rayed the animals to be sure they hadn't brought any stones with them. Next, I took a handful of stones, weighed them, marked each stone, and put them in with the crocodiles. That night, they ate the right amount of stones for their weight. We could see the stones perfectly in X-rays of their stomachs. No more stones were provided as the crocodiles grew. Finally, the time came, nearly a year after the crocodile's arrival, when it was presumed, from Cott's study, that one of the crocodiles, which had grown the most, would need more stones. The next batch of stones was, however, going to be special. The stones were of such weights that the crocodile could not eat them and still have inside its stomach the stones it had already eaten—not without varying significantly from that 1 percent figure. The next morning, not only had the right weight in new stones been eaten, but the crocodile had regurgitated some of the old stones. The crocodile had made change. Let's see a bird do that.

Over the years, I spent a lot of time with crocodilians. I've traveled for hours with alligators or caiman in the back of a station wagon, on the way to delivering them to the National Zoo in Washington, D.C., or to Louisiana. They make good riders and don't even snore. Old Pop, the change-making marsh crocodile, grew to be a ten-foot-long giant. Years after he left the Reptile House to be exhibited in the new Jungle Building at the far side of the zoo, I would go to the railing overlooking his exhibit and call, "Pop." Slowly his eyes would open from his sleep. At my second call, he would lie motionless for a moment. At the third call of "Pop," he would get up and walk directly to the railing where I called from, standing among dozens of other people. He knew his name and, years ago, responding to it always brought with it a reward of a fresh rat.

Crocodilians know where they live. One morning, we arrived at the Reptile House to find that nearly the entire group of adult crocodiles had left their pool during the night through a poorly latched door and now sat dreamily sleeping in the warm plant conservatory that surrounded the rear of the pool. "How will we ever get them back?" we wondered. At that time, Old Pop still shared the pool with about a dozen other animals. "Come on, Pop. Let's go," I shouted. To my amazement, all of the crocodiles got up and walked back through the open gate and into their pool. Today, like so many other animals, crocodilians are trained so they can enter a shipping box to be transported, receive medical treatment, or just be moved to another pool. It is no wonder crocodilians find people such easy prey; they outsmart us.

Most crocodilian-related accidents happen when people begin to feed them at a certain place, such as a fish-cleaning station on a lake or canal. The accident occurs when the human gets drunk and teases the crocodilian, or decides to go swimming in the evening at the same feeding place while the crocodilian is out hunting for food. In many of these cases, the crocodilian spits out the distasteful person—often too late, as the person may already have drowned. One victim drank a little too much and decided to punch a slowly swimming alligator in the mouth. The alligator won.

During my research visits to Palau, a small island country in the western Pacific, I learned that although a number of attacks by large crocodiles had occurred before 1928, in over thirty-five years, there had been only two attacks by saltwater crocodiles. These twenty-foot-long giants are the largest and most dangerous of the crocodilians. In 1965 a man who had been spearfishing at the edge of a mangrove swamp at night was seized by the shoulder in neck-deep waters. Unfortunately, he was killed. I was told that in the second case, a man fishing at dusk carried a bag of freshly caught fish strung around his neck. The man was seriously injured when he was seized by his rubber diver's face mask, then released by the crocodile. What self-respecting crocodile could resist such a feast? Many people are not so lucky, especially in Africa, where human corpses may become food for crocodiles, and lack of game makes the crocodiles more willing to take prey they would not normally be interested in.

Australia and New Guinea also have their share of saltwater crocodile attacks. However, these are rare, usually localized occurrences involving a single rogue crocodile. The majority of the twenty-three species of crocodilians that live in the tropical and subtropical regions of the world pose no special threat to people. Rather, crocodiles learn to fear and avoid people, since we are a threat to them.

My years of working with crocodilians came back to me in a rush several years ago. I had recently retired from the Central Park Zoo but was continuing my research and collaborations with the reptile department in the Bronx, where I had spent most of the best years of my career. The day after Christmas, my son and I went to the zoo on an errand. As we passed the front doors of the Reptile House, we noticed that it was closed. In all of my years at the Reptile House, it had rarely been closed, and then only for dire emergencies. This was particularly unusual for the busy season between Christmas and New Year's Day.

We cautiously entered by the rear door, only to have the handyman tell us, "The crocodiles are loose. Run. Run." Peter was about thirteen years old, and I was already pushing sixty-three. As we approached the crocodile enclosures, we saw that a cluster of veterinarians and administrative curators were watching as the keepers inside the exhibit battled to keep six hostile Cuban crocodiles separated from an equally ill-tempered twelve-foot-long Malayan false gharial, a slender-snouted crocodilian related to the long-snouted gavial of India. It was a toss-up as to who would tear whom to pieces.

It was a good old-fashioned crocodile fight, I thought, just like in the old days. The keepers, seeing me through the glass at the front of the exhibit, motioned for me to come inside and take over. I did; it was exciting, and it was my kind of fun. The object was to separate the Cuban crocodiles, one by one, using long poles and a stream of water from a hose, and drive them into a side holding pool. Crocodilians do not like water directed at their faces, and so they usually close their eyes and walk away. The technique was not going to work so easily this time, however, as each time one animal moved, several others raced to get away from it, usually up onto the rocks where we stood. They were more afraid of one another than of us. That did not make us feel any better, for each time a crocodile raced up between our legs, we had to quickly fend it off to keep from being bitten by its crushing jaws.

Finally, after about an hour of battle, the Cuban crocodiles were safely separated, leaving the monarch Malayan gharial alone in the pool. I was spent. The Reptile House temperature hovered at a humid eighty-five degrees Fahrenheit, and in the excitement I had neglected to remove my warm sweatshirt, worn over a thick woolen shirt. Sweat poured down my face. However, tears were streaming down Peter's face. As we left the building, I asked him why he was crying. He said, "One of the men"—he meant a curator—"said to the lady"— a veterinarian—"What do we do if the old guy"—me—"has a heart attack and drops dead?"

I laughed. I had never felt better in my life. Besides, we were only doing battle with a bunch of chickens.

11

ANNUAL MEETING

Each year, the members of the New York Zoological Society look forward to an annual meeting that truly follows in the traditions of the society's founders. From its earliest days, and for many years thereafter, "annual meeting," as the staff of the society referred to it, grew in scope and importance from a simple annual report to a gala event. More than just a presentation by the executive heads of a non-profit society to its membership, the annual meeting was a social event that was reported in the society pages of all of New York's major newspapers.

By 1954, the annual meeting had grown to a three-day affair held at the elegant and famous Waldorf-Astoria Hotel. There were after-noon matinees, evening performances of films, speeches and presentations by society staff and special celebrity guests, and elegant dinner parties where the cream of New York society, elegantly dressed in tuxedos, evening gowns, and fine jewelry, dined and danced well into the night for the benefit of the animals at the zoo. While partici-pating staff members were expected to dress in formal evening attire, keepers and other staffers were to remain somewhat invisible, wearing full dress uniforms, ties, and service caps. Eventually, the occasion was so well attended that the annual meeting was moved to the larger Avery Fisher Hall at Lincoln Center. Today, with a general democratization of the society, the annual meeting is open to any member of the public who joins the zoo as a member. Entire families may benefit from discounted admission to the zoos and aquarium, a zoo magazine subscription, entertainment, and educational events. Now filling the hall to capacity each year, the general members' portion of the annual meeting, however, continues only as a remnant of its former glory.

The annual meeting required months of preparation. Scheduled years in advance, the actual "meeting" was planned in the greatest of detail. Besides being a legal requirement of the New York Zoological Society's incorporation, this gala event was the single most important means by which the society displayed to its membership as a whole where and how their monies and donations were being spent. Between and after programs, important social events provided a special opportunity for generating new donations from wealthy patrons. It was *show-off* time.

Each year, the theme of the annual meeting was different, which meant that the props, labels, and films always had to be prepared anew. It seemed to be a requirement that each year's program outdo the previous year's. Once the meeting plan was set, carpenters and other artisans constructed elaborate portable exhibits that would hold live animals in natural settings for lobby displays that the members could enjoy before each performance. The sideshow of a sophisticated circus would not be much different. Each exhibit had to be built, inspected, and approved, then dismantled and reassembled on the day and in the place of the performances. The program itself included films and documentaries that highlighted the activities of the society and its staff throughout the world, presentations of special awards, and speeches by curatorial staff about the society and its work. For months before, it seemed as though the inner workings of the zoo suddenly ceased to function, as all priorities were superseded by the annual meeting.

To the animal-keeping staff, it was an exercise in making the impossible possible. Two adult sea lions could and did frolic in a pool in the lobby of the Waldorf-Astoria Hotel, followed by a herd of two-hundred- to four-hundred-pound giant Galápagos Island tortoises wandering through a forest of cacti. The day after the tortoises dined on a hundred-pound salad of fresh fruit and vegetables, including carrots, tomatoes, and bananas, the same spot might be occupied by a table of conference attendees from another organization, dining on their own salad of fresh vegetables. The difference was that the tortoises' fare was more nutritious, as it included the additions of multiple vitamin supplements and minerals—and the produce was higher quality.

The first captive breeding of a king cobra highlighted one year's events for the reptile department. So it wasn't a surprise when the director announced, "Wouldn't it be wonderful if we could bring the mother king cobra and her babies to the annual meeting this year, for the members to see?" We gasped. Mother was more than twelve feet long and had no interest in going to the annual meeting. Besides, although a mother king cobra constructs a nest and guards her eggs during the incubation period, she ignores her progeny once they've hatched. There would be little cute or endearing behavior to see. However, the offspring could be as deadly as their mother, and just as willing to deliver a potential bite to either a keeper or a velveteen-dressed patron, should the opportunity present itself.

Our cautious protestations aside, we were now directed to safely deliver an exhibit of king cobras to the fanciest hotel on Park Avenue. To make the display more realistic, the zoo acquired an expensive exhibit cage with special curved glass that became invisible when properly lighted. Not only would the members see a king cobra up close, but they also would not see anything separating them from the snakes.

Capturing the big venomous snake and getting it out of its cage at the zoo and into a large metal trash barrel for transport presented its own dangers. Traveling through the streets of midtown Manhattan with a king cobra and a dozen baby king cobras was also risky. We knew that we could predict the animals' behavior: mean, nasty, and aggressive. But who could predict the chaotic, erratic behavior of New York's taxi and bus drivers, or the consequences of a potential accident? What New York City police officer would accept "Don't worry about the accident—just let us take our king cobras and go to the Waldorf"? Besides, at the end of the final evening's events, and after the crowd of several thousand members left, we would then have to recapture the snakes and take them back to the Reptile House. Only this time, we would not be catching the snakes under the carefully controlled conditions at the Reptile House, but rather would be dealing with the animals in the lobby of a hotel, surrounded by curious hotel workers and our own mechanics.

As it turned out, at the conclusion of the show, the snake was as tired as we were after two days of being cramped in a cage that was just large enough for it to coil up in. The moment we showed her the dark opening of the mouth of a canvas transporting bag, the snake, instead of raising her hood in defense and threatening to attack, lunged for the hole and, in a blur of olive green, dived inside the bag, safely away from the annoyance of peering faces. The babies also went along docilely. It was anticlimactic, and a welcome end to the annual meeting.

Things did not always go so well. As the annual meeting was always held in early winter, we had to keep the snakes warm. The theme of one particular year was convergent evolution, or how animals from completely different regions of the world have evolved to look alike. Even though they are from different genera or even less closely related, both species evolved in the same type of environment, and therefore required the same adaptations, color, and behavioral patterns to survive. Our exhibit would contain emerald tree boas from South America and green tree pythons from Pacific Asia. Boas are from the Americas, while pythons live in Asia, Africa, Australia, and the Pacific Islands. While the python lays eggs, the boa gives birth to live young. Both emerald tree boas and green tree pythons look closely alike, in brilliant green with a white back stripe and crossbars. Both live in tropical treetops, and both animals coil on a branch in exactly the same way, with their heads pointing downward, their lips resting in the crook of their coils, which form a kind of natural basin. Rainwater collects in the crook of the coils, and the snake's head is then in a ready position to drink—all without the animal having to move an inch from its hidden resting place. The snakes are virtually invisible as their cryptic color patterns blend perfectly with the green leaves of their treetop surroundings.

Several hours before the exhibit would open, we prepared the snakes' enclosure with fresh leaves and branches. When it was ready, the head keeper decided we should all go to dinner, and he refilled the hot-water bottles that had served to keep the snakes warm as they were transported from the zoo to the hotel in the bitter cold winter. An hour later, we returned. The members would arrive imminently. To the horror of the head keeper, both of the snakes were dead. They had overheated. The hot-water bottles, which had worked so well at cold temperatures, had been lethal to the snakes in the warmer atmosphere of the hotel lobby. The head keeper now had the unenviable task of telling the curator that his and the curator's careers at the zoo might be about to end. We had an exhibit and a label, but no animals to show the members.

The solution was relatively simple, given my earlier expertise with stuffing the dead Texas horned toads and moving them around their cage to create the illusion that they were still alive. I coiled the dead snakes artfully in the exhibit, largely hidden by the leafy green fronds of the exhibit's plants. This would typify cryptic coloration at its best. Then I stood by proudly, answering the members' many questions, as the patrons and members oohed and aahed at the lovely natural display of snakes. My taxidermy skills had once more come to the rescue.

The following year called for the same vanishing-glass cage that we had used with the mother cobra. This time, a twenty-foot-long reticulated python was on exhibit. But unlike our experience with the king cobra, getting the python out of the display cage was a lot more difficult than getting it in. There simply was too little room for more than one person to grasp the powerful snake by the neck and overcome the twenty feet of writhing muscle. The snake had to be let loose on the lobby floor and captured quickly, before it made its way to the kitchen service area, where fresh chicken might be on the menu.

Eventually, the annual meeting moved to Avery Fisher Hall, and the original big python display gave rise to the notion that measuring a giant snake on the great stage would be a tremendous hit with the members. This soon became an annual event, with the members ecstatic that each year they could see and hear how much the snake had grown from the year before. Each year, a half dozen keepers would be fighting for their lives, wrestling on the floor, entangled in the coils of an angry python that was determined neither to make a spectacle of itself on the stage nor to be stretched out straight to be measured against its will. All of this would be going on just offstage as the zoo director announced, "Here comes the python."

Among the crowd in the front seats that year was Myrna, my wife-to-be, along with a group of friends and other staff members' wives. As dumb as I felt the performance was, I was somewhat pleased that I would no doubt have the opportunity to impress Myrna. However, when I got onstage I saw that a vacant seat existed where Myrna had once sat. During the entire episode, Myrna was in the ladies' room. It seems that the woman behind her had vomited all over Myrna's sweater, and Myrna missed the whole thing. Another year, I stuck a green plastic Monopoly house on top of my balding head, then went out to measure the snake. Myrna nearly fell out of her seat laughing, although to everyone else in the audience, it just looked like a green dot.

Labor rules at Lincoln Center dictated that only union stagehands could carry props and other items from the loading dock to the stage area. However, when we announced that we had no objection to union labor carrying our bags and boxes of snakes, a slight modification in the rules was quickly put into place. We could indeed carry our own snakes, the union ruled, as long as a union stagehand walked beside us.

As if measuring a giant python on the great stage was not amusing enough, some public relations genius decided that we should also measure a giant crocodile. We chose a ten-foot-long, two-hundred-pound crocodile for the event. With its jaws securely taped shut, the crocodile let us easily lift it from its shipping box and position it in the wings offstage without anything more than a minor twitch of defiance. While a half dozen keepers tightly held the crocodile securely against their bodies, the signal was given, and we headed out onto the great stage. As we walked in lockstep in front of a packed audience, the crocodile suddenly came to life, giving a violent thrash of its body and powerful tail that nearly carried all of us off the stage and into the first rows of the audience. Again it thrashed, and again, and each time we weaved toward the edge of the stage as the audience gasped. Fortunately, we managed to keep our grip on the animal and maintain some degree of control. We lowered the crocodile onto the floor of the stage and, as quickly as possible, measured it. For the return trip, I called for the animal's shipping box to be brought out onto the stage, to the animal, rather than risk vacating the first few rows of the audience in favor of a crocodile. The annual meeting always seemed to end with a story to tell, and not always from the reptile keeper. One time, the mammal department temporarily lost their binturong at the Waldorf-Astoria, when the thirty-pound bearlike carnivore from Southeast Asia climbed up its branch and out over the top of its exhibit. It was recaptured and deprived of a night in a hotel room.

But not all of the excitement took place during the meeting; some of it happened afterward. One year, a number of things had not gone well, and we were all tired and rather ill-tempered. As was usually the case, after putting in a full day at the Reptile House, the entire staff of the Reptile House would then have to work at the meeting. The afternoon performance was followed by the late-ending evening performance, after which the exhibits had to be dismantled and the animals returned to the Reptile House. The wives of the keepers would usually attend the late performance, see the show and the exhibits, and return with us to the zoo in one of our own vehicles. This night, although our wives left to retrieve the cars from the parking lot, they failed to arrive at the Reptile House, even after we did. Concerned for their safety, we now had to travel back to Manhattan from

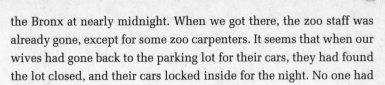

the Bronx at nearly midnight. When we got there, the zoo staff was already gone, except for some zoo carpenters. It seems that when our wives had gone back to the parking lot for their cars, they had found the lot closed, and their cars locked inside for the night. No one had noticed the sign that gave the lot's closing hours.

Unable to get back to the zoo at that late hour, the wives were directed by the carpenters to a room set aside for zoo staff members at a nearby cheap hotel. There they waited for us to figure out what had happened. They then joined a celebration party, honoring the end of the annual meeting and the extra work and overtime pay it brought with it. As we entered the lobby—a half dozen men dressed in official-looking uniforms—the clerk behind the counter, thinking the worst, dove under the desk and frantically called out the room number. He obviously thought we were a group of irate boyfriends or off-duty policemen coming to reclaim our errant wives from a hotel-room party.

Sometime after 2:00 A.M. we were collectively packed into the empty zoo van and headed once again to the Bronx, all in a fairly foul mood. One of the newer keepers, whom I'll call Dan, and his wife suggested that we should temper our hostilities and prepare for work the following day by coming to their Bronx apartment for a glass of wine. It seemed like a good idea, and soon we arrived at their sixth-floor apartment in a typical Bronx tenement. Before long we were all sitting on the floor talking and apologizing to one another for the mistakes we all had made.

Suddenly there was the sound of breaking glass, and the curtains flew from the adjacent bedroom window. A huge man in a black rubber coat with yellow bands, armed with an axe, stuck his helmeted head through what had once been the window. Close behind followed another rubber-coated apparition. From the kitchen, a loud *bang* came as the hall door was pulled off its hinges. Another rubber-coated apparition entered behind the shattered opening.

It was the New York City Fire Department, coming to rescue us. The street, six floors below, was filled with fire trucks, ladders, hoses, and police cars, their lights flashing red and blinding white in the night as people from nearby tenements filled the narrow street to watch the firemen climb the iron fire escape to the apartment where we now sat in total shock. Dan, still holding a half-filled glass of wine, suggested to the firefighter in the window that there were easier ways to stop by for a drink, such as knocking on the door. The firefighter appeared as stunned as we were.

Looking around the bedroom, he quickly seized on the cause for their intrusion. Dan and his wife had begun to assemble furniture and furnishings in anticipation of the arrival of their first child. One of the furnishings, a small table lamp with a rotating carousel-patterned shade, stood on the dresser top. As the carousel turned, the light cast flashing images of red and yellow tongues of color onto the bedroom wall, partly visible through the curtained bedroom window. People in the tenement apartment in the building across the street had mistaken the dancing colored lights for the flickering of flames, and had called the fire department. Not to be totally without purpose, as one of the firefighters turned to leave through the splintered doorway, he politely asked, "Sir, could you please extinguish that bedroom light?" Dan simply said, "Sure, no problem." It was an annual meeting to remember.

But that was not the annual meeting that I recall as one of the worst moments of my professional life to date. It was my first year as a curator of animals at the Central Park Wildlife Center, and the first time I was expected to deliver a ten-minute presentation on the great stage at Avery Fisher Hall. My talk would be about the illegal skin trade, conservation, and my forensic work with the Wildlife Conservation Society. I was expected to deliver my message flawlessly, supported by a series of slides that would be projected on the giant screen behind me. For weeks, I prepared my script, and I made several practice presentations before other zoo staffers and the general director, knowing that my life would be at stake if I failed to perform to the standards set by society speakers at a hundred annual meetings before.

Finally the night of the meeting came. I stood in line in the wings of the great stage, dressed in my new tuxedo, cummerbund, black bow tie, and black wing-tip shoes, waiting for my turn to step out in front of a filled-to-capacity house of nearly five thousand people. I could feel the sweat trickling down my back, inside my shirt. The stage manager held my arm as he spoke through the microphone on his headset to the technician in the projection booth at the rear of the great hall. The slides had to be in complete synchronization with my talk, controlled by the projectionist in the booth, which was barely discernible as a pinpoint of light at the rear of the hall.

As the speaker who preceded me left the stage, I braced to follow him at the podium, waiting for the stage manager to release my arm. Instead, his grasp tightened, and he hissed into the microphone at his lips: "What did you say? The slides are out of sync? They fell out of the tray? What the hell do I do now—send him out anyway, or what?" Then, as if responding to some whispered command, he said, "Go ahead" and thrust me into the limelight. I now understood how the Christians felt as they were hurled to the lions in the Colosseum.

I stood alone at the podium, before an audience that expected profound science and perfection. The world-class artists who had performed on that very same stage, some of them perhaps only the day before, seemed to demand it. The audience quieted and stage lights dimmed as the screen behind me sprang into light. Taking this as my cue, I began my talk. As I spoke, giggles and polite laughter began to bubble up from the darkness, where the audience sat. Soon the giggles also began to come from the balconies that encircled the hall. I turned to look at the screen behind me for some clue as to what was sending the audience into hysterical laughter.

The giant screen stood several stories high, and from my close-up perspective the image on it was nothing more than a sea of colored pixels, a bright blur. I spoke on, sweat soaking through my clothes. No raging king cobra or attacking crocodile had ever made my knees shake as they did then. I followed my practiced script perfectly, yet the giggles from the audience turned into great bursts of laughter.

Nothing projected related to anything I said; worse, these images were from a previous talk on birds. When I referred to a snake and its skin, a picture of the director holding a bird flashed on the screen behind me. Feeding flamingos replaced crocodile skins. An inspector of the U.S. Fish and Wildlife Service was represented by a penguin. All of which I could not see. Nevertheless, I knew it was the herpetologist's bird curse, come to exact its vengeance on me. I silently promised to repent and mend my bird-disdaining ways.

Finally, my torture was over. I thanked the audience and left the stage to polite, isolated clapping and numerous giggles, trailing a stream of sweat behind me. Moments later, I climbed to the balcony, where Myrna and Peter sat. A young boy in an aisle below pointed his finger upward, in my direction. Was there no escape, no place to hide, no sanctuary?

"How was it?" I asked Myrna. "Was it really bad?" I needed some little assurance that my nightmare was not as horrible as it seemed. Myrna looked at me with a smile, or perhaps it was a stifled giggle, and said, "Peter, it really sucked." Bill Conway, the general director, kindly broke from his usual expected criticism and soothingly offered, "Peter, you did well."

12

SNAKEBITE

The four-foot-long, yellow-and-gray-patterned Okinawan habu lay coiled in the silver feeding box. Its head pointed upward. Its yellow eyes, with their catlike pupils, seemed to be focused directly on me, ignoring the dead mouse I dangled in front of its face with a pair of twelve-inch-long, stainless steel surgical forceps. It was early in my zoo career, and I was about to learn one of the most important lessons of my life.

Habus are pit vipers; they belong to a group of venomous snakes called crotalids. These include rattlesnakes, copperheads, and water moccasins, found in North America, as well as other species from Central and South America, or Asia. All crotalids are characterized by facial pits. These deep holes, located on each side of the snake's face, halfway between its nostril and eye, are sensory receptors for heat. Using its facial pits, the snake can detect the body heat of even the smallest mammal or bird, locate its prey, and accurately deliver a lethal strike, even in the dark.

This particular species of habu is rather long-bodied, with a large, arrow-shaped head that is distinct from its rather slender neck. The species comes from the islands around Okinawa, and is known for the copious amount of toxic venom it can produce, its long fangs, and its relatively placid disposition.

This habu was tolerating a considerable amount of annoyance from me, as I rubbed and tapped its face with the mouse, trying to arouse the snake to bite it. I hoped that once the snake tasted the mouse, it would decide that the mouse was a decent meal and eat it. This was a typical technique to use when a new snake was reluctant to feed voluntarily. It stopped short only of forcing the meal down the snake's throat.

I tapped and poked, and the good-natured snake first resorted to hiding its head to escape my harassment. Since I wouldn't stop, it turned to look at me, flicking its tongue slowly in and out in annoyance. Still I persisted. After all, I could not waste all day feeding one dumb snake, when I also had several dozen other, more willing charges to care for. For all of the snake's patience, I was getting impatient and more determined. I was also getting careless, and was about to make the same mistake scores of amateur snake fanciers make each year—and get bitten.

Suddenly, the game was over as far as the snake was concerned. I inadvertently gave it no choice but to defend itself. It could not flee to escape my harassments, nor could it hide from them. It struck straight up at my hand, past the mouse and past the forceps. In a flash, I could see the snake's mouth open, the long fangs reaching forward to make contact. My right index finger was extended along the forceps to steady it. In a blurred instant, as the snake struck, I pulled back my hand. As the snake's jaws engulfed the top of my finger, I yanked the entire snake, still attached to my finger, out of the box and onto the floor.

I was bitten. Blood oozed and dripped from several small puncture wounds on the top of my finger. My first thought was that I needed to get the snake safely back into its cage. As I picked it up on the end of the snake hook, now sticky with blood from my grasp, the snake eagerly cooperated. I had only to aim its head in the right direction, and it lunged into its cage to escape and hide. I wanted to hide as well, but for another reason. Keepers can expect to be bitten by a venomous snake at one time or another during the course of their careers. But I was barely out of my probationary period, and had only recently been allowed to care for venomous snakes. I was horribly embarrassed by my carelessness.

I hoped I hadn't really been bitten. Early on in my probationary period, there had been a moment when I was sure I had been bitten by a venomous snake. A number of newly born African puff adders had escaped their mother's exhibit by crawling through the holes in a perforated drain cover. They were recaptured easily enough, as they sat congregated on a second drain cover below, but we could never be sure just how many had been born or had actually escaped. Later that day, I casually placed my hand on top of a stone column and immediately felt a searing pain in my palm, which immediately began to swell and throb. Looking at the top of the column, where my hand had been, I found a dead honeybee. I had only been stung by a bee.

It wasn't more than a few seconds before my racing brain moved past the denial stage to confront the realization that the actual bite was not the end of the incident, only the beginning. From what I had read and heard, I knew what to expect. There was almost no formal training program about what to do in the event of snakebite, only a short talk by Dr. Oliver when I had first started working. I knew there was antivenin—serum prepared from the blood of immunized horses. The antivenin was kept at the animal hospital by the veterinarian. I also carried a Boy Scout snakebite kit in my pocket, which included three rubber suction cups that could be used to draw out the venom from a finger or an arm; a pointed scalpel blade to cut into the fang marks to promote profuse bleeding, and a length of red woven string to be used as a tourniquet to keep the venom isolated in the bitten extremity, so that it would not circulate further throughout the body. Today, such treatment is considered inappropriate.

Within minutes, I should have begun to feel tingling and pain. My finger and hand should have begun to swell to enormous size. I had seen pictures of the arms of men who had been bitten on the hand by a South American fer-de-lance, another type of pit viper. The venom literally destroyed their flesh, leaving them with massive gangrene infections, and eventually, with only the long bare bones protruding from below the elbow, beginning where the tourniquet had been placed.

So now, I thought, the pain should be excruciating. I might well lose my fingers or hand, or even die as a result of this simple, careless mistake. More terrifying thoughts crossed my mind. I worried that as the venom progressed through my body, I would begin to vomit blood, and perhaps bleed from my nostrils and gums. My face and abdominal muscles might begin to fasciculate, contracting frequently and uncontrollably. If the snake had not used its venom recently and I had therefore received a large dose of venom from the bite, the symptoms would be more severe and rapid.

It takes a while for people to die from snakebite—sometimes days, agonizing days. It is only in the movies that the hero takes out his dirty, half-dull knife, which he last used to skin a tick-infested rabbit, and cuts into the heroine's leg, carving a casual X deep into each fang mark, then alternately sucks out the venom-laden blood with his tobacco-stained lips and spits it out with great fanfare.

What would my mother say? She always told my father to wear clean underwear every day, in case he had an accident and had to go to the hospital. I wondered if my own underwear was still clean, given that my heart was now pounding in absolute fear of the consequences I was expecting.

I started to suck my finger. The blood tasted about the same as it ever had, I thought. The venom of the spitting cobra tasted bitter and puckered my mouth, as I knew from having received a spray of venom in my mouth from an irate spitting cobra as I cleaned its cage. This wasn't an unusual event, and it was relatively harmless. Snake venoms are complex proteins and are totally digestible—not that I would recommend that anyone make a habit of slugging down a nightly martini laced with snake venom. Venom has to be introduced into the bloodstream, as by injection during a bite or absorption into an open wound, to have an effect.

On the other hand, I had once rubbed my eye during a major staff meeting just after cleaning the cage of the red spitting cobras. I must have had a few molecules of venom on my hand, because my eye immediately began to tear and burn with an excruciating pain. I ran from the room, groping the wall for the door to the men's lavatory, as sixty staff officers watched in disbelief. There hadn't been such interest at the meeting since one of the senior staff members returned from the men's room trailing six feet of toilet paper from the back of his trousers. Holding my eye under the flow of cold water gave immediate relief. Actually, I was in the right place for a remedy that African veldt natives use when one of these cobras spits in someone's eyes from in the wild: the other men gather around and urinate in his eyes. I presume the victim keeps his mouth shut.

Suddenly I remembered the tourniquet. I wrapped the red string from my snakebite kit tightly around my finger, just above where the blood oozed from the presumed fang punctures, and then I decided I'd better go tell the head keeper the news. When I entered the passageway, Spencook was cleaning some rattlesnake cages at the opposite side of the building. An important rule was never to speak to a person when they had the door to a venomous snake's cage open. They could become distracted and get bitten. I decided to wait patiently, holding my bitten hand behind my back, until he closed the cage door.

"Steve, I have bad news," I announced. "I just got bitten by the habu." I held up my bleeding, red-string-wrapped finger. The smile on his face froze, and he paled. "When?" he asked. "Just a few minutes ago," I answered. "Let's go to the office and call Oliver," he said, leading me out of the passageway to the keepers' office across the way. I sat down in the green leather high-backed chair as he called the curator's office and mumbled something I could barely hear to Dr. Oliver: "Peter. . . . Bitten. . . . He's here. . . . Habu. . . . Just now. Okay, we'll wait for you." At least ten minutes had passed since the bite. Steve's reaction made my heart beat faster, and I began to sweat. My finger now seemed to be slightly swollen. It hurt a little.

Oliver arrived in what seemed like seconds. He must have run from his office in the administration building, at the opposite end of the zoo. The veterinarian showed up too; Oliver must have called him. There we sat, looking at my finger, waiting for something to happen, waiting for me to die or at least pass out. No one really knew what to expect or what to do next. We just waited. My finger was turning blue and swelling. Oliver peered closely to examine the wounds. Rather than the one or two deep punctures that long, thick venomous-snake fangs might inflict, there was a small row of several tiny perfect punctures. Sticking out of one puncture hole was a tiny fine-pointed snake tooth.

Oliver instructed, "Take the tourniquet off and let's see what happens." It was an easy thing for him to say. Whatever was going to happen was going to happen to me, not him. As I unwrapped the red string, color began to return to the rest of my finger below where the string had been wrapped around it. Within minutes, the swelling had begun to subside as blood flowed through the finger once more. I felt fine.

"It could have been a dry bite, or he missed you with his fangs and got you with his secondary teeth," Oliver speculated. "Be more careful next time. Call me if you feel anything else happening." By sheer luck, I had escaped the consequences of a crippling or lethal snakebite. The snake's fangs were so long and set so far apart in its large head, that when it struck forward and upward, the outstretched fangs straddled my finger on each side. Only the harmless rows of secondary teeth between the fangs had imbedded in my finger as I'd reflexively jerked my hand back from the strike, which had caused the snake to be pulled out of the box, as well. I was lucky. How lucky remained to be seen.

In the early 1900s, when Raymond L. Ditmars was the curator, a reptile supervisor was bitten by a rattlesnake. It was a serious bite that could have resulted in his death. Antivenin (also called anti-venom or anti-snakebite serum) was not well known; by chance, a representative of the Brazilian Instituto Butantán was in New York to introduce a new antivenin that had been developed to treat snakebites from pit vipers. These early samples of serum were the first used in the United States to successfully treat a snakebite victim— the reptile supervisor.

From my own experience in 1955, it was apparent that the reptile department was poorly prepared and poorly trained to treat a serious snakebite. The head keeper had experienced several snakebites. Once he'd been bitten by a copperhead, which he had mistaken for a cottonmouth, not that it made much difference. Copperheads have a relatively mild venom that causes localized swelling and pain, while the venom of cottonmouths, or water moccasins, is much more potent and destructive to tissue. He had reached into the cage with his bare hand to retrieve a dead, uneaten mouse, and the snake bit his intruding hand. It was a very mild envenomation. He washed his hand in cold water to promote bleeding, then concealed his swollen hand for several days to hide his poor judgment.

Actually, one animal or another, both venomous and nonvenomous, was regularly biting him. Spencook had a fifteen-foot-long nonvenomous anaconda named Andy that he regularly allowed to crawl over his shoulders—usually to impress women—as he cleaned the Reptile House. Every now and then we would hear a bloodcurdling scream coming from the central island area, where the anacondas were caged, and we speculated it was Spencook being bitten again by his snake. He would soon appear with a number of deep lacerations and anaconda teeth embedded in his hand. He never caught on that his pet anaconda couldn't tell him from a meal of fresh guinea pig.

It was not until a new curator came on the scene, years later, that any serious consideration would be given to implementing a formal snakebite emergency procedure. We would stock a complete line of antisera at the Reptile House, in quantity sufficient to treat several potential bites from any species in the collection. We would formalize an arrangement with the emergency room of a local hospital, so doctors would be both trained and prepared to handle a snakebite emergency.

As for me, the lesson was well learned. The habu bite would be the first and last venomous snakebite of my forty-four-year zoo career. Unlike many other herpetologists, I would end my career with all of my digits intact. I would not be clearly recognizable in a crowd by missing fingers as the result of a snakebite.

Once a young tattooed man wearing a leather shoelace with a rattlesnake's rattle and a snake fang around his neck came to the door of the Reptile House and proudly announced that he was a member of "the white-fang club." He felt he had achieved success by having been bitten by a rattlesnake at a rattlesnake roundup. He believed that the experience now entitled him to be included among a select group of morons as a mark of distinction. Instead of being welcomed into our fold of very professional people, who daily risked their lives caring for the most dangerous snakes every day of the week, he received quite the opposite shocking welcome. No professional keeper handles dangerous snakes unless there is a genuine reason involving the health and welfare of the animal. Showing off or bravado is never a reason. The keeper who answered the door that day listened for a moment, took a long hard look at the man, and responded quite appropriately with "So what else have you done stupid in your life" before slamming the door in disgust.

Most people are afraid of all snakes as evil harbingers of the Devil, as endowed with magical powers, or as expressions of sexuality. The Judeo-Christian tradition and the biblical story of Adam and Eve in the Garden of Eden have seen to it that the concept of snakes being allied with the Devil still persists today. Snakes are a good scapegoat for anything bad, and they provide a generic slur that can be loosely applied to politicians, in-laws, and anyone else held in extremely low esteem. Nonetheless, my benevolent feelings about snakes are the same as I might extend to any unjustly maligned underdog. I have never once seen a devil, nor has any snake ever offered me an apple. I often ask people who are revolted at the thought of a snake if they have ever heard a snake bad-mouth its mother, steal a hubcap from a car, rob somebody, lie, or cheat. So why pick on snakes?

There are about three thousand species of snakes worldwide. Snakes live in just about every environment on earth, other than the frigid polar regions. While most snakes live on the ground, some snakes never come out from underground. Some never descend from the treetops, and some of those can "fly," or glide from tree to tree. Some snakes constantly swim and never leave the oceans. Some snakes give birth to live young, while others lay soft leathery eggs, and still others can do either. That's pretty neat. And all snakes have one thing in common: they don't eat plants.

All snakes can bite, but whether they do so depends on their size and willingness. Snakes possess about two hundred backward-curving, needlelike teeth aligned in four rows on the top jaw and two on the bottom jaw. A snake's tongue, although thought by some people to be a "poisonous stinger," is really only a harmless organ for tasting and sensing, much like our own tongue, although the snake's tongue also aids in the sense of smell. Some snakes are venomous, which means they possess special glands in their head that produce a venom or poison that they can inject into their prey to kill it, through a pair of hollow, specialized teeth. These are the snakes that are potentially dangerous to humans. The venom of poisonous snakes is composed of a wide range of proteins and other organic compounds that produce an equally wide range of catastrophic effects when injected into animals or humans. Depending on the species, and even the local population the snake represents, the effect of the venom can range from minor swelling and nausea to complete tissue destruction (necrosis), advanced gangrene, heart damage, hemorrhaging, kidney destruction, collapse of the central nervous system and breathing, loss of limbs, overwhelming toxic shock, and death. Only a small percentage of the world's snakes are venomous. Yet not all venomous snakes are particularly dangerous to humans; some are too small to bite through a person's clothing or skin, and others are unwilling to bite under any circumstances.

The rest of the snakes are nonvenomous species and considered "harmless." That doesn't mean they can't bite. It just means that they don't have any venom to inject. Harmless snakes range in size from several inches long to more than twenty-foot-long giants that may weigh hundreds of pounds. Such a giant may have inch-long teeth that can cause numerous deep, severe lacerations, perhaps even more destructive than a snakebite from some of the less toxic species of venomous snakes. I've seen male pythons bite other pythons, inflicting wounds that required two hundred or more sutures to close.

We once had a seventeen-foot-long anaconda that refused to feed on anything we offered it, from fresh-killed chickens to the favored food for anacondas, guinea pigs. Despite injections of vitamins and other stimulants, it held to its fast for nearly a year. While it was a giant in length, its emaciated body was little more than skin and bones. Finally we decided that the poor beast had to be force-fed, something we were reluctant to do for fear of damaging the snake's mouth in the process and, because of its already debilitated state, having it develop an infection. The snake was sure not to cooperate. Extra keepers were brought in to assist on the designated feeding day. We would have to overcome the snake's strength and stretch it out in a straight line. Even in its frail condition, the anaconda would coil and thrash unless absolutely overpowered.

The head keeper cautiously and quietly seized the snake with both hands at the base of the head, before the snake even knew it was in for a surprise wrestling bout. The snake's head was immense, fully ten inches long and five inches wide. It was like a volcano erupting, as the six other keepers piled onto the snake's body. One problem in holding a large snake is that there are no handles to grasp. Besides, the snake is apt to defecate, spreading vile-smelling musk over everything and everyone and turning its body into a giant, writhing, greased sausage in a natural casing. The keepers battled these difficulties, and finally the snake became exhausted. (Real keepers never admit to being exhausted.)

My job, once the snake's body was stretched out straight, was to force a dead rat down the snake's throat with a three-foot-long pair of veterinary forceps. As I pressed the dead rat to the snake's lips, the snake suddenly opened its jaws wide and lunged forward, carrying with it the army of surprised keepers who held on to its body. In and down went the rat, followed by the forceps and my hand. The jaws closed, imbedding dozens of its three-quarter-inch-long teeth into the top and bottom of my hand. Snakes have teeth that are curved and pointed like a fish hook, and once they're imbedded, there is only one way to escape from them: by pushing the object they are holding in the direction of their curve—that is, farther down into the snake's throat. The snake clamped its jaws shut tight, driving the teeth deeper toward my bones. Everyone knew that the snake had to be held still to prevent the teeth from tearing through tendons and blood vessels. The veterinarian, who was on hand, produced four flat wooden tongue depressors. Carefully, the wooden depressors were inserted between each row of teeth, separating the teeth from my hand and preventing more teeth from getting imbedded. I was lucky. A swollen, sore bandaged hand complete with punctures that made it look like an old-fashioned canceled check—banks used to cancel paid checks by making little rows of holes in them—was all that resulted.

Giant constrictors are favorite pets. The desire to have one usually starts when someone buys a baby two-foot-long python from a local pet shop. Within a year, with proper feeding and warmth, the snake will be nearly six feet long and growing. Soon, it is ten to twelve feet long and may weigh 125 pounds. At only ten years of age and twenty-one feet long, it can weigh two hundred pounds, with teeth to match. It may be docile at lower temperatures, but bite viciously as its body warms up. It is unusual for someone to be killed by their own pet python, but it does happen with some regularity. A forty-two-year-old, Winchester, Missouri, man was found dead by his wife on her return home from an overnight stay with her mother; he had been strangled by their eighteen-foot-long Burmese python. A thirteen-year-old Colorado boy was also strangled by his eight-year-old, twelve-foot-long, eighty-pound python. In New York, a thirteen-foot-long, forty-four-pound Burmese python, a very docile species, accidentally coiled around and killed a nineteen-year-old boy. And perhaps most tragically, a twenty-one-month-old infant was killed in his crib by his parents' eight-foot-long pet python in Sparks, Nevada; and a couple's three-year-old son was killed in Carlyle, Illinois, by their seven-and-a-half-foot-long python.

These sample cases do not represent attacks by vicious snakes.

Rather, they reflect potentially dangerous snakes being kept by people who have no idea what they are doing. Snakes are simple animals and respond predictably. One man was killed when he placed a rabbit under his chin so he would have his hands free to open the door of his python's cage. The hungry snake struck out and seized the man's head instead of the rabbit. To the snake, the smell of a rabbit plus movement equaled a live rabbit meal. The man, of course, struggled, which made the snake think the rabbit was still alive and needed to be killed. It then did what it was supposed to do: it coiled around the "rabbit"—that is, the man—and killed him. Similarly, pet venomous snakes will bite people who have the smell of a food mouse, pet dog, or cat on their hands.

To be sure, working closely every day, even in a zoo, with a large variety of venomous and nonvenomous snakes always presents the potential for an accident, even if one takes every safety precaution, under the most stringently controlled environmental conditions, in a secure facility. Herpetologists work with snakes for scientific or conservation purposes—for a living. A professional herpetologist may have an advanced degree in the study of reptiles and amphibians, or a related scientific specialty with a focus on reptiles. Sure, almost every professional herpetologist started out as an amateur, a young person who simply liked snakes, like me. But somewhere along the line the interest took on a serious bent and, along with it, a sense of responsibility, as the potential for injury or death from an accident became apparent. I would never consider keeping a venomous snake as a pet.

It's on this point that the professional herpetologist separates him- or herself (yes, there are female herpetologists, but not many) from the self-styled or amateur herpetologist. The person who keeps snakes and walks through the park with a python around his neck to attract attention is not a professional herpetologist but someone who desperately needs attention. Lower, in my opinion, is the individual who keeps venomous snakes as pets, disregarding the danger to themselves and to the innocent people with whom they may come in contact.

Snakes are masters of escape. What happens when an illegally kept poisonous snake escapes from the home of a private collector? Does that person knock on their neighbor's door and say, "Hi there. My pet cobra has escaped. Let me know if your toddler finds it. By the way, can I borrow a cup of sugar while I'm here?" Worse, what happens when the neighbor is bitten by someone's escaped snake and finds him- or herself in a hospital being treated by a doctor who has no inkling that there could be a snakebite from an exotic species in the middle of a modern city? Does the owner of the snake come forward, risk prosecution, and say, "Hey, it was my cobra that bit you. I sure am sorry."

In other cases, doctors more used to exotic species may err on the side of unnecessary caution. After I explained to one doctor that the young patient he had in the emergency room had been bitten only by a harmless garter snake and required nothing more than a bandage and some antiseptic, he persisted in his ignorance. The child was subjected to a very dangerous treatment that, in itself, could cause death. "In my country," he said, "the cobra puts the venom on the leaves of the bacca plant. I will give her the serum."

Unbelievably, there are those who, having been bitten and escaped death, wear their experience as a badge of distinction and learn nothing. Many nonprofessional snake handlers who get bitten end up getting bitten many times over. It seems their snakes know what they are doing, but the handlers evidently lack some basic brain function that should tell them to stop handling poisonous snakes. Most professional herpetologists strive to never experience snakebite, harmless or venomous, and look with disdain on private individuals who keep pet venomous snakes or are bitten by them. I recently met a young woman at a conference who proudly showed pictures of herself holding her pet adult king cobra and eastern diamondback rattlesnake in such a careless way that they could easily have bitten her, or anyone else. Her boyfriend, another self-styled herpetologist, depicted himself with his penis exposed, presumably to complement the size of the snakes in his friend's collection. I was not impressed with either of their accomplishments.

While many municipalities have regulations to control or ban the possession of noxious or dangerous animals, including venomous snakes, few of these regulations are enforced until an accident actually occurs. No one goes around checking to see if your grandmother has a cobra or two tucked away in a kitchen cabinet—that is, until Grandma shows up in a hospital emergency room suffering from snakebite. Because most venomous snakes are not endangered or threatened species, and may well be very common in the wild, their importation into the United States is not prohibited unless the country they are being shipped from bans their export. Therefore, it frequently falls to untrained state or local authorities to enforce ordinances against the owning of venomous snakes.

Many more hundreds of venomous snakes are imported into the United States than are found in zoos. Where, then, do the rest of them go? Many go to the Asian food markets for human consumption, or are used to make folk medicine or aphrodisiacs. One Asiatic cobra came to us at the Bronx Zoo from a passerby who happened to see some kids teasing it on a street corner in New York City's Chinatown. He felt sorry for the snake and took it away—in a brown paper bag—to give it a better home.

Other snakes go into the hobbyist market or are offered for retail sale in the pet trade. Virtually every commercial reptile dealer who has a mail-order list or a Web site—and there are hundreds—states they "do not [knowingly] sell venomous snakes to minors." How nice. Parents everywhere can rest assured that their twelve-year-old child cannot use their credit card to buy a deadly African black mamba over the Internet. However, little Jimmy or young Mary can buy a deadly snake from one of the hundreds of underground amateur or hobbyist reptile breeders who sell baby snakes, produced from a plastic shoe box, bedroom, or snake farm—perhaps in the apartment next door to you.

I was once taken by police to the apartment of a thirteen-year-old boy in the Bronx who was being treated at a local hospital for a snakebite he'd received from one of his pets the night before. As his mother escorted us into the boy's bedroom, I saw that there was an open-topped aquarium at the head of his bed. Inside were thirteen

African puff adder babies the boy had purchased from some local pet dealer. For weeks, the boy had fed the snakes a small mouse each, using a pair of tweezers. The snakes grew rapidly, but the tweezers, initially long enough to keep his fingers out of the snakes' reach, did not. One of the snakes had grown big enough to reach the boy's finger. The bite was not fatal, but the destructive effects of the venom caused the loss of part of his finger. His mother had never known that the snakes were dangerous, having only been told they were harmless "garter snakes." Without a cover on the tank, the snakes could have escaped as the boy slept and bitten him on the head or face. Because of her ignorance of the danger, his mother could also have easily been bitten. Did he ever bring friends over to see his snakes? They, too, could have easily been bitten.

There are about ten thousand venomous snakebites in the United States each year, and of those, about fifteen fatalities. People who keep venomous snakes as pets incur many of these bites, and many bites are from species that are not native to this country. The average snakebite victim is male, white, between the ages of twelve and forty-five, and is bitten when trying to catch or handle a venomous snake. Many cases involve alcohol or drugs. Keepers in professional zoos are rarely bitten by their charges because of the importance placed on safety, and the general dictate that no venomous snake should be handled except for medical or health reasons, and never for show.

A credentialed zoo has in place an emergency snakebite protocol, trained staff, and an affiliation with a medical facility that has been well indoctrinated in the treatment of snakebite. In addition, a continually updated supply of anti-snakebite serum, imported from manufacturers all over the world, is kept on hand. Serum is expensive. Each ampoule may cost from several hundred to several thousand dollars, and a hundred or more ampoules may be required to treat a single bite. Zoos purchase serum to protect their staff members in the event of a snakebite accident. Now comes the drunken moron who has a pet cobra and gets bitten showing it off to his friends on New Year's Eve. Although zoos are not required to provide serum for such emergencies, they always do so for humanitarian reasons. I don't necessarily subscribe to the practice. Such incidences often deplete these exhaustible supplies of serum, leaving the keepers, who must care for snakes on a daily basis, at great risk.

Our snakebite protocol initially involved intravenous preparation training at Roosevelt Hospital in New York City. In later years, a closer facility seemed to be desirable. One evening over dinner, I was lamenting the difficulty a snakebite victim might have in being transported in dense traffic from the Bronx to Roosevelt Hospital in midtown Manhattan. Our guest, a radiologist at nearby Jacobi Hospital, suggested, "Why don't you talk to Dr. Stanley Levenson at the Albert Einstein College of Medicine, of which Jacobi is a part, and see if he can set something up? I'll arrange a meeting."

A few days later, Bill Holmstrom—the senior keeper—and I were in the offices of Dr. Levenson, in the department of surgery, giving a presentation. As we stood in the corridor afterward, I reiterated, "We need a doctor who will learn about treating snakebite, keep up with the literature, and develop new techniques." At that moment, a young surgical resident sped by on his way to teach a class. Levenson called him back, saying, "Ah, Dr. Wetzel, come here. You are the new expert on snakebite for the Bronx Zoo." At that moment, Dr. Warren Wetzel became a friend, a colleague, and the most wonderful, crazy man I've ever met.

When treating his patients, Warren considered nothing to be outrageous or impossible. He was soon deeply involved in snakebite research, training new doctors in snakebite protocols, and gaining the trust of every snake fancier, would-be victim, and snake handler in the New York metropolitan area—and there were dozens. We soon had a printed, formal treatment protocol, a list of emergency numbers, and a team of physicians on call twenty-four hours a day, ready to respond to snakebite emergencies. The Bronx Municipal Hospital Center Jacobi Hospital snakebite trauma center, networked with poison-control centers throughout the United States, was born. U.S. Fish and Wildlife Service inspectors risk venomous snakebites daily as they inspect shipments of live reptiles, and the service became part of the program, providing funding for a variety of sera that we could not otherwise afford.

Within days of the establishment of our snakebite trauma center, the first accident occurred. A snake dealer importing a shipment of venomous snakes at Kennedy International Airport was bitten on the thumb as he opened a bag containing a king cobra—one of thirty such bags—for the benefit of the wildlife inspectors. Within minutes, he had been rushed by helicopter to the Jacobi center. Treated by injections of dozens of ampoules of king cobra antivenin from Thailand, he miraculously survived a bite that could easily have killed an elephant.

As the center's expertise became widely known, calls for assistance began to come in almost weekly. If the victim was not transported to the center, Wetzel provided counsel, while the Bronx Zoo provided serum and coordinated the response.

On many evenings I received a call from one of the poison-control centers and ended the night with Warren and the victim at the hospital. Most victims had one thing in common: they lied. They lied about the kind of snake that bit them; usually, it was their pet. They lied about their use of illegal drugs or alcohol. And they lied about how they were bitten.

On one occasion, Warren called to say he had an older biker coming in. The man was unconscious after being bitten by a rattlesnake. Warren asked if I would bring antivenin. Within an hour, I was at Jacobi—just as the victim, a forty-five-year-old man wearing a black leather jacket and motorcycle boots, arrived at the emergency room. His girlfriend, dressed in the same type of outfit and sporting a white-brimmed police cap, was at his side.

"What happened?" we asked as the medical team began to take his vital signs. The girlfriend said they'd been riding near Ellenville, New York, about fifty miles northwest of New York City. They were on a back road after dark when they saw a three-foot-long timber rattlesnake crossing the road. Not wishing to see it harmed, the biker picked it up, put it in a makeshift bag—his T-shirt tied up—and took it home to Queens, one of the boroughs of New York City, about two hours from Ellenville. When the snake was let out of the bag, it bit him on the right hand, just above the thumb. It is quite unusual for someone having been bitten only four or five hours before by that species of snake to be unconscious. The venom destroys cells, but it usually does not affect breathing. He was also experiencing fasciculations, small, ripplelike twitches of his facial muscles.

Warren asked, "What do you think, Peter? Something isn't right here." I agreed. This was not the kind of medical presentation one would expect from a rattlesnake bite. Furthermore, the story didn't jibe. It was late February, freezing cold. Ellenville was covered in deep snow. There was no possibility that a rattlesnake would be crossing the road under those conditions. Taking a closer look at the so-called bite wound, I thought it resembled the kind of skin dent and gouges made from a pinch with fingernails. There was no swelling, discoloration, or, apparently, intense burning pain. Whatever he had done, the man was faking snakebite. It made no sense to us, but neither of us was a psychiatrist.

Warren decided to give him a placebo and keep him overnight. The man's recovery was miraculous. He was up, hungry, and ready to go home the next day. Some months later, his girlfriend arrived at the trauma center to be treated for a genuine snakebite from a pet Mexican water moccasin, called a cantil. We thought it was an intentional bite. Months later, we heard that she had died of a drug overdose.

One of the most bizarre snakebite calls I ever responded to came from the Atlanta poison-control center. An African Gaboon viper in Washington, D.C., had bitten a teenaged boy on a city bus. I immediately called my counterpart at the National Zoo, Reptile Supervisor Michael Davenport, at home. His companion, Melanie, answered the phone. "I have a snakebite call from poison control about someone being bitten by a Gaboon viper," I said. "Where is Mike?" "He just got called by the D.C. police and is on his way to the zoo," she replied.

At the zoo, Mike found police officers in front of the now darkened Reptile House waiting with a black garbage bag. As Mike walked up to them, one of the officers dumped the contents of the bag onto the ground. Mike recognized two huge, deadly Gaboon vipers. To Mike's horror, one of the officers bent down and picked up one of the snakes behind the head. Going into the building to get a container for the snakes, Mike found the glass of the front door and of the Gaboon viper exhibit broken, his two vipers gone, and, left behind, some bamboo plant sticks and a brick. The snakes were from the zoo.

A sixteen-year-old boy had walked into the zoo and picked up a black trash bag from a zoo garbage receptacle, some natural bamboo sticks used to support plantings near the Reptile House, and a brick he found on the ground. Smashing the door and then the glass of the exhibit, he used the sticks to ladle the snakes out of the cage and into the plastic bag. He then casually walked out of the front gate of the zoo and waited at the zoo bus stop, with other riders, for a city bus to arrive. He sat on the bus with the bag in his lap until he came to his stop. At that point, he rose, slung the bag of deadly snakes over his shoulder, and was bitten by one of the snakes through the plastic. Gaboon viper venom causes excruciating pain, swelling, tissue destruction, and nerve damage. The boy screamed in agony. Just then a police car approached the bus. The driver of the bus was able to hail the police, and the boy was rushed to the hospital, while other officers took the snakes to the zoo.

Meanwhile, I contacted the Special Operations Unit of the New York City Police Department and had our entire supply of African viper serum shipped by police helicopter to Washington. The boy survived one of the deadliest snakebites known.

Another call was equally unusual. A man was bitten by his pet yellow cobra on a Saturday night and, within hours, was totally paralyzed, unconscious, unable to breathe, and near death. I arrived to find that Warren already had put the man on life support. For all practical purposes, the man seemed to be dead. But Warren had treated just such a bite not long before, with the victim following the same pattern of ceasing all voluntary bodily functions and appearing to be dead. At that time, another surgeon had arrived on the scene and, believing the man to be dead, began to comment aloud about whether the man's organs were still good and if he could be used as an organ donor. As the surgeon spoke, a tear formed and ran down the supposedly dead man's cheek. He could not move or respond, but he could hear everything, including the possibility that he would be cut up for his organs.

Warren was not to be fooled a second time. In this case, he asked a new intern who had just arrived to assess the cobra-bite patient's status. The intern did a quick examination and pronounced the man dead. Warren winked at me as we prepared the serum for injection. A certain number of vials of South African serum, manufactured to counteract the effects of a yellow cobra bite and given in one dose, would have the man awake and up in twenty-four hours. Warren instructed the intern, "Watch! Perhaps you'll learn something. In the meantime, don't leave the hospital or this guy for the next twenty-four hours. I'll be back on Monday!"

Warren and I attended to many snakebite victims. The one who made me the saddest was the fellow who tried to kill himself by having a venomous snake bite him after he'd ingested drugs and alcohol. As Warren and I worked on this man, who survived, another man, who had suffered a heart attack while making love to his girlfriend, arrived in the adjoining section of the crowded emergency room only to die without recovering consciousness. As I helped lift the huge dead man to a better-looking stretcher—one not spattered with blood—the man's heartbroken girlfriend came in to see him one last time. One man wanted to die and didn't, while the other wanted to live and could not.

Warren was an avid softball enthusiast. He formed his own team, the Cobras, and would sometimes show up in the emergency room still dressed in his muddy baseball uniform. He was reliable to a fault and a good friend besides. One day, while I was away chasing crocodilians somewhere in Brazil, my wife, Myrna, stepped down from retrieving a book from an upper shelf in her office and drove a two-inch-long splinter deep into her buttock. Not able to see or reach it, she called Warren. Warren soon arrived, wearing his baseball uniform, carrying a surgical kit, and with his accountant in tow. He surgically removed the splinter and stitched the wound closed, then left for his game. Warren's joke was that he had signed his initials with the sutures. Whenever I see the scar on Myrna's rear end, I think of Warren.

Warren died in 1996 at the age of forty-six, of a rare cancer. He is still loved and remembered. Amazingly, to this day, I'll find myself running into a doctor in a hospital in New York who'll say, "Wait a minute. I know you. You worked at the Reptile House when I was doing my surgical rotation with Warren Wetzel. Warren taught me everything I know about snakebite—and he stole my sandwiches, besides."

13

ESCAPE ARTISTS

There are innumerable snake escape stories worth telling. One of my earliest occurred on my first honeymoon. While most people select a romantic place for their honeymoon, I couldn't wait to take a honeymoon in Florida with my first wife, Winnie, to catch snakes. Winnie and I went to Bal Harbour, where her aunt and uncle allowed us to use their luxurious condominium on one provision, indicated by a small sign: NO SNAKES ALLOWED. Winnie loved animals, but loving animals and suddenly coming to the realization that her new husband had a close affinity to reptiles, snakes in particular, was more than she had bargained for. I was in love. I was in the Florida Everglades. Every flooded roadside ditch held a species of frog or snake I had never seen before in the wild, or at all.

One of our first stops was the Miami Serpentarium, famous for William Haast and his cobra show. Haast dragged an adult king cobra out of its cage by the tail and let it loose on the lawn, surrounded by a circle of picture-snapping tourists. He then, with great agility and concentration, proceeded to capture it with one bare hand by quickly seizing it behind the head as it stood raised in a hood facing the crowd of people. While the general public made grimacing faces at the mere sight of the snake, not knowing the real danger they could be in if Haast lost control of the animal, I was amazed that Haast had lived so long doing what he did. It was well known that Haast had experimentally injected himself with snake venoms in an effort to immunize himself against the bite of the most dangerous snakes. No one in his right mind would consider performing such a procedure on himself, nor would any physician risk a reputation by supervising it.

Haast was bitten a great many times during his career, and came close to death more than once. He had also become an icon and an idol to many snake fanciers, who, like him, inoculated themselves with snake venom, without medical supervision, so they could handle the venomous snakes in their personal collections with impunity. I considered these people morons. At least Haast had some legitimacy for what he did. His serpentarium provided difficult-to-obtain venoms for the production of sera to treat snakebites. He had helped doctors save the lives of many people, including children, who were severely bitten by Florida's giant eastern diamondback rattlesnakes or highly venomous coral snakes. He extracted venom from perhaps hundreds of snakes per day, and it was inevitable that he should be bitten often in the process. But despite my great respect for his contributions to snakebite research, whether from the numerous snakebites or the venom inoculations, Haast already looked dead to me.

Meanwhile, I was sure Winnie would enjoy a good night of snake hunting as much as I would. In retrospect, the adventure certainly did make an impression, as she reminded me of the lunacy of the trip and the ruination of her honeymoon for the remaining twenty years of our marriage. I never understood the problem.

Snakes abounded along the nearby Tamiami Trail. In the company of a young man from the serpentarium, whom we had met that afternoon, we set off as soon as it got dark. The first snakes we found crossing the road were huge, fat green water snakes. These nasty creatures, which bite when handled, are one of the most prolific snakes, sometimes giving birth to as many as one hundred live babies at a time, and the females were due to give birth within the very week. The next water snake we found was dead, having been hit by a passing car. As she was equally fat, we assumed she was pregnant and about to give birth. Ron, our friend from the serpentarium, produced a scalpel, and there on the side of the road we performed a caesarean operation on the snake. Sure enough, the dozens of baby snakes were ready and willing to be born and wriggled free of their embryonic sacs. We often wondered how many survived.

At one point, we stopped on the side of the dirt road so that Ron and I could explore the nearby canal and roadside ditches, leaving Winnie alone in the car. While we were gone, one of the large green water snakes we had already captured managed to struggle free of the cloth pillowcase it was held in and began to crawl around inside the car. Winnie vacated her seat out of deference to the snake, electing to wait outside for our return. This may not have been the best choice for her, as she then decided to walk up the road with a flashlight. She immediately came upon a glaring water snake of her own.

Eventually, we did return to the car. I assured Winnie that the water snake in the backseat was harmless and that she could have relaxed in the comfort of the car to wait for us, rather than suffer the hordes of mosquitoes outside. Ron was conciliatory, as well, and as I extolled the harmless nature of the escapee, Ron commenced to catch it and return it to a new pillowcase. The snake immediately turned, seized Ron's arm, and began to chew from his wrist to his elbow. Blood poured profusely from the dozens of needlelike holes the snake's teeth created. Many snakes have saliva that contains an anticoagulant factor, which makes the blood flow freely from the wounds, so the bites looked a lot worse than they really were. Bites from water snakes are not particularly painful, and Ron and I had experienced numerous such harmless snakebites in the past. I had, however, neglected to explain to Winnie that when herp people say a snake is "harmless," it means the snake is not venomous; it doesn't mean the snake is not capable of biting savagely in its own defense. I don't think the subtle difference in terminology held much interest for her.

We next stopped at a roadside bar and hamburger stand for something to eat. There, climbing the steps of the porch, was a glossy black-and-vermilion-bellied mud snake. We figured the snake knew the neighborhood, so the food must be okay. By the end of the evening we had caught a dozen or more four-foot-long green water snakes, an assortment of corn snakes and other rat snakes, some beige and red venomous copperheads, and several very fat black cottonmouth water moccasins, also venomous. I was pleased that our honeymoon was already a great success.

Back at the apartment, we wanted to photograph the snakes before releasing them several nights later. Not wishing to keep them confined in cloth bags for several days, we simply turned them loose in the spare bathroom shower stall, and went night swimming in the glistening blue pool. When we returned, we found, to our amusement, that the door to the bathroom was open and most of the snakes were gone. Now we could have a repeat snake hunt right here at home. We scoured the apartment. There was a rat snake under the sofa, another around the inside edge of the toilet under the seat, a cottonmouth behind the cushion on the love seat, and a water snake now in the swimming pool we had just left.

Finally, all of the snakes were accounted for except one, a fine orange-colored corn snake. Days passed, and it was nowhere to be seen. Winnie's aunt and uncle were due to arrive for their own vacation soon after we left. I better take one last look around, I thought. Upon close inspection of the wall heater, an orange-red snake's coil could barely be seen, deep inside. It was the missing corn snake. Once the snake was extracted—after we had dismantled the heater—we heaved a sigh of relief and liberated the snakes back into the Everglades. Then we reposted the NO SNAKES ALLOWED sign.

Anyone who works with snakes, whether in a professional zoological institution or in a private collection at home, and claims that their snakes never escape is a blatant liar. Any captive animal that is no longer under a keeper's control has, for all practical purposes, escaped. Whether it has managed to travel two feet from its cage or two thousand feet is immaterial. Snakes are notoriously successful escape artists. They have nothing to do, each and every night, but probe the corners of their cages for a loosened screen top, a frame that has slightly too much space around its edge, or a forgotten locking hasp or tie-down device. Even when snakes do not escape by virtue of their own wit, we humans tend to help them out. More than one baby snake has gotten out by climbing the corner of its tank, using droplets of water to allow its ultralight body to stick to the glass. Then, squeezing its body into the frame of the screen top, the snake is carried away to escape, unnoticed, when the keeper removes the top and sets it aside for cleaning. The snake simply leaves the scene after its free ride.

I recall a young Asiatic cobra that escaped an aquarium on the second floor of the Reptile House. The snake could not have gone far on its own, as the aquarium was one of nearly a hundred aquaria located within a snakeproof area called the screen room because of the double layer of screening that lined its walls. In this case, search as we might, the snake could not be found. As the head keeper announced he was going home to his apartment behind the Reptile House for lunch, I looked down at the birdcage he was carrying. For some reason, he had temporarily stored the cage in the screen room. There was the cobra, barely visible, coiled in the floor pan of the cage, under the newspaper liner. In another few minutes, the cobra would have been carried to the head keeper's home and left to wander around his apartment at will.

A young researcher was once hired to care for several hundred harmless baby rat snakes. The snakes were the annual offspring of a prized collection of different species of adult rat snakes that the curator was studying in an effort to understand the complex variation in scale color patterns that emerged when the animals interbred. In the days before DNA technology, it was an interesting question that could more easily be solved with captive managed snakes than by studying animals in the wild. Now such questions can be answered in the laboratory by comparing genetic material from a minute sample of blood or tissue. The researcher does not even have to know what animal it is, but only needs to provide the results of the comparisons to the investigator.

One species, the pilot black snake from the Northeast, ranges southward from New England. A second species, the yellow-and-brown-striped chicken snake, ranges northward from Florida. However, along a zone of integration in North Carolina and South Carolina, where both species come together and crossbreed, the snakes exhibit a variety of pattern combinations that are often referred to as entirely new species. Were they indeed new species or only hybrid forms? The implications had bearing on our understanding of the relationships of many other wide-ranging species. Caring for these experimental animals was a totally mindless job, but the collection represented many years of work by the curator.

Each baby snake, barely twelve inches long and about as thick as a pencil, was housed in a gallon jar, complete with a tiny water dish and a crumpled-up paper towel for it to hide in. These were temporary quarters, as the snakes grew so quickly that they could be transferred to larger cages by the time the next year's harvest of babies rolled around. The young man's task was mundane. He would place the jars with the snakes on a rolling cart and take them to the nearby sink. There, he would reach in and first remove the snake, putting it next to him on a table, then take out the paper towel and water dish. The jar would then be rinsed with clean water and dried with another paper towel, and a fresh crumpled towel, a water dish, and, finally, the snake would be added and the top replaced. The task became mechanical after the first hundred or so jars were cleaned. To his horror, one day the young man noticed that the jars he had just washed did not have snakes in them. Somewhere along the line, without thinking, the young man had changed the order of cleaning. He had removed the snake's furniture first, then rinsed the jars, pouring the rinse water down the drain. Unfortunately, he also poured the baby snakes down the drain along with the water. The curator was not pleased, and neither was I, because I had to have the plumbing system dismantled to find the little escapees.

There are other escape stories. One day, as a young research student sat on the toilet in the Reptile House reading a magazine, he was interrupted by a six-foot-long Asiatic cobra that had worked a rubber stopper loose from the drain hole in the floor of its cage. The snake had escaped through an opening barely half the thickness of its own body. Once through the floor of its cage, it had followed the wall into the nearby kitchen, then made its way under the open-bottomed partition that gave the 1898-vintage toilet some privacy. Upon seeing the snake at his feet, the researcher literally flew over the top of the stall, trousers and briefs around his ankles. The snake did not appear to mind.

Some escapees are amazing. A harmless twenty-four-inch-long milk snake escaped its tank twice in succession by squeezing itself between the aquarium tank frame and the screen top. Both times, it was recaptured several weeks after its escape, found by a mammal keeper, hiding inside the white-footed deer mouse exhibit in the Small Mammal House. The building was located across the green from the Reptile House, a hundred or so feet away. The great distance that the little snake had traveled and the choice of destination were marvels. Deer mouse babies are a food of choice for milk snakes, and the irony was that the associate curator of reptiles had collected both the snake and the deer mice.

It is not unusual for escaped animals, including reptiles, to remain near the familiar surroundings and smells of their home cage. A keeper left the sliding door of a second-floor cage unlatched by accident, allowing thirteen two-foot-long baby Burmese pythons to escape during the night. They weren't hard to find. All thirteen were discovered the following morning, neatly coiled on top of and under a bin containing dozens of white rats used for snake food, in the kitchen on the first floor. Perhaps the snakes, tired of waiting for a take-out order that did not arrive soon enough to satisfy their weekly hunger, had decided to go shopping on their own.

Our three huge reticulated pythons, on exhibit in a very large glass-fronted cage in the front of the main exhibit hall, were always content to stay at home, bathe in their large pool of warm water, and sleep the days away. The fifteen- to twenty-foot-long, 150- to 200-pound snakes rarely moved unless they had to. One night, the snakes were piled high together in a cozy bed, enjoying a snooze on top of a

The author's wife, Myrna Watanabe (right),
Venezuelan scientist Andres Seijas (center), and
Tomas Blohm (left) with some of the twenty-eight
baby American crocodiles captured, tagged, and released
at the Bahia de Turiamo in 1983.

PETER BRAZAITIS

warm heating coil, between the rock entrance to their cave and the glass front of their exhibit. Suddenly, the glass gave way under the combined weight of their bodies, or perhaps a snake or two had yawned, flexing their coils in a sleepy snake stretch. We arrived the next morning to find pieces of broken glass stretching for yards in front of the exhibit and the snakes nowhere to be seen.

They weren't far off, however. On finding themselves disturbed, tumbled unexpectedly onto a cold terrazzo floor, the snakes had done the next best thing to going home: they had crawled around to the back of the exhibit and gone back to sleep in the warm, moist space under their own cage.

Sometimes a supervisor can use a snake's escape as a learning tool for the keeper staff. I always taught that being bitten or bested, even by a harmless snake, was a mark of failure on the part of the keeper and a mark of success on the part of the snake. I had no sympathy whatsoever for the keeper and every respect for the snake. In one instance, a reticulated python taught the keepers a lesson they would not soon forget. That lesson was: Never place the tools needed to work with a dangerous animal in a spot where any advancing movement by the animal will put the tools out of reach. *Think ahead.*

That day the keeper, Joel, opened the door of the reticulated python cage and inadvertently aroused the snake as he cleaned. The snake responded by striking out at him. A fifteen-foot-long python can easily lunge nearly six feet. A bite from such a snake, with its more than two hundred sharply recurved needlelike teeth, can result in numerous deep lacerations that can sever muscle, penetrate to the bone, and require hundreds of sutures. Joel stepped back to avoid the strike. However, instead of retreating, the snake struck a second time, advancing as it did so, and leaving the front of its body hanging outside the cage. The tools now belonged to the snake, and there was no place left for Joel to go in the confined alleyway. Realizing that the situation was out of his control, Joel pushed the button on the nearest emergency bell, alerting the staff that he was in trouble. The other keepers responded immediately. However, they and Joel now found themselves trapped in a dead-end corner of the service

*The author (right) and Tomas Blohm in Venezuela
with a captured eight-foot-long tiger rat snake,
September 1983.*

area behind the snake's cage, with the angry snake in charge of the situation. Each time the snake struck, the keepers, lacking the tools to defend themselves, were forced to retreat farther into the corner.

At about this time, I was returning from lunch and decided to pass through the public area to check the crowd of visitors for any possible problems. As I walked onto the floor, something strange caught my eye through the small glass viewing port on the rear door of an exhibit. A human head suddenly bobbed past the port from the other side of the exhibit. In a moment, another head bobbed past, then another. This did not make any sense, I thought. Not wanting to walk in on an unknown situation, I took a circuitous route to the rear service area. By going to the second floor, I accessed a circular stairway that led opposite to where the snake and the keepers were having their differences of opinion. When I got halfway down the steps, the situation was clear. As the snake struck out, with its mouth wide open to bite whomever it could, the keepers jumped repeatedly to avoid the strike, their heads bobbing past the glass viewing port as they did.

I sat down on the steps, unnoticed, to watch the contest. One of the keepers said, "I'm sure glad Pete isn't here to see this. He would never let us forget—" as the snake struck again and they all jumped. "Wrong," I called out, to their chagrin. Realizing that my help was not going to be easily forthcoming, they resigned themselves to working out the problem on their own. One of the keepers seized on a momentary lapse of attention by the snake and leapt over it to reach a snake hook and a broom. With the tools finally in hand, the keepers safely wrestled the snake back into its cage.

"Why didn't you help?" one of the newer keepers asked. The others knew better. Borrowing a phrase from the staff artist who had watched as Larry the plumber throttled the head keeper during a historic argument, I replied, "Because I wouldn't help a bunch of dumbass keepers who don't know enough to think ahead to protect themselves. And the snake didn't seem to need any help; it knew what it was doing." To this day, Joel tells me he never forgot the lesson.

As a new keeper, I had learned the same lesson myself. Every night, a four-foot-long smooth-fronted caiman would climb out of its pool and wander about the building. I would have to find it the next morning and return it to the pool, where it would gladly stay throughout the day. One morning, I found it lying contentedly in a pool of water under a plant table in the conservatory behind the crocodile pools. Crawling through the water under the table, I reached the caiman and seized it by the jaws to keep it from biting. Unfortunately, I had inadvertently grabbed the animal with a concrete leg of the table inside the circle of my arms. Now I was stuck under the table with a ticked-off caiman that I couldn't let go of.

I called for help. The head keeper soon arrived, took one look, and said, "You don't expect me to get under there and get my new pants all wet, do you?" Then he left me to solve my own problem. I had to release the animal and get away from it before it turned around to bite me—which I did.

Myrna also fell victim to the little things that occasionally interrupted my life. On one memorable date, I announced that I had to stop at the Reptile House to catch a missing cobra. Myrna was no stranger to dangerous animals, having spent years in the swamps of Louisiana, South Carolina, and Georgia, devoting her nights to studying mother American alligators and how they defended their nests and communicated with their young. It was late, and the calls of exotic animals occasionally came through the night as I pulled up to the back door of the darkened Reptile House. Not fully confident of my intentions, Myrna said she would wait in the car. "I'll be back as soon as I can," I promised, and I went inside to begin my search.

That day, a keeper had found that the sliding track of one of the fiberglass cages in the snake nursery had come loose. A young black-lipped forest cobra had squeezed through the space in the frame and was gone. An immediate search of the area had turned up nothing. The search had continued until closing time without success. There were a million places a snake could hide undetected for months, or it might never be found. The best chance of locating the animal was at night, when it would be prowling about, possibly looking for food. We had arranged a schedule of keepers to search at various hours throughout the night, for it was essential to concentrate our efforts in the period immediately following the escape. The more time elapsed, the lower our chances of finding the snake, as it became more familiar with its new surroundings and discovered permanent retreats; or it might wander into the crocodile pools and be eaten, and we would never know it.

With a flashlight and a pair of snake tongs in hand, I began to methodically search passage after passage. Before long there was a knock on the door. It was Myrna. She had weighed her options and found that hunting for a cobra in the darkness of the Reptile House with me was preferable to sitting alone in the darkness in the car, listening to the strange night sounds in a not-so-good neighborhood in the Bronx. We were about to give up when I remembered a small steel plate covering a damp valve hole in the floor in one of the building's sections. As I slowly lifted the heavy plate, the beam from the flashlight caught the glint of shiny black scales on a snake's body. The cobra reared up in defense and looked up at us in defiance. Now, I did not have enough hands to hold up the plate, grab the snake with the tongs, and deliver it into an open plastic barrel. Myrna would have to hold up the plate while I captured the snake. "You want me to do what?" she asked. "Trust me," I said. "I won't get it near enough to reach you." After all, I pointed out, it was "only three feet long."

Within minutes, the deadly snake was safely in the barrel, and we were on our way home. Over the years, she and I would share many more animal adventures together—and they're not over yet.

14

THE KING COBRA'S GONE!

It was hot and humid as I made my way through the throngs of people milling in front of the Reptile House exhibits. As I came to the area by the crocodile pools, Bruce Foster, one of the keepers, frantically rushed to meet me. Sweat soaked his tan keeper's shirt, and he stuttered so badly I could not understand him. In his excitement, Bruce, a large, powerful young man, lifted me off the ground by my arms, so my face would be level with his as he attempted to blurt out the horrific news. I replied as calmly as I could, "Bruce, just put me down. What happened?" Finally, the words emerged. He was missing a king cobra.

Bruce was one of the most experienced and level-minded keepers on staff. I had known him since he was seven years old. His father, Charlie Foster, was a well-respected mammal senior keeper who had been in charge of the Zebra House for many years. Charlie would bring young Bruce to the evening meetings of our combined social and conservation group, the Northeastern Natural History Society. Years later, Bruce became a reptile keeper, a dear friend, and a colleague. There would be many times during our careers together when he would be at my side during some potentially dangerous procedure—capturing a large crocodile or handling a dangerous snake for medical treatment, for example. I had complete faith in Bruce, had in fact trusted him with my life many times over. I sensed that this was going to be another one of those times.

Bruce had shifted our three large king cobras out of the main exhibit cage into a side holding cage, through a sliding door that separated the two cages. Although it was common practice to work with venomous snakes left undisturbed in the cage during routine daily cleaning, any extensive cleaning or disturbance called for the snakes to first be removed to an adjoining shift cage. It was a matter of personal decision. While leaving the snakes in the cage as cleaning took place had certain risks, arousing the snakes to move them also presented its own dangers, since the snakes would become agitated and defensive. After safely shifting the snakes, Bruce had proceeded to clean the exhibit cage. Then he had left it empty, allowing it to thoroughly dry while he went to lunch.

Most permanent exhibit cages are essentially large, decorated concrete boxes, with a public viewing window on the front and a keeper's access door at the rear. Cages for particularly dangerous snakes, such as king cobras and mambas, are also fitted with a sliding door on one side leading to a separate holding cage, and a second trapdoor on the ceiling of the cage for special access. Bruce had taken advantage of the snakes' preference for darkness to encourage them to move—almost voluntarily, in this case—by darkening the shift cage and offering the snakes a place to hide away from the glass-tapping public and the bright lights of the main exhibit cage. It didn't always work this way, but by offering bright or dark lighting combinations between cages, you could sometimes enjoy good luck when the snakes went where you wanted them to go without any provocation on your part.

On his return from lunch, Bruce pulled open the sliding door by its cable-operated handle, allowing the snakes back into the exhibit. He watched through one of the small glass-covered viewing portals on the rear door of the cage as at least one of the snakes immediately entered the exhibit and began to search the cage. This was typical behavior. Most animals, especially snakes, will probe every nook and cranny of a "new-smelling" cage immediately after they are introduced into it, even if they have lived in the cage for many years. King cobras are fairly intelligent snakes, and nothing escapes their investigations as they prowl around the cage, touching every corner, branch, and stone with their tongues, as if to identify any new object in their cage or verify every old familiar one . . . or find a new escape route.

After securing the cable handle in its holder, with the door in the open position, Bruce then went to the front of the exhibit to watch the animals. Strangely enough, the exhibit was empty, even though he'd seen at least one snake enter the cage from the darkened shift cage. Puzzled, he returned to the rear keeper's area, turned on the lights of the shift cage, and carefully counted the snakes, pausing between each count to be certain that his eyes were not playing tricks on him. "One . . . two . . ." he counted. There should have been three snakes. The third snake was in neither the shift cage nor the main cage. Again he counted heads: one large brown head, two large brown heads. Counting heads is the only way to accurately count snakes; each snake has only one head, but when you're looking at the intertwined bodies of several snakes together, it's impossible to separate whose body belongs to whom.

One snake was gone. Disappeared. But how? There had to be a mistake. Yet again, he counted in disbelief, unwilling to comprehend that a twelve-foot-long, five-inch-thick, olive-green king cobra had vanished, literally in front of his eyes. It was no illusion. The snake was gone. It was then that he saw me walking in the public area and ran to tell me.

This was no laughing matter. King cobras are not small snakes. They grow to eighteen feet in length. Furthermore, not only are king cobras one of the most poisonous snakes in the world by virtue of the toxicity of their venom and the large volume of it they can deliver in a single bite, but the animal can, if cornered or angered by an intruder, be very aggressive.

An angry king cobra is a fearsome sight. Alert to any movement, the snake seems to concentrate intently on deciding what it wants to do. I have always felt you can see careful thought in a king cobra's eyes. It shows no fear, just a sense of awareness and confidence. It is as though it knows it can kill you whenever it wishes, if you will be foolish enough to persist in bothering it. It first calmly faces the intruder. Only a foot or two of its body is raised upward in a slightly spread hood. Its head and eyes are fixed on your every movement. If you move left or right, the snake turns to watch. It shifts only as much as it has to. The next move is up to the intruder. Another slight movement on your part, and the snake rears to its full height. A twelve-foot-long king cobra may lift fully half of its body off the ground, spreading a tapering hood that makes it look even larger and more formidable. The snake now stands facing you, literally eye to eye. It is enraged. Another movement by the intruder, or sometimes no movement at all, and the cobra rushes forward with its mouth wide open, its short fangs exposed, and growls loudly. It is difficult enough to retreat from the attack in an open room but impossible in the wild, hampered by branches and tall grass. The bite is delivered as the rushing snake reaches its enemy and strikes downward to seize and chew its victim, saturating the wound with venom. The snake may even press home a second or third attack, until the enemy is dead or gone.

The venom works quickly. It has to if it is to quickly kill the snakes the cobra feeds on, which themselves are difficult to kill. Within minutes, there is a tingling or burning sensation at the bite, followed by dizziness, blurred vision, difficulty swallowing and breathing, and then cramps and vomiting. The victim becomes limp and paralyzed. The victim's central nervous, respiratory, and circulatory systems cease to function. Some victims may survive with rapidly administered antivenin treatment; others are dead within minutes or hours.

People and horses have died after being attacked by an angry king cobra in the wild, when they unexpectedly came upon the snake in the bush. There are even old reports in the literature of working elephants in Southeast Asian teak and mahogany forests dying after being bitten on the trunk by a king cobra. In short, a person bitten by a large king cobra will almost certainly perish. Although we stocked sufficient antivenin to treat any bite from any poisonous snake in the collection, the serum to treat a king cobra bite, which is imported from Thailand, is of poor quality and not all that effective.

This particular king cobra was not especially aggressive, but it wasn't placid either. It would be irritable, and with little provocation could easily be aroused to anger and attack. Worse, we did not have the foggiest idea where it was. It could be hiding three feet away, watching us from the dark spaces under a cage. Or it could have escaped not only its cage but the Reptile House entirely, through the open doorway to the yards and service areas outside, not twenty feet away from the snakes' cage.

I first told the volunteers and work-study students to leave the building, giving no explanation other than "Take a break—have a nice day." Whatever was going to happen, we did not need extra people in the way, or to worry about. Besides, unlike the regular keeper staff, some of them were minors, and all were untrained and inexperienced.

While our first and immediate concern would have to be to protect the public, which meant evacuating the building, time was of the essence if we were to capture the snake at all. But how? What could we say to hundreds of people to get them to expeditiously and quietly leave the Reptile House without creating a potentially disastrous panic? Sometimes the summer crowd of visitors could be so dense that it would take fully fifteen minutes to wend your way the hundred feet from the entrance door to the exit. Today, the building was crowded to capacity.

I was always amazed that people would walk past an exhibit without giving it a second glance until someone else got the idea to stop and look. Then, almost immediately, a crowd would descend on the spot, people straining and pushing to see over and around the person in front of them. It was as though some aerosol attractant had been released, bringing with it a swarm of people, much like flies to dung.

Any hint of activity emanating from the mysterious environs of "behind the scenes"—even a simple thing, such as a keeper opening a cage door from the rear areas or simply walking out of the lunchroom into the public spaces—would have the same effect. A keeper walking among the visitors, carrying a pail full of stones, always elicited a call of "Look, they're feeding the animals." For this reason, we tried to keep staff activities as inconspicuous as possible on crowded days. On the other hand, I could walk unnoticed through the throng with a live snake coiled tightly around my hand, as long as I kept the snake at my side and did not obviously appear to be carrying anything.

The building was particularly hot and oppressive this day, with breathable air at a minimum among the overly perfumed women and smelly, sweating men. The pools of running water for the crocodiles added humidity, which was only increased by the artificial thunderstorms that raged three times a day, spraying sheets of water from nozzles over the pools, as strobe lights flashed simulated lightning and a huge speaker system filled the air with deep rumbles of thunder. The public loved it. I felt that the only thing that could further enhance the visitors' experience would be for us to have a static-electricity generator that could discharge a genuine bolt of lightning onto the aluminum guard railing. This suggestion, however, never met with much approval.

Even without the added stress that hunting for a missing king cobra would bring, doing anything in the Reptile House during hot weather was physically and emotionally draining. Assembling the keeper staff, we began at one end of the building simply telling the visitors that the building was closing for the day and they had to leave. Obediently, with little grumbling, and much to our relief, the people slowly but steadily meandered toward the exits. One man came over to me and said, "Ha. I know why you're closing up: there is a snake loose, isn't there?" I answered as calmly as I could, "Naw, we had a power failure and we have to turn off all of the exhibit lights. You know how Con Edison has been cutting back on electricity this summer, while raising our rates. We'll be open again tomorrow." "Yeah," the visitor replied. "Con Ed makes money for their stockholders while we suffer. Good night."

The public was finally safely out of the way. That is, if, in fact, the snake was still inside the Reptile House. Meanwhile, the keepers began, as discreetly as possible, to comb the bushes around the building. In the half hour from the time the snake disappeared until the public was evacuated, the snake could have traveled three feet or, for that matter, be on its way out of the zoo. We hoped that since the zoo was crowded, and since no one outside had been heard screaming in panic at the sight of a large cobra glaring at them, the snake was indeed still within the Reptile House. But the Reptile House was not entirely snakeproof to the outside world, and the snake could still find its way out of the building over the next several hours.

I next called zoo security and the police substation and asked them to post their people around the building's perimeter and quietly search for the snake. I also asked to have a police car standing by behind the Reptile House to transport a possible snakebite victim to our snakebite specialists at Roosevelt Hospital. I then informed the reptile department curator that his worst nightmare had come to haunt us all. Retrieving fifty ampoules of serum and several syringes from the refrigerator where the antivenin was stored, I carefully placed them on the oak table in the keepers' lunchroom. It was a good place to lay a snake-bitten, unconscious person down. I was certain that before this day and this event was over, one of us would be bitten. The last thing we wanted to do was evacuate the zoo, alerting the press to what was sure to be thought of as a sensational story, especially if a keeper or member of the public were bitten and died. The press was a swarm of locusts that we did not need complicating our lives. At that moment, my three-day migraine headache started.

I began by cautiously inspecting the top of the king cobras' exhibit cage for any hint of how the seemingly impossible had happened, how the snake might have escaped. Two keepers quickly began to check around the immediate outside of the building. It soon became clear how the snake had disappeared: the trapdoor on the top of the king cobra cage was closed, but its locking slide bolt was in the open position. Unknown to Bruce, two young people from the local high school work-study program had been assigned to vacuum accumulated dust from on top of the exhibit cages. One of the students had apparently inadvertently dislodged the slide bolt securing the aluminum trapdoor to the top of the cage with the wand of the vacuum cleaner, putting the bolt in the unlocked position. Like many design flaws I would see in coming years, perpetrated on animal-care workers by corner-cutting administrators and unwitting architects, self-closing security locks had been fitted to the keeper's access door of each exhibit during remodeling, while the unseen trapdoors on the ceiling of the most dangerous snake cages had only been fitted with simple sliding bolts. When Bruce had let the snakes back into their cage, the largest snake had simply followed a branch to the top of its cage and pushed against the trapdoor with its snout. The lightweight aluminum door had opened, and once the snake's body had passed through the open edge of the door, the door had closed behind it. The snake had then found itself loose, on top of the main exhibit cages. It now had several choices. It could go down onto the floor below and possibly escape the building through the nearby door to the outside; it could hide in the plumbing recesses under the cages; or it could climb to the second floor. We reasoned that a twelve-foot-long green snake should not be difficult to find. We were wrong.

If the snake acted true to form, we would have a short period of activity, perhaps several hours, when it would be in a strange new environment outside of its familiar cage and be actively looking for a place to hide. This would be the optimum time to find it, while it was still moving and active. By the end of the day, the snake would settle in somewhere for the night.

King cobras are diurnal, preferring to be up and about during daylight hours. If we failed to find it over the next day or two, it would soon select a place to hole up in and would move only when it had to, perhaps just for food and water. Strictly cannibals, king cobras feed entirely on other snakes. Although the Reptile House was filled with snakes, they were, we hoped, securely protected in their cages and not readily accessible to the cobra. However, we knew that the cobra was accustomed to being fed once each week, had not fed in several days, and would be hungry and actively searching for food again soon. It was important that it not find a meal, because if it did, it would then choose a place to hide and remain inactive for a week or more. Finding it as quickly as possible was paramount, both for our safety and for the safety of the public.

As with the lost black-lipped forest cobra, as time elapsed, the probability dropped that we would capture the king cobra before it hurt or killed someone. There was also the possibility that if it did prowl overnight, it might find its way into the large crocodile pools, perhaps to take a drink of water, where it would surely be killed and eaten by the crocodiles without leaving a trace. In that worst-case scenario, we might never learn what happened to it.

We immediately organized the four experienced keepers into two pairs of searchers and began a methodical search, expanding from the snake's initial point of escape. It was harrowing. There were dark recesses and corners everywhere on the first and second floors. There were tables and equipment, twisted plumbing, bags of bark, file cabinets, air-conditioning compressors, tubs, tanks, and dozens of places where even a large snake could secrete itself and remain unseen until you moved or opened the snake's hiding spot and looked inside with a light. It might then be too late, as the keeper would be very close to the animal and already within attack range. Besides the thousands of potential hiding places throughout the building and each of its sections, the basement of the building had been left as an unfinished crawl space with a dirt floor and a maze of new and discarded plumbing, old bricks, and stones.

Neither the original 1898 foundation, the cement slab that supported the first floor and was composed of cinders and concrete, nor the outside walls of the building had been replaced during the 1952 remodeling. Instead, the new interior of the building had been retrofitted into the old building. There were probably hundreds of unseen holes and accesses through which a snake could pass from the first floor, where the cobra had escaped, to the dark recesses of the extensive basement. During the remodeling, a second floor had been added as well, suspended halfway between the roof and the main floor. Over the public spaces from this second floor hung a hollow false ceiling, creating a two-foot-high inaccessible space in between, filled with wiring and plumbing that ran the length and breadth of the building. The hollow space was sealed with a plaster wall on one side, bordering the tops of the main exhibit cages, including the king cobras' cage. The entire building was an escaped snake's dream and a snake hunter's nightmare.

Our initial sweeps of the building turned up nothing. It was puzzling. We had started our searches within minutes of the snake's disappearance. In its initial escape, it would have to travel through the main keepers' passageways, immediately in front of the office and telephones, adjacent to the kitchen and food preparation room, and the bathroom. This was the most heavily traveled area of the building. Yet this twelve-foot-long snake had vanished in minutes. Bruce had opened the door, watched the snake enter the main exhibit, walked around to the front of the exhibit, and the snake was gone. Not more than ten minutes had elapsed before the immediate area of the escape had been searched. Even if the snake had gone promptly through the open door, the immediate area surrounding the building had been searched at the same time, within minutes. The cobra, an animal with a brain the size of a shriveled-up pea, was not only outsmarting us but causing great grief. Superstition aside, this snake had the makings of a new mythical creature with magical powers.

I decided to do the only thing I could think of. I walked back to my office and retrieved a familiar wooden block from my desk drawer. I had long ago cut the block in the shape of a coffin, from a small piece of lumber, to be used as the ultimate weapon in the fight against stress. Next came a well-used antique hammer and several nails. I then took a comfortable position, as I had on numerous occasions before, sat on my office floor, and proceeded to drive nails into what I thought of as "my coffin." An assortment of bent nails and depressions from maniacal blows of the hammer, along with corresponding dated entries, testified to the numerous trying events that had dotted my supervisory career. I would feel better tomorrow, I lied to myself, as I pounded in the next nail.

Darkness was beginning to fall, and although the entire building was illuminated, skylights, windows, and a glass conservatory provided additional light during the daytime. The recesses of the building were cast deeper into shadows as the sun set. No snake. By 8:30 P.M., we decided it was too dangerous to continue searching; plus, it was unlikely the diurnal snake would be prowling at night. Just in case we were wrong, we decided to sprinkle talcum and bath powder lightly across all of the entranceways and doorways between each keepers' area and exhibit section. In this way, we would see the trail left by the snake should it be on the move during the night. If we were lucky, we might be able to ascertain by the imprint of the snake's belly scales in exactly what direction it was headed. At this point, we were at a total, panicked loss. Everyone contributed his or her toiletries to the talcum-powder technique.

The next morning, we gathered outside the Reptile House at dawn. Everyone had been instructed not to enter the building until we were all together. For all we knew, the snake could be just on the other side of the door, an accident waiting to happen. We left an assortment of snake-catching tools outside the building so we would be well equipped from the get-go. Our plan was to open the door and clear an immediate safe zone. This zone would then be expanded throughout the day until the entire building was searched from roof to basement, much the way the military clears a minefield for advancing troops. Only in this case, even before it is touched, the mine can reach out and bite the searcher. There was never any thought that the snake might have any plan or intentions of its own. It would simply be terrified at being out of the familiar surroundings and smells of its own cage, and would defend itself aggressively only if it were startled or perceived itself to be threatened by someone approaching or coming upon it unexpectedly, or if it felt cornered and unable to escape.

I hate the term *snake attack*. It is difficult to fault the snake for biting or lunging at a person when that person is trying to capture the snake, is inadvertently standing on the snake's head or tail, or has found himself unknowingly between the snake and its escape route to its sanctuary. In the close quarters of the reptile building, however, these encounters, unfortunately, would be the most likely types.

The talcum powder gave little information. Tiptoe dotted trails had been left by mice as they scurried about during the night, picking up bits of popcorn left behind by visitors during the day. Two-inch-long American cockroaches left erratic trails of dots and streaks as they searched for food and ate the sweet-scented talcum powder. But there were no wide-bellied snake trails. By noon, we had still found no trace of the snake. The inevitable question arose: Should the zoo be closed? If it were, the press, anxious to grab such a meaty story, would surely complicate our efforts. I could see the possible headlines: "Escaped King Cobra Headed for the Sewers of New York"; "New Yorkers Afraid to Flush Their Toilets. An Army of Doctors Stands By." I was sure the snake was still in the building. But where?

I decided to take a closer look at the snake's possible escape route. There had to be a logical reason why the snake had vanished so quickly. There was. Adjacent to the unlocked door on the top of the cage was a light box that held the cage's illumination. These boxes were of poor design and overheated the lightbulbs inside, causing them to burn out too frequently. To help the boxes stay cool, the rectangular hinged box covers were left open for ventilation, and they leaned against the wall that made up the perimeter of the false ceiling between the first and second floors. There, hidden out of sight behind the box's cover, was a hole, left behind by an electrician, leading into the space between the false ceiling and the floor above. The snake could simply have passed from the cage's trapdoor into the hole in a matter of seconds. In all probability, half of its body could have been in the hole while the other half still remained in its cage.

We had to confirm our suspicions. Although it would be paramount to know that the snake was still in the building, it could be hiding in the worst possible place. The false ceiling was inaccessible for the most part. Tearing it down would mean essentially destroying the Reptile House for months to come, at great expense. We still might not find the snake in the process, and we had no idea what other holes and accesses to other areas and recesses had been left behind by workmen during construction. Now, however, I had a plan.

Calling in workers from the maintenance shops—at least those who were willing to come to the Reptile House—I had them chop holes at twenty-foot intervals around the entire perimeter of the false ceiling. If the snake were, indeed, in there, we wanted to give it every opportunity to get out whenever it wished, so we could capture it.

Next came the bait. The cobra would certainly be hungry from the activity of its adventure, and we had just the right appetizer. Succulent, pungent black racers were taken from the stores of frozen dead snakes we kept on hand for the weekly king cobra feeding. It was their favorite food. Once thawed in warm water, the black snakes were then tied with strong cotton twine at several places along the body and tethered next to the holes. The dead snakes were not about to move on their own, but we didn't want the cobra dragging them off either. With some luck, the cobra would be attracted to the scent of one of the dead snakes and begin to eat it. The cobra would then have two choices. As it couldn't entirely swallow the tethered snake, it could regurgitate the snake and give up its meal. In this case, we would then know that the cobra had been there by the saliva on the snake and that the dead snake had been moved. Or if we were really lucky, we might come in to find the greedy, hungry cobra with the snake still inside it, essentially attached by the same cord that held the dead snake.

Our searches produced other mysterious finds. While investigating one section, a keeper peered under an aquatic tank to find a phalanx of turtles snoozing in the moist darkness. Apparently, as the inattentive keeper had entered the turtles' cage to clean, the turtles, one by one, had left to explore the world on their own. Another keeper reported hearing scratching noises coming from inside the wall of the reptile nursery. We quickly gathered our forces and made our way down there, crawling crablike through the unfinished basement to that corner of the building. With our level of anxiety at high alert, we half-expected an enraged king cobra to emerge from any of a hundred dark recesses at any moment. We finally arrived at the ventilating duct that seemed to be the source of the scratching. Tearing open a small access port through which we could shine a light and cautiously peer inside, we were astounded to find a four-foot-long green iguana within the duct. The only problem was that we did not have any iguanas in the collection at that time. A visitor who no longer wished to keep it as a pet must have liberated it in the building. How it had managed to find its way into the closed ventilation system we will never know. The iguana was finally extricated, unharmed, from the duct.

Another encounter that day bolstered our hopes that the cobra was still in the Reptile House. Bruce decided to search the storage attic. Access to the attic was gained by climbing a stepladder placed beneath a trapdoor. By standing on the top of the ladder, a person could then pull himself up and into the opening. He would then be in total darkness among a sea of unused crates, shipping cartons, old cages, and boxes of lightbulbs. (A single lightbulb illuminated the space, but on this day, as usual, it was burned out.) The floor of the attic was made up of odd planks of wood, and unfinished walls and girders framed the interior of the roof. It was a conduit to nowhere and everywhere, but especially to the adjoining false ceiling. As Bruce shined his flashlight in the darkness, he immediately heard a low growl, mixed with the sound of hissing air, and followed by the rasping of scales as a body pushed and rushed through the empty boxes in a headlong flight to escape. The king cobra had undoubtedly been in the dark attic with him and had chosen to flee rather than attack. Bruce flew through the access door and down the ladder, calling for help. But it was too late: the cobra was once again gone.

Day three of a migraine headache and loose bowels. The morning was a repeat of the day before. The keepers met outside the Reptile House at dawn and began their safety-zone searches. But this time, it was different. A check of the dead snake traps disclosed that one of the black racers had, indeed, been dragged into the hole in the false ceiling. It was covered with slimy saliva and venom and punctured with tooth marks. Our cobra had not been as greedy as we had hoped, however, and had opted to spit the whole thing back out rather than be held to the spot by the cord. Unless one of our keepers had developed a fondness for old, smelly dead snakes, we now knew where our cobra was hiding—at least for the moment.

One by one, we cautiously peered as far as we could through the chopped holes. The beam of our flashlights barely pierced the recesses of the false ceiling. One hole after another brought renewed anxiety at the hopeful prospect that the snake—even just a coil or a few scales—would be visible. But there was also the danger that the snake would not be far into the ceiling, if it was there at all, but lying just inside the hole, out of sight. While kneeling in the cramped quarters between the end of the floor and a catwalk that spanned the top of the exhibits, there would be no place for a person to run, no escape or evasion, if the cobra suddenly charged from the hole. When it was my turn, sweat poured into my eyes and burned.

Then, at the last hole, far into the dark reaches of the ceiling, between two metal brackets holding up the ceiling below, lay a shadowy, barely discernible, scaled form. At first I could not focus my eyes enough in the poor light to recognize the convoluted shape lying in symmetrical coils, like a harmless fat green hose.

Once I had stepped into the north passage of the Reptile House, where the main exhibit cages held venomous snakes, and seen Chris, a burly mounted police officer who was assigned to the zoo and often visited the building. He stood in the passageway—motionless. I said, "Hi, Chris. What's up?" He said nothing, then forced his eyes slowly downward toward his side. Without moving, he mouthed the word *snake*. I burst into laughter. I wondered how long he had been standing there, motionless. Draped across the butt of his holstered pistol, holding him firmly in place, was a coil of the plastic garden hose used to clean the snake cages, which hung on a column in the passageway. As Chris had walked by, his gun butt had accidentally collected a coil of hose. Woven into the green plastic was a mosaic of reinforcing cords that resembled snake scales. The snake-fearing Chris had felt a tug that suddenly restrained him as he walked. He had glanced down, thought he had seen a snake coiled across his hip, and had frozen in fear, certain he was a dead man.

I was not looking at a garden hose. I had found the cobra. Its head twitched as the beam of light interrupted its solitude. I looked again to be sure of what I was seeing, and backed slowly away from the hole. The last thing I wanted to do was to motivate the snake into moving farther into the false ceiling, or leaving altogether. I called the curator to tell him that our nightmare might soon be over—or could get a lot worse.

It had been one thing to find the snake. But now that we had found it, the question was, How do we capture it? It lay too far inside the ceiling to reach easily. Neither did we know if there were any additional construction openings within the ceiling that would allow the snake to again escape our capture, should we disturb its resting place with too much noise and vibration from any extensive chopping away of the ceiling. The portion of the ceiling the cobra was in was actually part of a balcony wing that extended out over the crocodile pools, and was held up by a steel column located in the middle of the land area of an exhibit holding several large crocodiles, including a rather ill-tempered Cuban crocodile.

While we could see the snake, the angle was bad, and metal straps and hangers obstructed any clear approach to it from the second-floor hole we had previously made in the perimeter ceiling wall. However, if we could cut a second hole in the plaster ceiling wall from a place immediately above the Cuban crocodile pool, we might have a straight-line view to the snake. Even from there, the snake lay fully eight or more feet within the ceiling, and well out of reach.

I then had a rather stupid idea. By standing on the very top step of a stepladder, braced against the steel column in the Cuban crocodile pool, I might be able to quietly cut a second hole in the plaster wall and reach through it with a very long noose and pole and noose the snake. The problem was, what would the crocodiles be doing as I teetered on the top step of the ladder, standing in the pool among them? Second, any noosing pole I used would be too long for me to manipulate both ends of it at the same time. I couldn't hold on to keep from falling into the crocodile pool, manipulate the noose over the snake's head, and pull the noose tight by the wire at the opposite end of the plastic pipe all at the same time, and quickly. Once the snake felt the noose tighten around its body, it would erupt in a fury, twisting and turning to escape. I would be the closest thing to that fury. Even if I succeeded in reaching the snake without being rudely interrupted by the crocodiles, I would have to get the snake to attack toward my face, which would be framed in the hole, and, hopefully, get it to charge through the open noose. Once noosed, the snake could be extracted forcibly through the hole and thrust over the crocodile pool into the public area, where it could be taken in hand. I wondered why I had chosen this particular career. I was very accomplished at plumbing.

The curator arrived with his .410-gauge shotgun. The snake would have to be shot dead if there was any chance at all that it might escape our capture and take off at large again. In the meantime, we wanted to make every effort to capture the snake alive and unhurt. Neither the keepers nor I, however, enjoyed such caring protections in this gambit. The second hole I had proposed making, where my head would be framed in the opening, would lie in a direct firing line from the hole the curator would shoot from on the second floor. If he shot at the snake, there was a fair chance he might shoot me, as well. I didn't like that. In fact, the whole thing sounded like a flawed plan. I could either be bitten in the face by an enraged king cobra, fall from the top of a ladder into the jaws of an equally enraged Cuban crocodile, or be shot dead by an overly zealous curator. It seemed like the cobra was getting even for the choices I had given it earlier over the dead black snakes. Nevertheless, the plan could work.

The crocodiles seemed delighted, although resentful, that a whole army of potentially tasty people were entering their pool. Bruce held the ladder in place against the ceiling support column. Another keeper kept back the crocodiles with a broom, as though watchfully sparring with a combatant. I climbed the ladder to the top. As quietly as I could, I began to chisel away at the plaster ceiling wall, in a place I estimated was in the correct angle to reach the cobra. We had already fashioned a makeshift noose from a ten-foot-long piece of PVC pipe and a length of flexible electrical wire.

The soft plaster came away easily, exposing the underlying wire support mesh. Even through the mesh, I could now see the cobra in the beam of my flashlight, flicking its tongue and moving its head slightly in erratic jerks. It breathed deeply, its neck and body inflating slightly. It was trying to figure out what was happening; whatever it was, it wasn't happy about it. I quietly and cautiously cut away the mesh with a pair of shears, exposing a hole about one foot square— just big enough to drag the cobra through, if all went well. I would be the first to know if it didn't.

Sweat poured into my eyes, which burned from the salt. I inserted the open loop of the noose through the hole and pushed the pole toward the snake. If I succeeded in getting the snake to rush at me through the noose, I would yell, "Pull," whereupon another keeper, on the ground, would tug the noose tight around the snake and drag it through the hole. At that moment, I would have to vacate the ladder quickly, as otherwise I would surely be bitten as the enraged snake emerged; I would have to jump from the ladder onto the land area toward the rear of the crocodile pool, avoiding the crocodiles.

I prodded the cobra's coil with the noose pole. At first, it flinched spasmodically and turned to look at the offending spot on its body with a half-spread hood. I prodded a second time, and the snake growled as it expelled air from its lung in a burst of rage, catching sight of my face silhouetted in the plaster opening. It made a short rush in my direction, but only for a few feet, then retreated back to its coiled position. Again I prodded, this time harder, and now the snake had had enough. It opened its mouth and rushed full force toward me, lunging through the open noose as it did. I yelled, "Pull!" and leapt from the ladder as the king cobra boiled out of the hole with the noose tightly clamped around its body, thrashing, its jaws open wide as it attempted to bite anything or anyone within reach. I half-expected a shotgun blast to come from above. Fortunately, it never came.

In an instant, the writhing cobra was on the ground outside the crocodile pool. The curator, who had come from his shooting position on the second floor, rushed to grasp the snake behind its head. In the same brief amount of time the snake had needed to escape and become a lurking, deadly menace, it had once again become a captive.

We carried the subdued cobra, still growling in rage, back to the cage from which it had originally escaped. The moment its head was released and the cage door slammed shut, it darted to the front of the cage and faced the glass in sheer defiance, with us safely behind it. The cobra once again found itself in familiar surroundings. It turned, and in a blur of motion flowed onto the branch that led to the top of the cage and the trapdoor it had escaped through, and pushed on it with its snout. This time, the door didn't open.

Since then, every time we've found ourselves engaged in a stressful situation at work, either in the Bronx or, later, at the Central Park Zoo, Bruce and I have shared the same dream. It isn't a nightmare—and it isn't pleasant either. There is always an angry king cobra to catch.

15

NIXON GRIFFIS,
SEA SNAKES,
AND EELS

Nixon Griffis was well known as an important trustee and bene-factor of the New York Zoological Society whose gifts went well beyond simple donations of money and support. Tall and thin, a little hunched over, with his wispy gray hair combed back, he always wore a gray suit and small wire spectacles, and usually looked very much the part of a distinguished banker. Nick, as many of us called him, despite his importance, was a graduate of Cornell University and had served as an officer in the Signal Corps in the U.S. Army during World War II. He had then joined an investment-banking firm as a partner; later, as chairman and owner of Brentano's bookstores, he had expanded the chain to sixteen stores. After selling the business, he had devoted the remainder of his life to his real interest, wildlife conservation, which is how we got to know him.

New, rare, and unique animals were Nick's passion. His interest was easily aroused by a casual story in a newspaper or something he happened to see or hear. One day he could be taken with a rare scorpionfish inhabiting the reefs of Papua New Guinea, the next by a report of the capture of a supposedly long-extinct coelacanth in the

Indian Ocean, or the sighting of a giant squid carcass. Once his interest was aroused and he thought that having the species at the Bronx Zoo or the New York Aquarium would have scientific merit and generate public interest, he would go for it. Literally. His aides would soon be sent off to wherever in the world they needed to go to scope out the logistics, gather whatever information they could from local people, and set the groundwork for an expedition to capture and return with specimens. Nick frequently went on such expeditions himself, regardless of his failing health, accompanied by his friend and colleague Eddie Doles of the aquarium. He frequently completed the task by funding a special exhibit to receive the animals he had collected. For all practical purposes, Nick was a modern-day scientific version of Frank Buck, the man who had supposedly traveled all over the world to bring back exotic animal species. Nick was like an enthusiastic kid in a pet shop, only he could well afford to buy the entire street the shop was on, if he so desired.

I liked Nick. He was sharp and inquisitive, and he knew animals, especially fish. Often, when I was working on a Sunday afternoon, there would be a ring at the rear doorbell, and it would be Nick and his female companion, visiting the zoo and looking for a place to hide from the fawning attention of the upper-level administrators, and perhaps have a sip of coffee. The first question he always asked was, "How is Rosie? Can we see her?" Rosie resided in an off-exhibit holding tub on the second floor. She was a lovely coral pink South American boa constrictor that Nick had donated to the reptile department. Rosie gained special favor when he learned she had bred for the first time with a handsome, orange-hued male. Over the years, Rosie continued to breed, producing a dynasty of boas that were exquisite in their color and beauty.

Next inevitably came "And how are the frogs doing?" Nick was referring to the zoo's thirteen Lake Titicaca frogs, the product of another of his expeditions. He and a team of divers had collected them from the cold, high-altitude Andean mountain lake after which the frogs were named. The frogs were bizarre in that they were barely known to science, were entirely aquatic, lived at temperatures around fifty degrees Fahrenheit, and were thought to never have to come to the surface to breathe air. The chubby four- to six-inch-long green-and-white-spotted frogs have skin that hangs in great folds from their body and legs, like oversized drapery. This increased skin surface, combined with the frog's cold-water habitat, is supposed to allow it to absorb all the oxygen it needs directly through its skin from the surrounding water.

I panicked the day the frogs arrived unannounced at the back door of the Reptile House. Packed in an insulated box, they were handed over to me by Nick's driver from the aquarium, with the admonition, "You had better get these things in cold water fast or they'll die in a couple of hours." In little more than an hour, I had torn the refrigerated drinking-water fountain out of the staff office (much to everyone's regret), fitted it with a small electric pump to recirculate the chilled water through a long coiled plastic tube, and had several aquaria ready to receive the frogs. They lived at the Reptile House for many years, to Nick's amazement; most of the unusual fish he collected for the aquarium, he often said, soon died.

The yellow-lipped sea krait is one of the fifty species of sea snakes that inhabit the warm-water oceans of the world. It's a moderate-sized snake, with black and yellow markings on its head that form a mask and bright yellow lips, from which it gets its name. Its body is beautifully patterned in silver gray and jet-black bands from head to tail. While females are often more than four feet long, the male is diminutive, at best one-third her size. Although the snake's venom is particularly potent, and quickly paralyzes the central nervous system of its prey, the snake itself is very docile and literally cannot be made to bite when captured. That's a good thing, too, because there is no specific antivenin to treat a sea krait bite, should an accident occur. I must admit that I have never been able to bring myself to handle sea kraits in any way other than with extreme care, and with a sturdy pair of long-handled tongs. I never wished to be known as the statistic that might prove the exception.

Sea snakes, as a whole, spend their entire lives in the ocean. They hunt fish and other prey among the recesses of tidal pools, reefs, and floating kelp, and give birth to large numbers of live young at sea. Since they have no enlarged belly scales, they have difficulty crawling when forced to be on dry land. But their tails are compressed into a broad paddle, and their ability to swim and dive to great depths is remarkable. Thousands of sea snakes have been reported in the waters of the South Pacific, and migrating swaths of writhing sea snakes have been described as extending for miles.

The sea krait, on the other hand, is unique in that it is the only species of sea snake that has wide belly scales like those of land-dwelling snakes, which enables it to crawl out of the sea and onto the beach at night. The females lay about a dozen elongated, white, leathery eggs in these hideaways, and may guard the eggs by coiling around them. Large numbers of sea kraits can often be found hidden under palm fronds, among beach debris, and in coral caves, particularly in Fiji and the Pacific islands of Palau. Very little was known about the life history of the species—that is, until Nick decided that he and John Behler, the Bronx Zoo's curator of reptiles, would go to Fiji, where, while Nick languished in the sun, John would make a collection of sea kraits for a new coral reef exhibit at the Reptile House. My story is what happened when they returned with more than twenty of the snakes. Then my problems began.

First, although they will eagerly drink fresh water, sea kraits need to live in salt water. Second, sea kraits feed only on living eels of the appropriate size—a thing that varies with the size of the individual sea krait. These two primary requirements, we soon learned, posed a nightmare of logistical problems.

We had the resources of the New York Aquarium at our disposal, with its deep wells for pumping sea water. However, bringing many gallons of sea water from the bowels of Brooklyn to the zoo in the Bronx once or twice a week would be more than our staff could manage, particularly when we tabulated the time spent away from the care of the rest of the animal collections. Besides, we had no truck that could carry hundreds of pounds of water. Manufacturing our own sea water would be the only answer. At this point, saltwater aquaria were just beginning to come into the marketplace, and artificial sea salt, complete with a balance of minerals, was available, albeit at a very steep price.

Addressing their diet was another issue entirely, and not as easily solved. Eels? Where would I get a constant supply of live eels in New York City? My first stop was one of a number of local pet shops that carried Pacific Rim reef eels. I bought two, each about six inches long, for forty dollars apiece. We happily plopped them in the first tank with two snakes, and they were gone within an hour. This would not do. We had many more snakes to feed, and even after they fed they would be looking for another meal in a few days.

Then I remembered the Italian markets. I loved to eat eels as a kid, skinned and breaded and deep-fried with Italian seasoning. I raced to the Italian fish market on Arthur Avenue, a few blocks from the zoo. The Arthur Avenue markets had served us well for many years. Each Wednesday, two young boys could be seen wheeling a hand truck loaded with crates of chickens to the back door of the Reptile House, as their older brothers had done for years before them, making the weekly python food delivery. I will always remember how the accounting department at the zoo constantly complained about the bills they had to pay and then store in their files. Each weekly bill was the same: twenty to thirty pounds of chickens at $5.50 a pound, live, written in pencil on a letterhead envelope spattered with chicken shit.

There were eels—live beautiful green eels, eels in baskets of wet sea kelp, and eels swimming in huge tanks of water. I asked for a dozen—no, two. The fishmonger, in his white coat and black rubber apron, quickly scooped out several eels with his net, grabbed them one by one with his rubber-gloved hand as they writhed uncontrollably, then thrust them into a plastic bag. I had forgotten how when eels are irritated they give off a thick slimy secretion that makes them all but impossible to grasp. "How much?" I asked. "Ten bucks," he said. A bargain, I thought. I was sure that my troubles were over—fool that I was.

The eels were way too big for the snakes to eat. Eels for human consumption have to be large enough to make a good meal: at least a half dozen three- to four-inch-long sections of meat-covered verte-brae, after the head, viscera, and skin are removed. Our snakes, how-ever, would eat them whole. The fish-market eels had bodies fully an inch and a half thick. We soon found that even our largest, four-foot-long snake could only engulf an eel barely an inch thick. One krait that tried to eat an eel nearly choked to death. I began to call every-one I knew who might give me an idea, with absolutely no luck. It then occurred to me that the Italian markets had to get their eels from someplace. Back to Arthur Avenue I went, to my fishmonger. "The Fulton Fish Market, on the south end of Manhattan," he told me. Then, to my amazement, there in the Yellow Pages was a listing for a wholesale fish distributor on Long Island that advertised eels. I was cautiously ecstatic.

I called the "eelery," and sure enough, they not only stocked all sizes of eels but also were willing to open an account for us and de-liver. The next day, we were at the eelery with a purchase order in hand. I had never seen anything like it before. A huge run-down hangarlike building was set in the middle of a collapsing parking lot. The lot was partially flooded with water, and as we drove up we could see ripples made by eels swimming away. Or perhaps they were trying to park?

The building itself held rows of large wooden tanks, into which volumes of aerated water gushed, flowing out again through plastic drainpipes. Each tank held hundreds of eels. The building contained thousands and thousands of eels. Unlike the surrounding parking lot, the building was completely flooded with several inches of water. We were given rubber boots to wear to tour the facility. At each step we took, escaped eels fled through the water in every direction. From here, boxes of live eels were being shipped by air freight all over the world. We watched as a three-foot-long corrugated waxed box, about two feet wide and six inches high, was placed on a steel table. One man threw a pail of crushed ice into the open box as another held the top in a way that half-covered the open box, to limit escapes. Next, another man was ready with a five-gallon pail full of writhing eels, netted out of the water of a nearby tank. He literally threw them en masse into the waiting box of ice, whereupon the second man slammed the top shut and a banding machine quickly sealed the box. The next box was instantly readied as the first was loaded onto a truck for its trip to Kennedy Airport and some waiting European gourmet table.

The deal was soon done, and for the next several years our sea kraits thrived and bred. The hatchling babies, barely eight inches long and the thickness of a pencil, required elvers, or young eels. Born in the Sargasso Sea, some eels make their way into the mud flats of the coastal northeastern United States to grow. We found ourselves sending expeditions of keepers to the mud flats of Staten Island at low tide to seine for eels. On any given trip they might find several or none, along with discarded guns, drug paraphernalia, and old rusted cars. Eventually, our supply eelery moved to Maine, but it continued to ship us eels. This time, the boxes of live eels were put on a bus that stopped on a street corner in midtown Manhattan, where our keeper punctually waited each week. I often wondered what the regular ticket-holding passengers might have thought if they had known that their trip was being shared with throngs of live eels on the way to be fed to a horde of hungry, venomous South Pacific sea snakes.

16

GOLIATH FROGS

In April 1981, I was about to add a new dimension to my life. This would be my first major involvement in field research. John Behler sat down at the big oak table in the Reptile House seminar room. "So," he began, "are you ready to go to Cameroon?" I hadn't the foggiest idea what he was talking about, but I reflected for a moment, then said, "Sure." Little did I know what I was getting into, or that both of us would come close to losing our lives before our adventure was over. The trip John was talking about would officially become known as the Nixon Griffis Goliath Frog Expedition to Cameroon, West Africa. This time, Nick had his eyes set on the giant Goliath frog of equatorial West Africa. The frog is the largest in the world, grows to the size of a small dog, and can weigh as much as ten pounds. Nick's appetite was up, and plans quickly became reality with Nick: by the time John and I were recruited into the expedition, not only had Nick begun to investigate the feasibility of the study but a new exhibit to receive the frogs was already in the planning stage. Our destination would be the forbidding mountainous jungles of Cameroon, where reportedly, the Goliath frog inhabited the region's fast-moving rivers, waterfalls, and rapids.

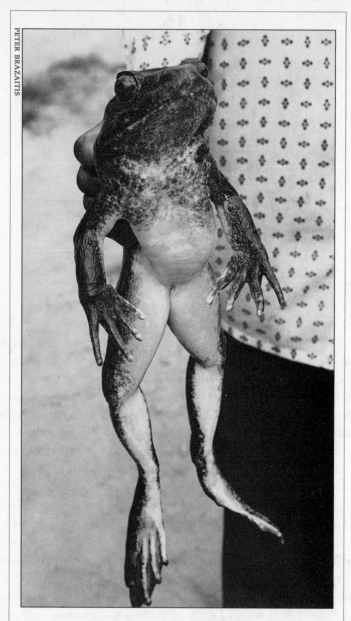

A captured Goliath frog.

Nick had connections all over the world, and he used them. The basic operational plan was simple: go to Cameroon and secure any necessary permits; rent four-wheel-drive vehicles for transportation; establish a base of operations within the Goliath frog's home range, from which we could foray into the field in several directions; house and care for the frog collections we hoped we would capture; and rest and resupply between local expeditions. We would first fly to Douala, then make our way to Yaoundé, the capital of Cameroon. There we would meet with our in-country contact at the U.S. embassy, obtain our vehicles, and jump off into the interior in search of the frogs. After collecting as many frogs as we required, we would return to Yaoundé, then backtrack to Douala, where we would fly with our live cargo to Ivory Coast. In Ivory Coast, Nick had arranged for us to board a Pan American 747 cargo plane bound for New York, which touched down in the port city of Abidjan once a week. Even our stopover accommodations in the most elegant hotel in Abidjan had been arranged. The whole expedition would take less than a month. It sounded simple enough. We were idiots.

I had a special problem: I couldn't swim. Yet I was going to hunt frogs in the middle of the night from some kind of small boat on rivers that swirled through forests, hundreds of miles from any serious medical help. I had barely three weeks to learn to swim, or at least to be reasonably sure I could survive in a river accident. When I told the instructor at the YWCA that I needed to learn how to swim in a couple of weeks, then explained why, the look on his face was priceless. This would be my third attempt at learning how to swim, and despite the boasts of Bob, the instructor, that he "had never found anyone he could not teach to swim," just as I had in my previous two attempts, I got progressively worse with each lesson. Midway through my trials, someone stole my bathing suit from the men's locker room as I showered. I've always suspected it was Bob, attempting to get rid of me to protect his unbroken record. He finally conceded defeat and spent the last few lessons teaching me survival skills, which would later help save my life by giving me confidence in the water.

As quickly as our plans had begun, they changed. Unknown to us, an old research associate, Dr. Victor Hutchinson of the University of Oklahoma, was already well advanced in planning a similar expedition to Cameroon to capture Goliath frogs. Vic had postulated that these giant frogs, with such a primitive respiratory system, could not possibly sustain stress and high levels of activity without collapsing, or even dying. He was eager to study them in his physiology laboratory under highly monitored and regulated conditions.

The historical literature included information on where a few scientists had captured these frogs—usually dead—for museum collections. Since we were both intending to use these data as a kind of road map, our individual plans immediately merged into one effort. Independently, we probably would have visited the same places, done the same things, and given the natives twice the amount of entertainment as we eventually did.

I had worked with Vic some sixteen years before, during a course of studies on how pythons incubate their eggs and keep them warm. Unlike most reptiles, some pythons can contract their body muscles as they coil around their eggs, thereby raising their body temperature enough to incubate the eggs. I knew Vic as a very professional scientist. He always dressed in a white shirt and tie, and he had an authoritative bearing about him, a holdover from years spent in the military. He liked being in a command position, and his midwestern drawl, jungle boots, fatigues, Vietnam cap with cartridge loops, and even his limp seemed to enhance the image. I liked him, and I planned to salute him as often as I could.

Although Vic would use this opportunity to take a well-earned sabbatical, he had received a sizable research grant to collect and study the frogs. He, in turn, had found a young graduate student, whom I'll call Ralph (after my lazy orange cat) for the purposes of this story. Later, I will refer to his wife as Zoë, after a difficult calico cat that lives under my dresser. Ralph had been in the Peace Corps in Cameroon. Vic gave Ralph a plane ticket and $3,000 and sent him back to Cameroon to prepare for our arrival. The money was to be used to secure four-wheel-drive vehicles, acquire permits, find lodgings, and generally pave the way for the expedition. The problem was that, unknown to us at the time, Ralph instead used much of the money to buy a bride and throw a month-long monster party, the likes of which the bride's village had never seen. Ralph sowed the seeds of disaster on our behalf, even before we left New York.

John and Vic would share overall leadership responsibilities as senior investigators, meaning they would pay all the bills. John and I were the best funded, so we could make things happen, while Vic had to pinch pennies. Of the two, John was the more responsible and serious-minded of our group, and the best looking, besides. This was an attribute that, on occasion, we would find as important as bribery. This trip was going to be a first in many ways for all of us; we could not have anticipated the political morasses or poor conditions we would have to deal with, or the full range of equipment we would need, to accomplish our mission. Some of us would forget to bring essential supplies or equipment, such as a mosquito net in which to sleep without disturbance from hordes of mosquitoes, nocturnal visitations from centipedes and spiders, or from equally sleepy lizards. Such omissions would mean the difference between some degree of comfort and sanity and mental depression. Some supplies, such as gallons of insect repellent, we erroneously anticipated would be available in Cameroon. They weren't. I enjoyed the only mosquito net, a completely enclosed pouch of my own design, which excluded all unwelcomed visitors. The others would often have to endure sleepless nights and swollen lips with great reserve and dignity.

The team would be complete with the addition of Ted Papenfuss from the California Academy of Sciences. Ted was easygoing, independent, a superb field scientist, and a survivor. I liked him immediately, and quickly surmised that I could learn the most about getting along in the bush and dealing with local people from him. I also figured that if there were ever a question of survival, Ted would be the person to be with. Ted had been to Africa before, and had even captured a Goliath frog. Once he had been arrested in some African country and had had his international driver's license seized by the authorities. At the last moment, he had traded his pass to a chain of

California movie houses for the license, then quickly left the country. At the end of our trip, he tried to give his worn and tattered field clothes to the natives, but they refused them. I really liked Ted.

The day finally arrived, and twenty hours after we left New York, we were in Cameroon. Our education began immediately. The immigration authorities ignored us until we figured out on our own that we had to make up some address of where we were staying in Cameroon before they would allow us entry. How would we know this information until we met our contact, after entering Cameroon? Immediately, hungry baggage handlers descended on us like swarming ants, while a shoeshine boy tried to polish my sneakers as I walked. The ticket agent ignored our tickets, threatening to make us miss our connecting flight, until we paid his baggage-handler colleague a gratuity for him to intercede on our behalf. We had just experienced the Cameroonian method of redistributing wealth.

The forty-minute flight to Yaoundé on Air Afrique was hot and cramped. I kept looking at the torn seats and debris strewn about the cabin, wondering how often the thing got serviced and hoping it would remain airborne. In Yaoundé, the customs inspector decided that John had too many cameras and should give him one. He then thought my tape recorder was an illegal two-way radio, until I played back the tape with Myrna's voice on it, jokingly berating me for my bad looks. He compassionately gave it back and passed us on, believing that since the voice was my wife's, I was already suffering enough.

Ralph, Vic's American student, had arrived. He was a younger and less educated man than I had expected. Also, he had brought a microsized Renault, driven by his brother-in-law, to transport the five of us plus a month's worth of equipment to the hotel. I was worried. The Hôtel Mont Fébé turned out to be huge and expensive. It boasted noisy music, a swimming pool, a lounge, Coca-Cola at three to six dollars a bottle, and prostitutes of various races and skin colors. One showed up at Vic's room that night and brazenly used his underarm deodorant before he could get rid of her.

Ralph had not been able to secure the essential four-wheel-drive Land Rovers we needed for our treks into the backcountry, nor had he arranged for any of our permits. He said he had set up our base camp in Ebolowa, a small town some distance away, which proved to be located inconveniently from all of our anticipated collecting sites. In six weeks, he had, however, been successful in spending the $3,000 Vic had given him, and he was now completely broke.

The success of our expedition was clearly questionable. I was sure of one thing though: if John and I did not survive, neither would Ralph. Ted continued our education by explaining that what we had so far encountered was what seasoned Africa travelers call "wawa," short for "West Africa Wins Again." It means that just when you think you are getting somewhere, you find out you have actually been led in a circle and haven't accomplished anything at all. We would use the phrase often during our stay. We would also learn that everything must occur as "wait," or "West African Internal Time," which means that in West Africa, everything moves at one-tenth the speed at which the rest of the world functions, including Mexico, New York City street pothole-repair services, and even the Louisiana bayous.

Our first visit to the ministry to inquire about permits led us to a questionable secretary who spoke to Vic while she looked coyly at John, smacking her crimson lips. Madame Tebbe measured her own importance by the number of times she could make people return to her office in pursuit of anything they needed. Our permits would not come easily, if at all. We soon learned that the more important the minister was, the less often he was required to come to work. To get him to sign or issue anything, we needed the approval of the crimson-lipped Madame Tebbe, in addition to paying someone a tip to keep our applications under his nose. I always felt that the ministers and their assistants were in absolute earnest when they welcomed us with warm smiles and handshakes.

By midmorning we had met Simone Paul Nwanak, our Cameroonian contact and escort and the commercial assistant to the U.S. embassy in Yaoundé. Simone was everything Ralph was not: intelligent, self-assured, and fluent in English, French, pidgin, and a number of African languages, including Bulu (a local language). Simone was handsome, slight of build, impeccably manicured and dressed, and could live for weeks out of an ordinary attaché case without wrinkling his clothes. He read everything and anything, knew how to handle any situation, and was more civilized than the rest of us. We had been told before we left New York that Simone was a "frog man," and particularly liked them. He did like them well enough—but to eat, not to study. He and I shared a reputation for being able to fix cars with few tools and fewer spare parts, an important talent in Cameroon.

Our first lunch in Cameroon inadvertently consisted of hard-boiled eggs and sodas; the barkeeper handed us a handful of hard-boiled eggs in lieu of change.

The next morning, we met Simone at the embassy and again tried unsuccessfully for the elusive permits. We had, however, made some progress in securing vehicles—a rather luxurious Renault 12, rented from the hotel Hertz dealer, and a dilapidated Land Rover with balding tires, worn-out steering, a bad transmission, and almost no brakes. John, Vic, and Simone commandeered the Renault, while Ted, Ralph, and I were relegated to the Rover.

Ralph was already a growing problem. He was becoming belligerent at not being given the authority and respect he felt he deserved, as a white man, over Simone, an African. Luckily, the noise level in the Rover was so high we could barely hear each other speak across the front seat, much less hear Ralph from the back. Ralph's mind seemed to be an interesting pile of rendered fat; he fixated on simple things and responded to any problem with "No problem, Doc," repeated several times over. We speculated that he was on drugs, had had a nervous breakdown, suffered from some tropical parasites that had invaded his brain, or was an alcoholic. We collectively decided to use Ralph as a gofer, a calling more in line with his abilities, although John and I really wished to use him as bait to study carrion-eating beetles.

The road to Ebolowa was in no way related to the bold red marking on the map, which indicated a primary route, drivable in all weather. In reality, the road soon diminished to a twisted, winding dirt road with deep ruts and washed-out crevasses. Any rain turned the dirt to a slick and slippery deep mud, especially dangerous with our balding tires. The road crossed many forest streams via bridges made of hardwood logs and planks. Heavy rains often washed them away, or they had collapsed unexpectedly from rot under the weight of heavy trucks. The rainy season was coming; would the road and bridges still be here when it was time for us to return?

Our digs in Ebolowa were not what we had expected. We would live with Ralph and his bride. Ralph's wife was a tall, lean Cameroonian who spoke no English. She was to be our cook and housekeeper at our base in Ebolowa, which turned out to be Ralph's house and the house next door, which belonged to one of his equally dysfunctional friends. We wondered why Ralph had chosen this inconvenient place for our base camp, and the reason soon became obvious. He wanted us to pay for his wife's services, and for his overdue electric, water, and rent bills.

The houses were a mess; they were filthy and needed to be cleaned up. Actually, they really needed to be burned down in the name of sanitation. In contrast, most Cameroonian houses were neat and swept clean, despite being made of adobe mud with palm-frond or sheet-metal roofs. Each house usually held a host of residents: brown-and-white dogs, which were kicked often by all members of the family; pigs, which were inquisitive intruders to every conversation; and visiting goats, chickens, and an assortment of uninvited spiders, scorpions, and beneficial lizards, which roamed the walls and ceilings. The houses and villages alike reflected the pride of the people and the leadership of the chief. People strolled, chatted, and visited with friends in the evening, dressing up on Sundays in traditional sarong-like wraps and gorgeous print shirts. We were the grubby scrounges and the dirtiest people to be seen, day or night.

Our first excursion into the bush would include Monsieur Bomba, the prefect of forestry and game, a short, toadlike fellow who would assist us by exerting his authority over the village leaders. The road seemed to be a continuous series of huts, giving the impression of lots of people. Actually, one had only to walk fifty feet off the road to be in dense jungle with miles of impenetrable forest ahead.

We reached the end of the road at a small clearing on the river. Several half-rotted dugout log canoes, or pirogues, waited as a public paddle-it-yourself convenience. Simone immediately began a negotiation with a villager and the local chief, and we soon arranged for a frog hunt that night. Darkness arrived instantly—as it does at the Equator—and the biting flies came out in droves. While we relied on our insect repellent to keep from going insane with annoyance, the chief seemed simply to ignore the pestering. No stranger to high finance, the chief quickly set the rules of the game, producing a notebook and a pencil and recording our "contract." We agreed to pay 3,000 francs for the first giant frog and 2,000 francs for any others, with something extra for the chief's services. The chief then said we should not catch frogs ourselves; we were to let his people do it. (I think this was to save face in case we caught frogs and they did not.) The frogs, although living free in the wild, fell under the domain of the village, and were therefore theirs. We also had to bear in mind that the frogs served as human food, too, an important source of protein to the people. We were really taking food off their tables. This was sustainable-use conservation at its grassroots best. The deal, however, was not binding on another boatman Ted had found, for he was from another village, and this chief did not rule him. We could hunt frogs with him.

At about 10:30 that night, Vic and Ted left the landing for the first sweep of the river in the chief's dugout. They captured our first Goliath frog and saw at least six others. Although Goliath frogs inhabited the splash zones of waterfalls and rapids, as we had read in the literature, they, like our native bullfrogs, were just as apt to be found sitting under a bush or at the edge of a rock in someplace quiet. One was even found in the middle of the cleared gravel boat landing on the other side of the river. Once disturbed, however, they were slow to return, if at all, for the rest of the evening. It was hard work to manipulate the heavy boats in the swift current, even with two additional paddlers. These boats, which weighed hundreds of pounds, were hand-cut and hollowed into shape from a single tree trunk, and took weeks to produce.

After a restless night on the front seat of the truck, I breakfasted the next morning on bananas and iodine-disinfected water. Simone spent the night at a friend's house; he told us that here in the bush he could stop at any house and be given food, lodging, and a woman if he so desired. Simone was totally uninterested in catching frogs. Rather, he felt his job was as liaison and facilitator only, and getting wet and muddy was not his responsibility.

We all felt groggy, dehydrated, and tired, and were in no condition, either emotionally or physically, to embark immediately on another trek. That evening, we decided to take a walk to some old, artificial fish ponds, once used to raise tilapia, and immediately spotted a harmless snake eating a four-and-a-half-foot-long file snake as it slid into the water. The file snake gets its name from its distinctly triangular-shaped body and rough textured scales. Vic and I stood near a banana tree to watch the snake and soon discovered that we had gotten into an army ant nest. The ants acted as though they were all programmed to bite on cue. We began to dance around in concert as the burning sensation from the fiery attack hit both of us at exactly the same time.

At dawn the next morning, we found that Ted's one Goliath frog was dead. It appeared to have suffocated in the wet snake bag we had used to keep it moist and quiet overnight. It was a big frog, with a body nearly ten inches long—almost two feet long with its legs extended—and weighed nearly two and a half pounds. To our disbelief, as we examined the limp body it slowly began to move. We quickly washed it off in clear water to rinse away any excreted toxins from its skin, and gave it an injection of a synthetic epinephrine stimulant. Ted then tried giving the frog mouth-to-mouth resuscitation, but the frog was dead. Next time, we would bring foam-rubber chips and a cool chest. The foam rubber would cushion the frogs against abrasions and keep them moist, and the cool chest would protect them from overheating. We knew we could buy a foam-rubber mattress just about anywhere. These pads were very popular because, unlike other materials, foam did not rot in the tropical heat and wet, and they were cheap. We would also try to house the frogs in the bathroom, if we could get the water turned on and running, and if we could get the place clean enough.

We were in the field only five days, yet we found ourselves routinely talking loudly, overenunciating, and gesticulating with our hands, even when we spoke to one another. It seems to be what happens when one is in a foreign country and does not speak the language. We were trying to make ourselves understood. It's very rude.

After lunch, Ralph fell asleep somewhere, and we quickly sneaked off to visit a friend of Simone's in a nearby village. John was a short but huge man—about five foot two and bald, with huge arms and hands, a great barrel-like chest, and a friendly smile he flashed often. He worked the land for another owner, like a sharecropper back in the States. His village was very neat, beautifully landscaped with colorful local forest plants. His crop was cocoa beans, and he told us that green mambas, deadly snakes belonging to the group that also includes the cobras, liked to bask on the tops of the cacao bushes. The pickers must be very careful, he said, because despite the snake's great length, its slender green body blended perfectly with the green leaves of the plant. The bean pickers could easily disturb it before they even knew it was there, and the aroused, irritable snake would bite at the slightest provocation. In this part of the world, so remote from real hospitals and antivenin, a bite usually meant death.

When I inquired further about snakes, John said that he had killed ten Gaboon vipers on the very trail we now traveled. Gaboon vipers are short, fat-bodied snakes, up to six feet long and eight inches wide. Their body pattern is designed to make them invisible among the debris of the forest floor, as the snake waits for a forest rat or other small mammal to pass within range of its short strike. Its fangs are among the longest of any venomous snake. Its wide and swollen-looking head has glands that produce great quantities of highly toxic venom. A person bitten is usually a person dead. My God, I thought, the trail is only twelve inches wide, and I can't see the ground two inches off of the path. How many benevolent Gaboon vipers had we passed close to without knowing it?

As John swung his machete to clear the overgrowth in front of us,

I saw that his hand was badly swollen. He had a filarial parasite infection, as many people there did, transmitted by insect carrier bites. These worms plug the small capillaries and blood vessels of the tissue immediately under the skin, often leading to internal organ damage, great pain and swelling of the hands and feet, or even death.

Back at camp, supper was tough zebu beef, mushroom-nut soup, and baked bananas. Simone was going to meet John and go to a movie in town, while we decided to return to John's village to walk the Gaboon viper trail, hoping to spot one of the snakes as it prowled its nocturnal haunts. We soon stopped at a small bridge in a dense section of jungle. I walked slowly down to the stream's edge, on one side of the bridge, and was instantly attacked by hundreds of army ants. The bastards pinched everywhere. I had stupidly stepped right into a column of ants nearly a foot wide that seemed to go on endlessly. Their speed was amazing, and once I got out of their way, we watched them carry the carcasses of crickets, moths, and anything else unfortunately small enough to be overcome. John and Vic played with the colony, spraying them with insect repellent, which made them reorganize themselves into different columns.

When I had had enough of them, I walked farther down the road. Soon I saw a path leading down toward a swamp. This time, I told myself, I was not going to be victimized. I was quite careful, scanning the bushes and the ground with my light before each step. Suddenly, I felt bites and stings all over again on my neck and back. More army ants. I ran up on the road flailing wildly at my shoulders. John came over and helped me get my shirt off. I was covered with ants, and he quickly saturated me with insect repellent. While I had been intent on watching the ground for ant columns, these ants had been swarming in low-hanging branches overhead. One ant, a particularly pugnacious beast, remained to wreak its vengeance an hour later by attaching itself painfully to my scrotum as I carried equipment into the house. A guy could learn to hate ants in a place like this.

Another trail wound eerily into a dark palm forest. It was close to midnight, and our headlamps and flashlights cast patches of light here and there, creating ever-changing shadows. It was as though we were in a cathedral with high arching ceilings. The forest was composed of one botanical giant after another. We felt as if we were microorganisms in a vast exotic greenhouse. We had all seen palm trees with leaves several feet long, sitting in a pot next to a hotel entranceway. But these were something else entirely. Each palm grew from a collective trunk ten feet in diameter. Each leaf stalk reached fifteen feet or more above us before the leafy fronds emerged, spreading and arching to form a cavernlike ceiling forty or fifty feet above our heads. Then there was the *Schefflera,* another common houseplant at home, with a brown woody trunk from which thin green stalks that terminate in a fanlike cluster of five elongated leaves combine to form a single multilobed leaf. Here this plant grew up and through the dense forest canopy a hundred feet above us. A stilt-root tree, before me, was beyond belief. The root system formed a series of stiltlike supports, each as big as a tree trunk itself. These joined with secondary roots, which intertwined to form an elevated gnarled and twisted mass covering an area at least twenty feet across, at least five feet above our heads. From this natural gigantic platform, high above us, began the actual trunk of the tree, a forest giant, six to eight feet in diameter and reaching straight up through the palm canopy and out of sight more than a hundred feet above us. The forest floor was covered with a thick, spongy mattress of leaf litter, soaked with water from a stream that ran beneath and welled up pools here and there. Broken palm fronds lay in impenetrable masses around each trunk, while curled vines descended from nowhere and returned.

A small mouse scampered across a downed palm stem, froze in the beam of a headlamp, composed itself, and was quickly gone. From everywhere, glistening clusters of spider eyes reflected the light of our headlamps like sapphires. It was eerie, unnerving in its magnitude, and beautiful. We walked carefully, for the tan and diffused markings of a Gaboon viper or an equally deadly rhinoceros viper would be nearly impossible to distinguish if it lay half hidden in the debris of the forest floor. Frogs called from the darkness everywhere. We would isolate one call and try to triangulate our light beams until we came upon the vocal source, only to be distracted by a new and more interesting chorus from another direction. Often the direction of sound was deceptive, bouncing from the hollow of one tree to the recesses of another. Once, as I hunted a sound that I perceived to be several feet away, I turned to speak to John and found the tiny perpetrator, a frog, not more than a few inches from my face, sitting confidently on a palm leaf.

Native workers had been in the forest during the day, cutting palm branches. Palm stalks are hard, absolutely straight, and uniform for their entire length, and are used as cross bracing for adobe walls and thatched roofs. I suddenly noticed a thin nylon thread, extending from a bent palm frond and angled to a tie at the ground. We froze and examined it carefully before going on. In the forest, natives frequently set such trip traps to capture game. Disturbing the trip string or wire may release a falling log or a pointed shaft, or fire a shotgun. This one appeared to be unarmed. As we continued through the forest in awe, hardly speaking in the humility such a place demands, bats careened crazily in and out of our light beams. We did well in the forest, capturing several species of frogs, a rear-fanged *Boiga* night snake about six feet long, and a small orange-and-black mottled Calabar python. These small nocturnal snakes have a blunt, rounded head and a blunt, rounded tail that resembles the head. The clever creature coils itself into a tight ball when bothered or attacked by a predator, leaving the tail to act as the head on the outside of the coils, and protecting its head by hiding it deep within its coiled body.

We had to get back into the field to look for Goliath frogs if we were to fulfill our mission. It's often too easy to get bogged down in the trivia and detail of one's base of operations in a comfortable town or small hotel, and end up spending little time in the field. The truth is, for city people such as us, several days in the bush were so exhausting that we had to recover back at base camp, not only for ourselves but to care for and maintain the frogs, tortoises, and other reptiles we had collected. The equation was simple: the more animals we had, the more time it took to care for them. The more time that required, the earlier we had to arise so as not to impinge too much on our fieldwork and the search for our primary target, Goliath frogs.

Our next stop was Lolodorf, a dirty little town whose waste left the streets only when the rains washed it into the river at the bottom of the hill. Young African children with reddish-tinged hair, a sign of protein deficiency, and albinos with unpigmented skin, hair, and eyes, appeared to be common. There was a beer truck parked in front of a noisy cantina, and none of us liked the rowdy group of semi-drunk soldiers who gave us a scrutinizing stare. It was clearly not a good place. We left Ralph there for three days, with only 5,000 francs and our best wishes. I think he found a basement to sleep in.

Monsieur Bomba made good use of his importance to us as regional prefect. He indeed opened doors, leading to cooperation from local villagers and leaders that we otherwise would not have enjoyed. At the same time, we provided the opportunity for him to demonstrate to his constituents that he was a man of the world and brought cash-paying customers—us—to the villages under his dominion. Besides, he also stopped to visit his numerous wives at many villages along our route, a trip he could not easily have managed on his own resources. Whether his house was really located near the end of our trek, or whether he chose to bring us there at the end of a circuitous route along which his many wives were located, I'll never know. In any case, after his visits to his wives and our driving for numerous hours over tortuous roads, we were all exhausted, although perhaps for different reasons.

We eventually arrived at Monsieur Bomba's house, an upscale cement ranch-style building with a corrugated metal roof that denoted his importance. As we ate a dinner that included canned sardines, rice balls, and some kind of bony catfish heads and backs in a greasy red sauce, I noticed the chunks of slimy, chewy meat in the spicy avocado stew and asked what it was. There was no response. I asked again, and finally Simone said that Monsieur Bomba did not wish to tell us, but it was some kind of bush meat: crocodile, monkey, jungle cat, or porcupine. Monsieur Bomba spoke little as he engulfed his food, even when a large fruit bat flew in the door, circled the room several times on two-foot-long wings, and exited through a window. It seemed as though we were the only ones who noticed.

After dinner, the conversation turned to forestry and illegal hunting. Simone said that even to speak of killing a gorilla was to ask to be put in jail. Monsieur Bomba told us that gorillas and elephants sometimes entered this village to raid the banana trees. The people were not particularly afraid of them or of elephants in the forest, he said, but he added that gorillas did harm many hunters who tried to kill them. The Scotch whiskey he offered stayed in my throat for a very long time.

After dinner, we split up. It was getting late, and we needed to prepare for the night's hunting. Vic and Simone would go with Monsieur Bomba's men on the river, in Bomba's big pirogue. It was a monster boat, hewn from a single log fully forty feet long and weighing hundreds of pounds. Ted and I found another boatman, who had a small one-man pirogue he had just carved at his house and knew where he could get another boat. A man named Tembe also came by. A few nights earlier, Ted had hired Tembe for a night of hunting, which had proven fruitless. We had terminated the hunt after only a few hours. Ted had then paid him a fraction of the amount he expected, proportionate to the number of hours we'd hunted. Tembe had felt cheated, and I'd agreed with him. Tembe had returned later, with his wife in tow. A rather large woman, she had managed to extract at least a little more of what she felt her husband was due, but neither she nor Tembe had left completely satisfied. He now said he would show us up and hunt the giant frog alone. We gave him a hand light and a small net and wished him good luck. He would soon become our good luck.

At 8:30 P.M. we arrived at the village, where our new boatman was waiting with his friend, who owned another boat. Triumphantly, we headed for the river, carrying one of the boats on our shoulders. It was a beauty, as newly hewn pirogues go. The charcoal on the inside was fresh enough to rub off at the brush of a hand, and the fresh edges of the gunwales showed the intrusions of a deftly wielded machete. There were, however, some points lacking in quality control. The cut edge of the gunwales had been carved with little concern for a straight line; it dipped and rose at the whim of the carver or the grain of the wood. It would also allow for varying degrees of freeboard.

Our crews tried to convince us that we should sit on the top of the boats and hold them together with our feet. Instead, we astounded them by cutting some bamboo stalks and splitting them into planks, which then became a platform that could hold together an outrigger-style canoe with a double hull. Bear in mind that, altogether, we are talking about a combination of two hollowed-out logs, the sum of which was approximately six feet long and two feet wide, with hulls not more than twelve inches deep. The car battery used to power the handheld spotlight was now placed in the center of one boat. One paddler straddled the rear of the boats; I came next as the net man; Ted, holding the high-intensity lamp, followed as the spotter; and a fourth man acted as forward paddler. A wise centipede scurried from the bottom of the boat, disappeared over the side, and swam for the adjacent bank. The boatmen kept saying, "Dis be fine! Dis be fine!" I doubted that.

Before we could explain that we first wanted to try out our dubiously river-worthy craft, we were pushed off into midstream. The river, swollen by recent rains and running in powerful swirls, eddies, and, here and there, white foam, quickly engulfed the front of the boat. I remember asking myself if the water was going to feel cold as the river rushed in through Ted's kneeling legs and the double pirogue slowly began to turn over. It was like watching it happen to someone else, in slow motion, or as if I were outside the boat looking on. I recall seeing the face of my wristwatch under water and wondering if the water would ruin it.

In a flash, I regained reality. My watch, hell. The water had a good chance of ruining a perfectly good life—mine. I hugged the hulls and groped for a handhold as the river took over. We were moving fast. The car battery had already gone to the bottom of the river, as had my $125 Wheaton headlamp and its battery. I watched it glowing courageously for a moment before the river claimed it, too. Fortunately, we had not lashed the batteries into the boat, for their weight in the now flooded double pirogue might have pulled it down, leaving us without anything to hold on to. Somehow, the three of us managed to cling to our matchsticks as the river took us its own way. We were moving fast, heading for the rapids and waterfalls not far downstream. I was still gripping the frog net, while Ted kept hold of the spotlight. The paddler, too, had kept his wits about him and now managed to climb onto the overturned craft. He attempted to control our headlong flight downstream by paddling with one hand.

Somewhere beyond the swirls in the darkness lay the bank. Our paddler began shouting, and suddenly, out of nowhere, another boatman appeared. Paddling furiously, he caught up to us. A second voice now came over the river sounds. It was our disgruntled friend Tembe. He had heard our shouts, and he, too, paddled out of the darkness to help us. To my surprise, my other headlamp, which I had donned at the last moment, was still working. "Loosen your boots," Ted shouted, although I was only a few inches away from him. He didn't know I had failed Swimming 101 just before leaving, so taking off my boots would hardly help me swim out of this predicament.

Using their boats like minitugs, Tembe and the other boatman paddled us diagonally across the current, while our paddler pushed from the rear. Ted and I kicked with our feet, although mainly to feel like we were doing something other than lying in the water like bloated fish. I kept thinking of the rapids and waterfalls, now so close that we could hear their distant roar. Slowly, we approached the bank, and finally there was footing. We dragged ourselves from the water and, with our boatman, collapsed exhausted on the bank. Tembe and his friend pulled the boats to safety. In a moment, though, there was a giggle from someone, then a grunt, and soon all of us were pounding one another on the backs and laughing uncontrollably.

Soaking wet, Ted and I walked back to the village. The villagers, having heard the commotion, came out to see us. Tembe and the others began talking rapidly, with great gestures and excitement, describing what had happened. Soon everyone was laughing and taking turns patting us on the shoulders or shaking hands. Few people survive such ordeals on the river at night, and we had obviously been bestowed with some degree of magic or luck, which they hoped would rub off on them. Someone gave me a silver-colored dead fish as a gift. I thanked him profusely, then, knowing how valuable any protein was, made a grand gesture by holding the fish up high and offering it to his wife "for the children." It immediately disappeared amid many thanks. Our friend had lost his machete, as well, so we made a big thing about paying him 1,000 francs for it, as well as 1,000 francs each to the men who had risked their own lives to help us.

We had begun to walk, dripping, back to the cabins, when Tembe caught up to us with his wife and their small child and, with machete proudly in hand, insisted on accompanying us. He said he wanted to go back out to catch frogs (thankfully, he had so far caught only us), so we loaned him a net. Meanwhile his wife, promising that he would not drink up the money, promptly took it away from him. I really liked these Egoumba tribespeople. We would never expect this type of behavior from Americans. In Tembe's eyes we had cheated him, and in return he had risked his boat and life on the river to save us. We were learning many lessons about life and people here in West Africa.

Ted and I were still laughing. We had almost bought the *grande grenouille,* as he put it—the big frog. When we got back to the cabins, they were open, but Vic and John had our dry clothes in their car, so Ted and I decided to take the lantern and go for a walk in the equally wet jungle.

Simone came home around midnight, out of breath and anxious to see us. He had stopped in the village to see how we had managed, and one of the villagers had asked, "Have you not been to the camp?" When Simone had said, "No," the villager had said, "Well, you should go there now." We related our story and as Simone listened, he shook his head in disbelief that we were still alive.

John and Vic arrived a little after midnight, saying, "Boy do we have a story to tell you guys." They, too, had had their share of excitement. They had gone onto the river in Bomba's larger pirogue. In an instant, the river had turned the boat around and sent it crashing backward downriver and into a murderous, broken-down stand of bamboo. The force of the water literally propelled them through the thicket like a huge torpedo. John dove to the bottom of the boat to avoid being decapitated, warning Vic just in time for him to avoid being torn out of the boat. On the plus side, they had captured one small Goliath frog with a cast net.

We all were very lucky that night. The torrential rains were upon us, it seemed, and the rivers would become worse with each day. I felt that our future attempts should be only under the best of conditions, which might mean no more small boats, if we could help it. When we finally went to sleep that night, I didn't even care if there were lizards in bed with me.

Despite our misadventures, we were slowly accumulating Goliath frogs with each successive foray into the bush. After several days in the field, we returned to base camp for a few days to recover and restock supplies, batteries, and fuel. Nevertheless, we were suffering from exhaustion, hunger, headaches, diarrhea, dehydration, and emotional stress.

Soon we were back in the field, searching for frogs. About fifty yards downstream from a boat landing, we came across what appeared to be a small inlet, largely obscured by a barrier of downed and splintered bamboo and raffia palm leaves. As Ted and John's lights flashed into the hidden recesses of the inlet, a pair of glistening coals sparkled back. It was a Goliath frog, sitting calmly in the shallow water.

The boatmen saw where we were focusing our interest and nudged the nose of the big pirogue into the bamboo. But between fighting the current and the tangle of bamboo and vines, it was apparent that we would not be able to approach close enough to use the net. I decided that if we could get me close enough to the bank, I would make my approach over land. We all pulled and pushed the pirogue as close as we could; then I slipped over the side into the waist-high tepid water.

Ted and John still had the unmoving, smug frog full in the beam of

The author with village frog hunters in Cameroon, 1981.

their spotlights. The river bottom was soft, but with a firm base. I struggled through the bamboo and hanging branches, then climbed onto the bank. "The frog still hasn't moved," they called out, although I couldn't see it from where I stood. As I followed the direction of the beam of their light, another Goliath frog suddenly bounded out of the shallow water and disappeared. It was unexpected, and I jumped uneasily in the darkness.

Inches outside of the narrow beam of light from my headlamp, it was absolute black darkness. I concentrated intently on the first frog, which I could now see sitting just ahead, still out of net reach. Scanning with my headlamp to the left disclosed another frog on the other side of the inlet, and at the same time, John spotted a fourth frog at the edge of the bank opposite me. He also saw something else—a glint from large eyes, moving rapidly through the vegetation toward me, past the frog. The six-foot-long black forest cobra slipped into the water and disappeared in the soft muddy bottom mere feet from where I stood. I wondered where it had gone. Incredibly, my frog had still not moved an inch.

I now began my approach, slowly, down the bank again, deeper into the inlet and up to my ankles in mud. We all held our breath, for we had come this close before without success. Somewhere in the recesses of my mind, I began to realize that the feeling of the water on my body trickling down my legs was different. I sensed that the water was now running in the wrong direction, not draining down but moving up, on the inside of my left leg. At first I didn't believe my own sensations, that tickling feeling that your brain has difficulty maintaining control over. But it was true; the "water" had now reached my thigh and was still moving. Part of my brain said, "Panic," while another part insisted I should grab at the moving spot in a frenzy. Still a third said, "Be calm. It could be worse than you imagine." I was now standing motionless as my emotions argued over which signals would be sent to what part of my body first.

John and Ted called, "What's the matter? Is the frog still there?" I knew full well where the damned frog was, and at that moment I couldn't care less. Just then I felt the movement inside my shorts, several inches below my belt. I knew this could not be a good thing. My mind argued further. Whatever it was, it was alive. It could bite. My brain computed the possibilities, all bad. In one rush, the indicator on my tolerance meter went off the scale. I grabbed at the movement through my pants, then tore at my belt buckle, ripped at the button, and tore open the zipper on my fly. In an instant, my pants and shorts were down. John and Ted stared in disbelief as I stood bare-assed in the jungle; I was supposed to be catching a frog. I slowly released my grip on the handful of clothing. A ten-inch-long, gray-and-red-legged centipede boiled out of the cloth, writhing as it hit the ground, and scrambled into the debris of the forest floor.

The frog still waited, no doubt amused. Laughter rose from the boat, but I failed to see the point of it. Readjusting my pants, which I hoped I alone now occupied, I again concentrated on the frog that sat just ahead. Slowly, I picked up the net and brought it into line. As I made a short, uneventful sweep, the frog jumped forward, right into the oncoming mesh. I had him.

I had my frog, but I had also exhausted my desire to hunt anymore that night. Besides, it was now quite late, and there were no more frogs to be seen. We returned to the pirogue landing. The boatmen, too, were tired, for the heavy boat was difficult to maneuver in the strong current, and we had gotten hung up on rocks in midriver several times.

We never seemed to be getting enough rest to recuperate from the activities of the day before. Part of our problem was that, for want of food, we were eating moldy French bread and local chocolate bars, which seemed to separate freely into coconut oil and cocoa-bean residue. I would have given anything for one of Zoë's cooked flat chickens, so tough and stringy that we could hardly wrench the meager flesh from its bones with our teeth.

That night, we slept under the porch roof of the combined clinic and hospital, run by the tribal chief. There was a treatment room with a bucket of old, putrid wound dressings, rusted bent syringes, ancient bottles of carbolic antiseptic, methylene blue, and a broken stool. In the next room, there was a table with drugs: vitamin B_{12}, atropine, calcium gluconate, multivitamins, and vitamin K. The ward consisted of two rusted iron beds and no mattresses. In the clinic area, a foam-rubber mattress lay on a sheet of corrugated sheet metal on the floor. Another room, adjoining the maternity room with its rusted iron mattressless crib, was called "the Surgery." It was the most repulsive, for lying on the table were rusted and bent scalpels and forceps. The operating table was made of bamboo slats tilted toward the wall and covered with a black rubber mat. At the end of the table was a concrete catch basin, with a connecting hole through the wall at one end to allow blood to run off the table into the open sump outside. It had not been cleaned in some time. No wonder the life expectancy in Cameroon was about thirty-eight years. The chief, largely untrained, did the surgery.

John and I slept on the mattresses we found in the clinic, placed on the outside porch floor. It was better than trying to sleep in the stench of the operating room, and with the roaches, which abounded there. Simone decided to stay with friends in the village. Ted slept on one of the ward cots, on the bare springs, and didn't seem to mind the smell. He must have been extremely fatigued. At a little after midnight rain began to fall, and by 3:00 A.M. my mattress had become saturated by a stream of water that flowed across the porch floor. I felt as if I were lying in a sphagnum moss bog, and I was soaking wet when I finally abandoned my "bed" and moved onto John's mattress with him to finish the night.

Our plan called for us to return to the embassy in Yaoundé. When we arrived, Ambassador Horan came by with his kids and was thrilled with the novelty—as was the entire embassy staff—that we were using their library as a temporary frog house and staging area for our expedition. Heavy rains began to fall as we checked back into the only hotel with a room available, the Mont Fébé.

On the way back to our base camp in Ebolowa, the Land Rover broke down with a burned-out wheel bearing, so we left Ralph behind, once again, at a local garage, to await its repair. By nightfall, however, we'd had no word from Ralph. Simone was pissed off; he could not understand how we could trust Ralph to drive the Rover back on his own. Ralph had demonstrated over and over again that his ability to follow instructions and stay focused was very limited.

We suspected that both the hardships of living in Cameroon and alcohol had taken their toll. Simone was very afraid of the ramifications of Ralph either wrecking the vehicle or, worse, stealing it. If the latter occurred, we would all end up spending the next years in a Cameroonian prison, eating bugs.

John, Simone, and I retraced our steps back to the garage, where a small boy said he had seen both Ralph and the Rover leaving earlier in the day. After a fruitless search of some back alleys and saloons, we returned to the embassy.

Fatigue, sickness, and emotional stress were beginning to take their toll on all of us. Vic kept repeating the notion that we must return to the village of Bipindi. Granted, the frogs might be larger and more numerous there, but the roads were bad and the people disorganized and inefficient. Furthermore, the rains were upon us; once there, we might not be able to get out for months. Vic then said he wanted us to return to Nyabessan. This was not the levelheaded Vic speaking, and we all knew it.

By then, Vic had run out of money and was infusing his personal funds into the mission. Furthermore, we still needed more permits to fulfill export requirements that seemed to be made up at the whim of every official, in the hope of extracting more money from us before we left the country. Without satisfying each new requirement, we might not be able to make any shipments of frogs to the States at all. Besides, we had to deal with the issue of Ralph and the missing Land Rover, as the owner was getting antsy. He suspected there was something amiss. We had only about four days left in Cameroon, and we were not in good shape emotionally; nor were we equipped for two more field expeditions. We decided we could possibly pull off one more excursion at best, and the ambassador offered to help us with our permits and with any problems with the Land Rover, which was very reassuring.

The next day, as we approached the embassy after lunch, we saw Ralph and the Land Rover in the parking lot across the street, along with a young boy. Vic said we should go into the embassy while he talked to Ralph. John and I started to go, but halfway there we looked at each other and said, "The hell we will." What happened next was a blur of shared rage. I got to Ralph first. It made me happy to feel my hands around his throat. Vic grabbed me, and John grabbed Vic. I yelled at Vic to take his hands off me. All of a sudden the group of us realized what we must look like, a bunch of white Americans brawling in the street in the middle of an African capital, in front of the U.S. embassy. To make matters worse, we were directly across from a police station, where a group of policemen was watching us with great amusement from a doorway.

Ralph smelled badly of sour wine, and it seemed as if he had retched all over himself. His excuse was that it had been late when the Land Rover was fixed, and he had been so tired that he had figured it was best to leave in the morning; only he had overslept. Then he had run out of gas and couldn't start the Land Rover; after much trouble, he had found that the gas line had come apart. Of course, he said, he did not know we had gone looking for him.

His story was, we knew, mostly lies or hallucinations. John and I checked the gas tank and found that the reserve tank still had gas in it. The fuel line showed no evidence of having been broken or repaired. Ralph had been missing, or at least unaccounted for, for more than twenty-four hours. In reality, he had simply disobeyed orders and had chosen to go to his girlfriend's house, his wife in Ebolowa notwithstanding, and drink rather than come directly to the embassy. His sick hangover attested to that.

John, Ted, and I decided to leave immediately for Ebolowa and the field instead of waiting for the following morning. We returned the Land Rover and rented in its place a Russian four-wheel-drive Neva. Vic and Simone would remain in Ebolowa when we went into the bush. They would try to complete their shipping permits, then send Vic's share of the frogs on their way to New York. Ralph had to come with us, against our wishes, so we promptly told him to get in the back and keep quiet unless spoken to. He was afraid of us, and well he should have been.

The next morning, after a hard night of driving in the rain—and nearly plunging off a collapsed bridge into the raging river below—

we arrived back in Ebolowa. Late afternoon found us heading again to the clinic in the jungle. On the way, we saw one of our nets tied to a tree as a signal. We stopped, and the children came out shouting, "Frog, frog." The villagers had captured and kept twelve frogs for us, as well as three tortoises. The frogs were in pots and pans, and three escaped as the villagers rushed to show them to us. One large frog took several bounds, with a group of children hot on its hopping heels, then rolled over and died. We were amazed at what we now knew was happening to our frogs. Vic's premise was right: the frogs could deplete their blood oxygen supplies very quickly through stress, go into cardiac arrest, and drop dead. We decided to go to the other villages to tell them to hunt frogs, and on the way back, we picked up two riders. One man carried a relatively fresh baboon or mandrill leg neatly balanced across his head.

After our supper of sardines, bread, and iodine water, we went down to the pirogue landing and took some temperature readings. In the trees at one landing we saw huge glowing eyes in the beam of our headlamps. They turned out to belong to a group of tiny galagos, or bush babies. These tiny forest-dwelling primates with big ears and great eyes, which are especially large to allow them to see during their nocturnal foraging for insects and fruit, would peek around the tree trunks and branches at us in curiosity. Their eyes seemed to blink on and off like giant fireflies as each animal peeked, scurried around the tree, and peeked again. There were also other eyes, glowing like coals and moving quickly through the tree branches overhead. These belonged to a group of five palm civets, a kind of small cat, that were probably out hunting the galagos. In a tangle of branches next to the river, I looked high above into the canopy of vines. The beam of my headlamp picked up the glowing reflection of a single eye, gliding smoothly through the leaves, then doubling back upon itself. I wondered if it belonged to a tree cobra, like the one we had previously seen killed on the road.

John recorded our sightings under stress, as he had been attacked by army ants, and had them affixed to his cheek and chest. Tree hyraxes—small, shrewlike, herbivorous mammals that are unique to Africa—warmed up for another session of screaming and moaning.

The calls of these small mammals sound exactly like a woman being torn limb from limb. This would be our last night in the bush, and I would miss all of it. This completely alien world had captured me with its furtive shadows, suspense, and intriguing revelations.

Most of the remaining time would have to be spent caring for the animals. We planned to get up at 6:00 A.M., before the patients arrived at the clinic, to leave for Ebolowa. Ted moved a clinic bed onto the porch, to avoid the roaches inside, which were unabashed about climbing over your face as you slept, or nibbling at your toenails. The stench of old wound dressings still permeated the air. John chose the still-damp mattress I had used on our last stay, while I stretched the hammock between the porch railings. We all needed sleep badly, but we would not get it.

The Goliath frogs spent the night jumping in their plastic bags, and otherwise going wild. Three broke through and had to be recaptured. John couldn't sleep through the drone of mosquitoes and decided to take a predawn walk down to the river on the off chance that he might see a frog. He got back about 5:30 A.M. and noisily made getting up a necessity for the rest of us, except Ted, who remained sound asleep. Some chickens wandered by, and by throwing bread crumbs to them, I managed to entice a rooster to crow under Ted's cot. Ted still slept soundly. Two roosters, a chorus of "When the Saints Go Marching In" from the alarm on my watch, and a small herd of goats milling around his bed failed to wake him. Finally he rubbed his eyes, demonstrating that he was still alive.

It was full daylight by six-thirty when the chief arrived with his men and nine additional Goliath frogs, bringing our total to twenty-one.

We finally arrived in Ebolowa and immediately set to cleaning up the frogs. I was suffering from an intense headache and chills, as was Ted. We were all covered with mosquito bites, despite our insect repellent. Titos, a Greek businessman who lived in Ebolowa, invited us to dinner, and after a forty-five-minute nap and another frog wash, we went over to see him. Titos also told us the rest of what we wanted to know about Ralph.

Ralph had met Zoë and bought her a wedding dress before he left to go back to the United States to get the rest of his Peace Corps money. The other villagers had then convinced Zoë that the white man would not return for her, and she had nearly lost her mind. Titos said she put on her wedding dress and paraded up and down the streets of Ebolowa for weeks in a drunken stupor. At this time, Ralph met Vic back in the States, took the $3,000, and agreed to set up the expedition. Once back in Ebolowa, Ralph used the money to buy Zoë, as we had speculated, and paid for a wedding procession the likes of which Ebolowa had never seen. He bought gifts and blankets for Zoë's entire village, and had a wedding procession seven kilometers long. Titos cashed many of Ralph's traveler's checks himself, in exchange for goods, thinking it was Ralph's own money. Unbeknownst to any of us, our expedition had been subverted before our plane had even gotten off the ground in New York.

After a honeymoon at the expensive Hotel Mont Fébé, there simply was no money left to do the things he was supposed to do. Ralph decided to bluff, and nearly succeeded. We resolved that before the trip was over, Ralph would be forced to admit to Vic what had happened, for whatever little satisfaction was in it.

We were up washing frogs soon after dawn. It would be a miracle if we got any of them back alive. So far, those we had placed in plastic wine casks with foam rubber chips, covered with cloth, had fared the best. Zoë wanted to go to town to get soap, so we sent Ted to make sure she and Ralph returned. I set up a branch at one corner of the room for two chameleons we had purchased from a young boy and his friend who had shown up early one morning at our door. We didn't really want the little lizards, but the look of anticipation on the boy's face was so amusing that we paid him a few francs anyway. The money no sooner hit his hand than he turned and sprinted away—so quickly that he ran right out of his flip-flops, and had to return and put them back on his feet. The chameleons perched like cryptic Christmas-tree ornaments that changed color at any emotional whim. Each eye rotated independently on its own little turret until some insect caught its interest; then the two eyes coalesced intently on the target, as a prelude to a lightning-fast extension of the sticky tongue and the disappearance of one more insect. One chameleon hung on my shirtsleeve while I ate bread and water for breakfast. By noon, we had lost two more frogs, and Zoë, Ted, and Ralph were not yet back with the vehicle. As John so aptly put it, "It was a depression day."

When Ted returned, he told us he had contacted the embassy. He had spoken to the ambassador, who had said the frogs had been sent off; but he had not seen Vic since the day before. Much to our relief, Vic and Simone returned in the early afternoon. They told a story of not having been able to get the export document until the very last minute, and of having to get a tax-exemption letter from the commissioner of finance, which was an impossibility. The frogs would not have been shipped except that the head of customs at the airport had been raised in Simone's brother's house, and he cleared the shipment.

As we left Ebolowa the next morning, we passed Ralph on the road, and he sheepishly bade us good-bye. We paid Zoë thirty thousand francs for her work, but she sent us off with anger and insults. Too bad. We left another thirty thousand francs with Titos to pay our electric bill for us, rather than trust it to Ralph. We figured Ralph had been paid enough, or had not really been paid back enough— depending on one's point of view.

While we were on the road, Simone had us stop so he could purchase a long-dead spotted jungle cat from a passerby. The cat, he said, was food for men only, as he tossed it into the hot trunk of the car. His wife would prepare it for him as a special treat. We hoped we would not be invited to dinner.

Once we arrived at the embassy in Yaoundé, we again turned the library into a frog hotel, and prepared for the trip home. Ted and Vic would carry three frogs in their baggage and go through France. I think Ted was eager for a night in Paris. When he got home, Vic wanted to call Ralph's father back in the States and try to get Ralph home, one way or another. We were all sure Ralph would die in Cameroon. Vic, to the last, and much to his credit, felt sympathy and cared deeply for his student's well-being.

We ate steak and potatoes at the Marseilles restaurant, a sleazy, somewhat dirty second-floor café with a balcony overlooking the street and the town movie house. The steps leading up to it were lined with derelicts, lepers with half-bandaged oozing sores, and sick beggars. This was certainly not the atmosphere one wished to deal with before and after a meal. The steak was particularly spicy and tender and, for Yaoundé, reasonably priced. It wasn't long before our bowels began to rumble; we should have remembered that tender beef does not exist in Cameroon. There, tender beef is rancid beef.

The marine guard let us into the embassy at about 9:00 P.M. The wooden boxes we had had constructed in the shop around the corner from the embassy were well made, lightweight, and lacked air holes. Into each box, we fastened five plastic wine cask liners filled with foam rubber on the bottom. In each of these, we put a cloth bag lined with foam rubber, and one or more frogs. Then came a sheet of rubber to cover the cask liners, and finally the wooden lid.

Vic was very jumpy and had been emotionally stressed for days. The Ralph situation had taken its toll, and he was having difficulty accepting that, despite the great cost, he had been in the field for only three days out of his entire trip. Both John and I told him to rest and let us pack. Vic insisted on doing his share, however, and began boring air holes into the sides of the boxes with the blade of my large folding knife. I told him to mind the blade, as it had a loose blade lock. I had no sooner spoken the words than the blade closed on his middle finger, cutting it to the bone along its full length.

Vic wrapped the wound with a handkerchief and quickly said it was all right, insisting that he would continue and we shouldn't call anyone. Recognizing that his fatigue had compromised his reasoning, I quickly called the marine guard. Even when the embassy doctor's wife arrived (the closest thing to a doctor that was available, but quite competent), Vic still insisted that the wound need not be treated. I told her my knife had been used in the bush for every conceivable purpose, including probing dead carcasses. Infection was sure to follow, and the wound was very deep. Vic's finger needed stitching, which she was not prepared to do. Instead, she cleaned the wound with antiseptic, put a butterfly bandage on it to hold the edges together, then splinted and bandaged it. Vic was experiencing tingling and some minor pain, so we suspected that he had severed some nerves. Even then, he continued to insist on helping us carry the boxes to the lobby downstairs.

Afterward, we decided to spend the last few hours together at a kind of late-night snack bar serving French cakes, beer, and pastries. The anticipation of going home brought some emotional relief of its own, as we drank beer, laughed, and recounted stories that few people at home would believe. The cashier (and apparent owner, from the way she browbeat the waiters) was a hefty Frenchwoman who wore her bleached-blond hair piled high on her head, and a black dress cut so low it showed her cleavage down to her knees. We all thought of home, and wanted to take nothing with us from Cameroon except our hard-earned frogs.

After a few restless hours of sleep, we arrived at the embassy well before dawn, collected our cargo of frogs, and were soon at the airport. We were all parting company. John and I said good-bye to Vic and Ted, as their flight was to leave the next day. We would see Vic in New York, and would care for his frogs before he continued on to Oklahoma. We all regretted saying good-bye to Simone, who among all of us was the most professional, easygoing, and personable. He, in fact, was the one who had made the expedition a success. We landed at Douala at 8:40 A.M., and watched as the boxes of frogs were loaded onto the Air Afrique plane, which we hoped would take us to Ivory Coast without a hitch.

Customs exiting Douala was about as bad as getting in. The customs officer wanted, of all things, John's alarm clock. He didn't get it. The consulate people showed up to help with our tickets, and we were soon in the air again. I could feel John's and my relief as each successful step brought us closer to New York and home. Our flight landed briefly at Lagos, Nigeria, and lastly Abidjan, Ivory Coast. There, our frogs were immediately impounded by customs.

One of us had unthinkingly labeled the boxes with Abidjan as their destination, not New York, because we had to pick the boxes up from cargo, clean the frogs, and hold them overnight for the Pan Am clipper cargo flight due in from Johannesburg at noon the next day. However, because the boxes said Abidjan, they were now technically imports and tomorrow would be new exports, for which we had no documentation. To add to our miseries, John and I were now suffering in full from the steak we'd had at the Marseilles. We had food poisoning. Both of us immediately swallowed large doses of anti-diarrheal medication and began taking tetracycline, anticipating the long painful flight that lay ahead. We were going home, and there was no way we would miss that plane.

The Pan American Airways office was a tiny pair of rooms hidden in the recesses of the Abidjan airport. Once found, they were easily lost. We learned from the Frenchman who ran the office that Pan American Airways in Ivory Coast flew under the auspices of Air Afrique. Inexplicably, our Pan Am tickets were no good on Air Afrique. We would need help, which they assured us they were all too willing to give. Edward, a smiling, pleasant young native manager, was determined to take care of us and get us in the air—with our frogs. He had been notified of our arrival by the people in Pan Am public relations, via telex, and had learned, as we did, that they intended to have press coverage of the frogs as we arrived in New York. They wanted us to hold a frog on the ramp of the plane for pictures. We figured that if we weren't very lucky, it might well be a dead frog.

Edward spent most of the remaining part of the day with us following at his heels, as he argued first with one official, then another. They were insistent that the frogs be admitted through customs, and that we then secure export papers before they could be released. That could not be. If we missed the noon clipper, it would be a week before the next flight. The frogs would surely die. Customs personnel remained sympathetic but unwavering. At 7:30 P.M., Edward's supervisor arrived, and assured us that no matter what it took, the frogs and we would be on the plane. At that moment, the frogs were under customs' control, locked up in the customs section of the cargo building. It looked hopeless, just when we were so close to getting them home. The cargo building was hot, and we at least got permission to wash the frogs. Two more looked poorly.

There was nothing else we could do, and as it was then dark, the building would cool. We took a taxi to the hotel at which Nick had made reservations for us some time before. We nearly passed out in amazement. The Hotel Ivoire Inter-Continental was the finest, most luxurious hotel in all of Africa. The hotel sat in the center of the largest swimming pool in the world, complete with palm-tree covered islands, suspended restaurants, and impeccably manicured gardens. The hotel boasted a theater and Africa's only ice-skating rink. We were sick and went to bed.

The alarm woke us at 6:00 A.M., and neither of us spoke very much as we got ourselves together. After all of our work, everything was to be lost or gained that day. We had slept for nearly ten hours as though we were dead. As we walked out of the front door of the lobby, we were dwarfed by two ivory tusks that crowned the entryway, white and gleaming for what seemed like seventy-five feet in the air. We were duly impressed. Neither of us had found any place to purchase souvenirs during the entire trip, so we decided to take a short walk to the native quarter we had seen from our window. It was fruitless, and the garbage-saturated sand around the houses made the village smell sickeningly sweet. We went back to the hotel, awkwardly close to the village squalor, and checked out.

At the airport, we received both good and bad news. The good news was that the supervisor, who would not have such important frogs die under his responsibility at any cost, was going to make up a phony set of bills of lading showing New York as the destination, as should have been done in the beginning. He then told us they were going to load the frogs, along with twenty tons of pineapples, and the plane would leave with us aboard. Once off the ground, it would not be called back. The bad news was that our plane tickets were, indeed, worthless. Our Pan American flight to New York was on a 747 cargo plane that normally carried only a flight crew. Our tickets called us "attendants." Air Afrique did not recognize the role of attendants on cargo flights. Instead, we would have to buy new tickets from Air Afrique, as passengers. Worse, they would not accept traveler's checks or American Express credit cards as payment.

Edward had the answer. He took us to the bank and, vouched for by Pan Am, John got his remaining traveler's checks cashed into $1,700 worth of Ivory Coast francs. The enormous volume of near-worthless money could fill a bushel basket, and did. We quickly returned to the ticket window and stuffed the money at the clerk by the handful. She seemed bewildered at the prospect of counting it, but at long last our tickets were in hand and we were another step closer to home.

We had only a few short hours left before we had to be on hand for our flight. Edward sent us to the Trashville Market, a crowded bazaar, where we bought silver bracelets, dresses, scarves, and coverlets for the folks back home. This excursion also took our minds off the possibility of further disaster. It was fun. John and I bargained like professionals, and one merchant was so embarrassed that John had negotiated such a low price that he had John pay him behind the sales counter, away from the sight of the other merchants. We were astounded when one blue-and-white-robed old Muslim gentleman, surrounded by his wares of silver jewelry, produced a nineteenth-century handheld brass balance. He placed the bracelet John wanted on the hanging pan on one side, and a counterweight in the opposite pan. He then read the weight as the pointer moved along the embossed scale, with the balance held at eye level. Once the weight was read, the old man produced a modern electronic calculator and figured the current day's rate of exchange on the international silver market.

At 3:00 P.M., we were back at the airport. Our "bird" had landed on schedule, and stood like a great white gull on the field in front of the waiting room. It was a 747, and it was good to see the U.S. flag painted on its tail. But we were not yet aboard. Edward came and told us to wait at the doorway; when he motioned to us, we were to walk onto the field as though we had every right to be there. We watched as twenty tons of pineapples were loaded into the gaping cargo hold. We saw our boxes of frogs come next, and wondered how Edward had managed to get his hands on them. Edward waved. John and I walked casually to the plane, took a few quick pictures, and said good-bye to Edward. He, too, had risked a great deal for us; the

Pan Am people had stolen our frogs from the Ivory Coast customs warehouse for us. Quickly, the cargo door was closed. There were six seats behind the cockpit in the dome, and after strapping our precious frogs onto the deck below, we settled in. The ship was like a huge empty whale, and we felt like a few tiny sardines rattling around inside its belly. The pilot welcomed us aboard, and when I asked about the mysterious cargo of frogs among the pineapples, he said he had no intention of going back.

To add to the tension, the takeoff was momentarily delayed, as the small plane in front of us blew out a tire as it taxied down the runway. But our wheels left the ground as darkness began to fall, and we were on our way to our next stop, in Senegal. Once in the air, we rechecked the frogs. The boxes were warm, and it made us gulp to think that we might indeed find all the frogs dead. We tore the lids off. One frog was dead, but the others were in good shape. As the foam bedding smelled of ammonia and urine, we immediately began washing the frogs in fresh water from the crew's lavatory. The frog that had died was one that experienced a prolapsed bowel back in Ebolowa. I had massaged the bowel back into the frog's rectum with my pinkie covered with antibiotic ointment. The temperature in the cargo hold was barely 65 degrees Fahrenheit, for the benefit of the fruit, but the skipper raised it to seventy for the frogs.

At 7:24 P.M., we were sitting in the cockpit of the 747, behind the pilot and copilot, watching in awe as the giant bird glided in a whisper toward the lights of the runway that tilted and swayed ahead of us. Slowly, the world settled, and we bumped and squealed as the wheels touched the runway. We taxied down the runway and, like a car in a supermarket parking lot, began looking for a parking space big enough to accommodate our bouncing wings. The Dakar airport used no ground guides, even for 747s. A repair crew came on board, and the captain told them the radar was out and would have to be repaired before we could leave for home. It was touch and go, but the radar was somehow fixed, although the repair-crew chief said he had his doubts that it would work with "whatever we did with the antenna." Will nothing ever go right again? we wondered.

At 10:00 P.M., we left Dakar in the darkness below and headed out over the ocean for home. I asked the captain, who, coincidentally, knew John's father, how much water was in the tanks, as we would again have to wash the frogs. He consulted the manual and said, "Plenty, about a hundred gallons." Two gallons and four frog washes later, we ran out of water with a hiss of air pressure. The ground crew had not refilled the tanks. The captain volunteered the crew's bottled drinking water, which we stretched as far as we could. We could do no more. Whatever frogs would survive was now out of our hands. We had done our best. We went back to the cockpit and looked at the stars for a while. The engineer showed us how to program the on-board computer, to select a new course and plot new bearings. We then slept on the floor for a few hours, for it had been a very, very long day.

At 1:04 A.M., New York time, the clipper ship *Carrier Dove* touched down at John F. Kennedy International Airport, with two dazed men, eighteen Goliath frogs from the equatorial rain forest of Cameroon, and twenty tons of pineapples.

After arriving home and resting for several days, John and I met in his office at the zoo. We hugged. We had survived.

Seven months after Ebolowa, Nyabessan, and Bipindi, Ted Papen-fuss traveled to the jungles of Peru, having gotten one frog back alive in his baggage. Vic's shipment, which had been sent out before we had left Cameroon, had been seized in Paris by the customs authori-ties, because it had no papers with it. The papers had been attached on leaving Douala, but were said to have disappeared between there and France. The frogs were finally released after more than two weeks and arrived in New York, all dead. Their papers were still af-fixed and clearly labeled on the outside of the shipping box, just as they had been when the box had left our hands in Yaoundé.

Vic still did not have feeling completely back in his injured finger. Simone was well and, ever the entrepreneur, was now in the auto-repair business on the side. He got several people—including me—to ship him Volkswagen parts from the States. He was also trying to get into the animal or tropical-fish business, and wanted to hire Ralph as a worker but failed. Ralph and Zoë were still in Cameroon. Vic tried to talk to Ralph's father, but to no avail. Simone wrote that Ralph had first tried to go north and get a job as an interpreter with the oil companies but hadn't been hired. He and Zoë had then gone back to Ebolowa and lived with her villagers for a while, but he could not find work. They were now living in extreme poverty and misery somewhere in Douala.

John and I came through with our treasured Goliath frogs, a dozen tortoises, and most of the small frogs. Nine Goliath frogs were sent to Vic Hutchinson for his studies, replacing the frogs lost in France. The remaining frogs resided for many years in their tropical-forest exhibit in the Reptile House and Aquatic Birds House at the Bronx Zoo. But the story doesn't end here for the frogs and me.

Word spread throughout Cameroon that Goliath frogs were extremely valuable to zoos around the world. Soon an enterprising new legion of Cameroonian animal dealers began sending letters, offering Goliath frogs at thousands of dollars per pair. Another U.S. entrepreneur imagined that the world's largest frog had to be capable of the world's longest frog leap. He figured he would not only buy Goliath frogs but would also enter them into the Calaveras County Fair and Jumping Frog Jubilee contest, held each May at Frogtown, in Angels Camp, California, and win thousands of dollars. He didn't know that one or two even moderate leaps, the most a Goliath frog was capable of, given its great body weight, would in all probability cause the frog to roll over dead. Concern grew for the future of the Goliath frog as a species, with this developing commercial market and the lack of trade controls in Cameroon. The U.S. Fish and Wildlife Service officially listed the Goliath frog as a threatened species on December 8, 1994, after one of the service's biologists put his career at risk—with just a little help from me—to establish its protection from unscrupulous traders.

17

SPECIAL PLACES

Tomas Blohm sat at the head of the table as the maid, in her gray uniform, arranged silver trays on the white linen tablecloth. This was our first breakfast in Venezuela, and we were surprised to see that they ate cornflakes here. As we ate and drank, and became acquainted, for neither Myrna nor I had spent much time with Tomas before, Tomas reached onto his plate for a small morsel of roll. Still engrossed in telling us about his interests, he half-turned in his chair and casually held the piece of roll in the path of a column of army ants that streamed from somewhere in the darkness of the floor, marched up the white wall behind him, and disappeared behind a beam of the vaulted ceiling. The ants milled around the bit of roll for a moment. Then, as Tomas released his grip, the roll seemed to develop a mobility of its own, as dozens of ants joined forces to carry the piece, like a newfound prize, up the wall, toward some secret destination. Tomas turned back to face us and continued the conversation, as though he had just fed a pesky cat rather than a swarming horde of army ants. Here was a man we immediately loved.

Tomas was a moderately tall, thin man, and perhaps a little bent over, more from hard work than age. His wrinkled face spoke of years in the blazing Venezuelan sun. The tinted lenses of his thin-rimmed glasses seemed to be a necessary complement to his narrow, angular face. His distinguished-looking wisps of platinum hair looked surprisingly untidy, in contrast to the manicured man I had seen pictures of, dressed in a white dinner jacket and bow tie, receiving an international conservation award. Tomas most often wore a long-sleeved tan field shirt and a wrinkled visor cap straight out of a farm catalog. He would sit with his legs crossed at the table, deep in thought, holding a cigarette in the V of his fingers near his lips as he spoke.

It's hard to explain how we had come to Venezuela in the first place. Myrna and I were both crocodile people and had been communicating with other crocophiles around the world for years, including Tomas. She was teaching anatomy and physiology at a boring local college, and I was going about my daily routine as a superintendent of reptiles at the zoo. We needed a vacation badly.

Myrna had become quite friendly with our local travel agent, a lovely woman with long dark hair, who had arranged Myrna's many trips to Georgia and Florida to study alligators. My travels and work at the zoo had made us some of the agent's more interesting clients, and she liked to ask us, "Where in the world am I sending you next?" So when we had despaired about where to go on vacation, Myrna had said, "Let's go see the travel agent."

We had walked into her office and sat down at her desk to brood. "Okay, what do you want?" was her inevitable question.

Myrna started with "We need a vacation."

The agent asked, "Well, where do you want to go?"

"Someplace warm," we replied in unison.

"Preferably with crocodiles," Myrna added.

"Any reptiles would be all right, I guess," I sighed.

Myrna suggested, "How about a resort hotel, a club, or even a spa on a Caribbean island?"

The agent shook her head. "No. I know you two. You would be bored to death. You'll have a terrible time and blame me. I won't send you to a club or spa. Try again."

"I hate Florida," Myrna groused. "I want to sit on a beach and read."

"No, you don't." The agent shook her head again.

Meanwhile, I pawed indifferently through a travel magazine. I don't know whether it was a blue-and-white banner hanging on the wall or an advertisement in the magazine for Venezuela, but the thought came to both of us at the same time, and we both said, "Let's visit Tomas Blohm!" We remembered that at the last Crocodile Specialist Group meeting, Tomas had urged Myrna to come visit him in Caracas so he could show her his special pair of Orinoco crocodiles.

Within minutes, we were back at home calling Caracas. The Blohm maid answered the phone, then quickly handed it over to Tomas. As soon as he heard it was us, he asked, "When are you coming to Venezuela?" In minutes we had a plan, and our happy agent could begin to make flight arrangements. A week later, we were in Caracas, with Tomas meeting us at the airport.

Venezuela is a beautiful country, with great winding rivers, high mountains and plateaus, tropical rain forests, arid plains, and vast grasslands. The tall, monolithic Blohm building, which then dominated downtown Caracas, testified to the important role the Blohm family played in Venezuela's economy and development. The family had been in Venezuela since the mid-1800s and had been instrumental in developing the early rubber trade. Cecilia de Blohm, Tomas's wife, is an important figure and spokesperson in the international conservation community. She and Myrna seemed to be cut from the same cloth, outgoing and dedicated to whatever cause they've taken up, to the last gasp. For Cecilia, it was the preservation of wildlife. For Myrna, it would always be the cause of the week.

The Blohm house was located in the middle of a walled compound, on a street where embassy residents lived in homes with manicured gardens that reflected a very comfortable lifestyle. But the similarity between the Blohm house and its neighbors ended there. The house was a large, sprawling stucco affair with an upper floor and outbuildings. The main house was encapsulated in an octopus of iron bars, which formed a continuous cage that extended from the garden at the side of the house, went past the kitchen door, climbed vertically to the roof, and spread across the roof in a complex of barred rooms, walkways, runs, and canopied resting areas. Within the cage complex lived a family of adult chimpanzees. A huge male hung by his massive arms next to the kitchen door, waiting to throw banana peels at anyone he didn't know. He was particularly delighted at Myrna's visit, because she reacted so actively to wearing a used banana peel or a gob of saliva on her shoulder or in her hair. An equally large female chimp and a clinging baby completed the immediate family group. It was a wonderful chimp family home, for the animals could entertain themselves by looking in the windows at the people inside, scampering through the runs and walkways on the roof, or lounging in the shade of a canopied chimp veranda. Tomas explained that the chimps had arrived unexpectedly; traveling circuses had left first one, then the other, as sick animals.

During our tour of the house and garden, Tomas asked if we would like to see his grandchild. There, in a crib, cozily nestled in a baby blanket, was a newborn chimp. Not only did the baby have his own room in the house, but the serving maid was assigned to care for it, changing its diapers, feeding it, and hugging it.

The garden, far from manicured, hosted dozens of waterfowl, chickens, small mammals, macaws, and other native animals, as well as pens of basking Orinoco and American crocodiles and caiman. Tomas next brought me into his bathroom to see a five-foot-long American crocodile with an injured jaw, residing in his bathtub. Tomas commented that taking a shower in the morning had become somewhat difficult, in that he had to share the tub with the snapping, growling crocodile. "No matter," he added. "We've come to an understanding. When I get in, he moves to the far end of the tub until I'm done." Tomas had become well known as a benefactor to all living creatures, in Caracas and throughout the world.

The Blohm ranches, particularly Hato Masaguaral, located in the llanos, or grasslands, to the south of Caracas, had been kept largely in their wild state, and consequently had become havens for populations of wildlife that had all but disappeared from the rest of Venezuela. Scientists from all over the world could find a welcome research center to study everything from ants and plants to birds, jaguars, monkeys, crocodilians, mollusks, fish, and anything else. Wildlife lived side by side with cattle, as a model to show that agriculture and cattle ranching did not have to evict wildlife to be profitable. Although the house in Caracas was Tomas's primary home, Hato Masaguaral was his real home, where he felt most comfortable, even though it lacked electricity.

Tomas knew that Myrna and I wanted to see crocodilians, particularly Orinoco crocodiles—not that we would object to seeing American crocodiles, or even the more common spectacled caiman—and he had a tour plan already waiting. He was as excited as we were.

Orinoco and American crocodiles had been all but exterminated in Venezuela, but the situation for the Orinoco crocodile was much more dire, because it inhabited only the inland basin of the Orinoco River and its tributaries. A few isolated individuals survived. Most of those were in the large open rivers that drained from Colombia into Venezuela, and on the large, private, guarded cattle ranches that lay in the llanos through which the Orinoco River and its tributaries flowed. The number of Orinoco crocodiles had dwindled to the point where it was not entirely clear if there were enough individuals left to sustain the species.

American crocodiles, on the other hand, could be found over a much greater coastal and oceanic range, from Mexico and the southern tip of Florida to the northern and western coasts of South America to Peru. The belly skins of Orinoco and American crocodiles lack bony plates in their scales, so when tanned they make extremely fine, soft leather, ideal for handbags and other accessories for the fashion trade. The depredations of skin hunters over many years had succeeded in making Orinoco crocodiles one of the most endangered species in the world, with the American crocodile not far behind. Both species are big crocodiles, by any standards. Males can reach six and a half meters, or over twenty-one feet long, and weigh nearly a ton. Females are a little smaller. These giants can catch and kill cattle or humans, as they had done in the past.

One of our first stops would be to try to find American crocodiles in the coastal mangroves at the Bay of Turiamo, a paradise of white crystalline sand beaches and blue sea. The land approach to the bay was isolated by a navy base, whose commandant had no interest in killing the crocodiles that lived in the estuary of the river that flowed into the bay on the far side of an exposed coral reef. Tomas knew the commandant, so along with Andres, a young biology student from the university who was studying the crocodiles, and an aluminum rowboat with an outboard motor, we were soon on the beach preparing to set out across the bay. Despite the submerged barrier reef that blocked the entrance to the bay, the surf rolled onto the beach in rough, high waves. The rusting hulk of a large tanker lay stranded at the edge of the water, driven to ground by a violent storm years before. We held on to the sides of the boat as the small outboard motor strained, trying to push the boat over the incoming waves, and reach the relative calm of the bay beyond. Finally, we escaped the surge of the sea and made for the shore, diagonally across the bay.

It was not yet dark, so we decided to search the mangrove swamps and the beaches for signs of crocodiles. It didn't take long. There, at the edge of the water, was a dark, moist half moon, and a checkerboard-patterned scaly track in the sand. Flanking it on each side were several dinner-plate-sized footprints that dug deep into the sand, each with four large clawed toes, and a long tail drag mark that extended into the water. A large crocodile had emerged to bask at the edge of the water, then had quietly left, probably as we had noisily walked toward it along the beach.

Farther along the shore, the soil changed from white coralline sand to orange-red loamy sediment, accumulated as soil washed downriver from far inland at the end of the rainy season each year. Mangrove roots grew thick and impenetrable along the bank, with overhead branches that sheltered hordes of insatiable mosquitoes. We climbed to the top of a rock-and-soil mound overlooking the water. There, in a shallow hole, were the egg fragments of a recently hatched crocodile nest. A mother crocodile had climbed more than fifteen feet up to lay her eggs in a nest overlooking the water. One could hardly imagine a twelve-foot-long female crocodile plunging headlong, diving into the water from such a height. Our excitement was barely contained as we ate crackers, drank water, told crocodile stories, and waited for dark.

At 9:00 P.M. we approached the mangrove-covered bank below where we had found the crocodile nest earlier. Tomas played the piercing beam of a high-powered light ahead of us, sweeping the water as we slowly approached the bank. Tiny white diamonds of light, reflecting brilliantly in the beam of the lamp, came into view, first two, then six. Sweeping the water farther along the bank, he found more eyes. Ten, twenty, finally another eight, for a total of twenty-eight baby crocodiles. It was the entire clutch of babies that had hatched from the crocodile nest above. But where was the mother? Mother crocodiles vigorously defend their babies and will attack any intruder, particularly any predator who seizes a baby crocodile. When seized, the baby emits a high-pitched distress call. Not only was the mother nowhere to be seen, but the water was so heavily laden with silt that we figured she could be inches away, underwater, and we wouldn't know until she was upon us. Or, having been hunted before, she could have been watching us from some nearby secluded place.

Tomas, Andres, and I slipped into the thigh-deep muddy water while Myrna assumed the job of continually searching the surface of the water with the light for any sign of the returning female. The sky had darkened during our trip to the bank, and now, to make things worse, it began to pour; lightning flashed downward, and rumbles and cracks of thunder followed moments afterward, just beyond the bay. Myrna stood upright in the aluminum boat, clutching an oar, as she shined the light. As we captured each baby crocodile, holding their mouths shut so they couldn't call mom, we passed them back to the boat to Myrna, who put them into a burlap bag. Curiously enough, when one baby would be captured, the others nearby would try to escape by running out of the water and hiding motionless in the tiny forest of emerging mangrove roots that protruded from the mud. It made sense, for the tiny twelve-inch-long hatchlings would face a much greater danger from marauding fish, birds, or other crocodiles if they tried to hide in the deeper river water.

The wild baby American crocodiles were an important find. Myrna was terrified that the mother would suddenly boil up from under the water and jump into the boat—something crocodilians can easily do. But the babies were silent. Each baby was weighed, measured, and marked by clipping a tiny scale from the top of its tail in a numerical code, so that Andres could return over the years and monitor the babies' growth and survival. At one point, there was an unusual great swirl of water close to the boat, which could very well have been the unseen mother. Our work with the babies done, we returned them to the water, none the worse for their experience. We were elated with our own experience of at last seeing—not to mention capturing—wild American crocodiles.

Next, we decided to travel up into the mouth of the river that emptied into the bay. There, we believed, we would find young crocodiles, too large to be with their mothers and too small to be out where the adult crocodiles roamed. Before long the eyes of a five-foot-long crocodile reflected back in the beam of our light. A little farther on, another shone, and farther on, a third. Each time we attempted to get close enough to slip a noose over an animal's head to capture it, it dove underwater and vanished, only to resurface several yards away. This was a sure sign that the animals were wary and had been exposed to hunters before, perhaps not people hunting them for their skins but people raiding nests for eggs for food, or simply shooting them for sport.

Andres, who spoke no English (and Myrna and I spoke no Spanish), kept telling Tomas that he wanted us to catch "a big one," a large adult crocodile. Knowing how dangerous such animals could be, Tomas, Myrna, and I agreed not to risk spoiling our vacation with a possible hospital stay.

It was still raining and thundering late that night, when the sea started pounding into the bay over the barrier reef. Tomas said that we would have to leave the boat—which was taking on a lot of water—behind, rather than risk losing it, and walk back through the surf in the dark. I was a bit dubious of this plan. We would have to walk back to our camp and the trucks by wading through the water for several kilometers, around the perimeter of the bay. As we sloshed along, keeping our headlamps and flashlights playing on the surface, I could remember only one statistic I had read: that most shark attacks occur in water that is less than hip deep. Myrna, recalling the barrier reef outside the bay, was more sanguine about sharks. Tomas was worried about venomous pit vipers dropping from trees. More than tired, we were happy to finally get back to the trucks and the meal of bread, roast chicken, American cheese, sardines, and coffee that Tomas had thoughtfully packed for our trip. Hammocks were soon suspended in the overhanging mangrove, to the resentment of a four-foot-long iguana that had chosen the same place to spend the night. Myrna elected to sleep in the back of Tomas's Toyota Land Cruiser.

The sun glistened on the bay as morning came—along with the smell of fresh coffee. Tomas was not one to be without his basic comforts. We would now have to walk back through the surf to where we had left the boat the night before. Still tired, we spoke little. Myrna decided to remain on the beach, which was so exquisite (and the young Venezuelan navy men so handsome). Determined to get in a day of reading yet, she said that she'd decided to relax and read until we returned. "Tomas," she asked, "do you think it will be safe with the navy base so close?" "No problem," he replied. "You needn't worry." She later admitted that she was hoping some of the handsome navy men who visited the beach with friends would notice her. Tomas knew better. The women who accompanied the navy men were so exquisite in their beach dresses and bikinis that none of them ever noticed Myrna, dressed in jeans and a T-shirt reading *See It and Say It in Spanish*. Poor Myrna.

Hours later, we reached the boat and began our return across the bay. As we neared the point at which the waves, probably six or seven feet high, were breaking toward the shore, Tomas shouted something in Spanish, to Andres, above the roar of the water. I held on, but I didn't understand a word of what he said. As we came closer to the crest of the waves, Tomas again shouted something in Spanish. "What did you say?" I yelled as loud as I could. Tomas turned to me as the waves sprayed in our faces, and said, "I forgot you don't speak Spanish! When we come to the crest of the waves, jump out of the boat and hold on to the sides to keep it from capsizing!" At that moment, all of us jumped over the side of the boat and held on as the crashing waves carried us to the shallow water and shore. I still wonder what I would have thought if I had not known what was said, and suddenly, at the critical moment, Tomas and Andres had jumped from the boat and left me alone, behind.

Although we were exhausted when we got back from our foray, Tomas was not going to let us rest. We said good-bye to Andres and continued our adventure. Tomas took us through high cloud forests where the treetops remained perpetually shrouded in the dense fog of low-hanging clouds. He clearly loved his country. He took us inland to a reservoir, the Embalse de Camatagua. It was on the shore of this reservoir that Tomas owned a cattle ranch. Although he had an important position in his family's business, professionally he was more a rancher than a businessman. A graduate of Cornell University's College of Agricultural Sciences, he had devised new methods of handling cattle that made it much easier for ranchers. Tomas had built a kind of ferry, a platform on floating pontoon drums, that anchored on the lake at this northern ranch, not far from Caracas. He hoped that it could be used as a base to study migratory waterfowl. He suggested that we sleep on the ferry, out of the way of jaguars or humans.

After arriving at the ferry, we settled down in our camp to eat and listen to the night sounds. The maid, Maria, had packed us a dinner: bread, soup, sardines, and cheese. Maria was Tomas's nemesis, and Tomas was convinced that she purposely did things to enrage him. We heard Tomas grumbling as he began to unpack the food and stoke up the gas burner to heat the soup. Soon the grumbles became Spanish curses. Tomas was beside himself as he continued to empty the contents of several small glass jars into a saucepan. The soup was hot, but it was watery and tasteless, with barely a hint of green-pea flavor. Tomas ate in silence.

The first course done, Tomas opened the cans of sardines and a loaf of sliced white bread, then began to unwrap a package of sliced

American cheese. Suddenly, he could hold his rage no longer. Slices of white bread and cheese flew into the air as Tomas raged in Spanish, his curses punctuated here and there with the name Maria and more flying cheese. Finally, he calmed down enough to speak English. Maria had packed jars of split-pea baby-food soup, originally intended for his young grandchild, who lived with Tomas's son and daughter-in-law in the house next door to his. Tomas had to use it to make our flavorless watery soup, hoping we would not notice, as he had plotted Maria's firing. But the ultimate insult had come when Tomas had addressed the cheese, which had turned out to be enclosed in the type of packaging in which each slice is separated from the next by a sheet of paper. It was absolutely beyond Tomas's limit of patience to separate the slices from the paper, and Maria knew it.

The next morning, just before dawn, we were awakened by the sounds of men talking in the darkness on the far shore. Tomas was already awake and had his ever-present pistol at his side. "Shhh," he whispered. "Poachers." Soon the voices faded into the forest. Tomas explained that he had two adult Orinoco crocodiles isolated in an oxbow lake on the river at his ranch, and would have to move them to the safety of Hato Masaguaral, his ranch many miles south in the llanos, to keep them from being killed by poachers or squatters.

Tomas had been troubled many times by squatters and others who had tried to build on his land. There had been several attempts on his life, and for several years he had a contingent of National Guard soldiers living on his ranch in the llanos to protect him. Once, as we traveled a back road, we came to a roadblock, manned by several young boys in uniforms carrying rifles. Tomas told us not to speak to or look at them for fear that they would construe it as disrespect and arrest us; he placed his pistol close to his seat, just in case. Bandits often wore army clothing, he explained. Then, to his relief, he recognized an old friend of his—the sergeant who was in charge of the soldiers posted at his ranch. We were soon on our way. In my opinion, the democratic way in Venezuela left much to be desired.

While at Camatagua, we got to see his prize Orinoco crocodiles. Myrna, in fact, almost got to see one of them from the inside out. We arrived at the caretaker's house in the early afternoon. Tomas knocked on the door of the rough wooden house. The caretaker emerged from the dark inside, probably disturbed during his afternoon siesta. After a few words, the man went around the house and came back holding two live chickens upside down, by their feet.

Tomas explained to us that he had hired the man to live on the ranch, protect it from squatters, and, once a week, feed the crocodiles a chicken apiece. He was convinced, however, that the man was not feeding the crocodiles often enough, because whenever Tomas came to check, the crocodiles seemed inordinately hungry.

The caretaker with the chickens led the way as we started off down a path toward the water. The path followed the top of a kind of berm, or low dam, with a bank that sloped about twenty feet, steeply, down to the water's edge. Tomas walked behind the caretaker, followed by me, and Myrna pulled up the rear. Both she and I carried 35-millimeter cameras around our necks, hoping for some good Orinoco crocodile shots. Myrna also carried a pair of compact binoculars around her neck, next to her camera. The grass grew knee-high along the path, and here and there a liana vine snaked its way through the grass. As I passed a place where I could look down to the water's edge, I suddenly made out the two-foot-long head of a crocodile—a large animal, probably more than eleven feet long. The end of its snout was twisted to one side, probably having been broken, then healed, after a fight with another crocodile.

Just at that moment, a chicken squawked loudly as the caretaker and Tomas, who had now found the male Orinoco crocodile, approached it. Hearing the chicken squawking, the crocodile in front of me at the edge of the bank lifted its head. It was a movement I had seen many times before, when a crocodile is suddenly intent on locating and attacking prey. I turned to Myrna and began to say, "Be careful. The crocodile is right here." The words were barely out of my mouth when the huge crocodile saw Myrna, who was now standing where the chicken had been when it had squawked. Thinking Myrna had a chicken for it as well, the crocodile left the water and ran the few feet up the bank, coming directly at us.

Myrna turned and ran. The crocodile lunged past me, only a few feet away fixed on attacking Myrna. My new Olympus camera was safe, I thought, thinking only secondarily about Myrna's safety. Suddenly, with the jaws of the crocodile mere feet behind her, Myrna tripped on a vine and fell into the tall grass, over the edge of the berm, momentarily out of sight of the crocodile. "Stay down. Don't move," I shouted. "Don't move!" The crocodile stopped in its tracks, waiting for any new sign of movement from Myrna, as she lay barely hidden in the grass, well within a single lunge from the terrible jaws. Myrna later said the only thing she could think of as she was lying there in front of the crocodile was "This is going to hurt a lot."

At that moment, another squawk came from the chicken being eaten by the male crocodile farther up the path. Our attacking crocodile, not wishing to miss out on the advertised meal, turned and again charged past me, on the way back to the water. With the crocodile gone, Myrna emerged from the grass, blood streaming down her chin. As she had fallen into the grass, she had smashed her mouth on the protruding "hot shoe" of the camera, landing facedown with the camera under her chin, driving the shoe through her lower lip. She had barely escaped with her life. We continued on to Hato Masaguaral—there was no medical care here—and Myrna had a swollen, purple lip and a new view on her value to me versus the value of a cherished camera. Years later, when she was interviewing a bee and wasp expert for a story, he related to her how he had gone to Hato Masaguaral and had heard from Tomas Blohm the oft-repeated tale of the woman who was almost eaten by the female Orinoco crocodile. "That's me," Myrna told the astonished man.

We saw our wish list of crocodilians and had our vacation. There were other adventures on this trip to Venezuela, and many more to come when we would return the following year, and I would help capture the two Orinoco crocodiles to send them to a safer place, even though one of them nearly ate Myrna.

18

THE GREAT
REPTILE HOUSE
ROBBERY

It was December 26, 1974. At 7:45 A.M. I sat sleepily at my desk, sipping a cup of cold coffee from an uncleaned pot and reading the log entries from the previous two days before starting my daily rounds of the Reptile House. Bob Brandner, the senior keeper, who had been in charge during my two days off, entered and sat down. "I found the plastic flashlight inside my wall locker yesterday morning," he said. "The one from your desk drawer. I left it on top of my locker." He seemed to be merely passing on a bit of information, and I barely registered his observation as he proceeded to check the posted daily work assignment schedule and left. One by one, the other keepers arrived, checked their assignments, and left to change into their uniforms.

I always liked to start checking the building from the second floor. This allowed me to scan the temperatures that were automatically registered on thermometers located in the air ducts of the various independent environmental systems, check the operation of the bank of compressors that maintained these environmental conditions, and generally get an overview of what might be, mechanically, going wrong that would require calling in service personnel early in the day. Detailed reports of individual animals or problems would come in as the keepers inspected their sections and the animals in their care. This route also took me past my own locker.

The desert cage, the rain-forest cage, the riverbank exhibit, and the amphibian section all seemed normal. Lights, ventilation, and temperatures were all functioning properly in the quarantine room and the two environmental holding rooms.

As I came around the corner of the quarantine room and approached the keepers' locker area, there was the flashlight Bob had spoken of, sitting on the coping of the balcony in front of the lockers. I had thought he had said that he had put the flashlight on top of his locker yesterday, I pondered, picking up the flashlight to return it to my desk drawer. The location of a flashlight could be important in an emergency. Every tool had to be where it was supposed to be so it was available if you needed it in a hurry. I was a stickler for that, and everyone knew it. I made a mental note to remind Bob. As a supervisor, I was a pain in the ass. Then I noticed that my locker door was ajar and the locking hasp was broken. Something was very wrong. I called on my ever-present two-way radio and alerted the keepers to check their sections carefully.

One by one the keepers reported their findings. Juan's wall locker had been closed but unlocked; a ten-dollar roll of coins was missing. Bob's entire set of keys was gone from the belt of his uniform trousers that had hung in his locker, but several single dollar bills obviously sitting in the locker had not been stolen. Tools and equipment had been disturbed throughout the building, but no power tools were missing. It appeared that someone had been in the Reptile House during each of the previous two nights, using the flashlight from my desk drawer in the process. I shuddered to think of what else they might have been up to.

Snakes and a lizard were missing as well. Although the door to the rainbow boa cage in the main exhibit passage was closed, it was now unlocked, and one of the three brilliantly colored snakes was missing. Surely it had not left on its own volition, closing the cage door behind it. A six-foot-long boa constrictor was missing from one of the center-island cages in the large constrictor exhibit area. A three-foot-long boa constrictor was gone from the quarantine room on the second floor, and two more boas were missing from a holding room. A six-inch-long ameiva lizard was gone from its aquarium home, and a five-foot-long pilot black snake was missing from the quarantine room. A six-foot-long African rock python was no longer in its galvanized metal tank in the outside holding area, although the screen top of the tank was not only closed but locked shut. Snakes certainly don't escape and tidily lock their cage doors behind them. Not only that, but a carrying case was also missing, and the snake certainly had not taken it with him. Its feeding records had also been neatly stacked on an adjoining cage. All in all, a total of seven snakes and one lizard were missing. Animals had been stolen from sections throughout the building. It was as if someone had spent many hours on a shopping spree, carefully picking out the particular animals that suited his fancy. Thankfully, none was poisonous, but all were fairly irascible—that is, except for the African rock python, which was downright nasty and somewhat aggressive. We had been robbed.

Mike Gallo, the head of zoo security, was quickly notified. As a retired New York City police officer, he had worked for many years at the local police precinct. His connections with his colleagues brought quick results, and two detectives arrived in short order. These were two street-smart cops who found that a case of burglary at the zoo involving a bunch of missing snakes was a somewhat humorous diversion from their usual fare of shootings, murders, beatings, and robberies. They took in every detail as we showed them each area where animals were missing. It was cold outside and fully eighty degrees Fahrenheit inside the Reptile House, but the detectives never removed their topcoats or hats. It was as though they knew that this crime scene would not take long to investigate.

Together, the detectives soon added more elements to the puzzle. They had found scratches on the lock and adjoining wood of the office door, suggesting that someone had tried to open the door without a key. There were two sets of exit doors leading from the public space to the outside; the inside set of doors had their slide bolts pulled back in the open position, while the second outside set of doors, equipped with dead-bolt locks, showed signs of tampering on the inside but remained locked. Whoever had been in the Reptile House had either tried to break out of the building or was trying to make it look as though he had tried to break in. Most puzzling was that the perpetrators had apparently been inside the building trying to get out. How had they gotten in to begin with? None of the glass windows on the perimeter of the building was broken. Neither had the doors been pried open from the outside. It did not make sense. However, at that moment, we believed that they had in their possession the keys from Bob's locker.

It also seemed clear that more than one person had taken part in the entry because of the amount of disturbance and the number of animals involved. What seemed equally mysterious was that the Reptile House was located in the center of the zoo, and immediately across the walk at the rear of the building was the residence of several curators and a veterinarian. Zoo security guards patrolled the zoo throughout the night, and night watchmen checked the furnaces, as well. None of them had heard or seen anything. Could several people have climbed over or through the high perimeter fencing, walked hundreds of feet through the zoo, and spent two consecutive nights stealing snakes before they had retraced their steps while carrying a half dozen bags and boxes of animals—all without being heard or seen? The detectives, still in topcoats, with their hands stuffed in their pockets, listened to all of our speculations. Finally, the detective who seemed to be the senior of the two said they would be back. They would also send a fingerprint team over, he added, giving us an offhand look that said, "We have to do this, but it's a waste of time." He ended his site investigation with a simple pronouncement. As he turned to go, he said, over his shoulder, "Kids. It was kids that done this."

Several hours later, probably well after their shift should have been over, a fingerprint team of several disheveled men arrived and began to dust a fine powder, with a small feather applicator, over the walls and doors of each section in which items had been disturbed or where snakes had been taken. I wondered if it was worth the effort, as some of the doors involved were located in the public spaces and probably had on them the fingerprints of several hundred thousand people—including ourselves. They soon left, looking as tired and detached as when they had arrived. We later learned that although they had gotten some complete fingerprints from some of the aquaria that had been disturbed, none had proven to be associated with anyone whose prints were already in police records.

Our suspicions seemed to immediately evolve in a different direction. Could the perpetrators have been zoo staff members? Could they be persons who had access to keys and did not have to break in? They would only have to make it look as though that is what had happened—and they hadn't been very smart about it, at that. Did these persons have enough knowledge of snakes to avoid the poisonous animals and concentrate on those snakes that might have sale value as pets? How had they so easily avoided the zoo security and night watchman patrols, unless they had knowledge of them? Mike wondered, as well.

Mike was a highly skilled police officer who had inherited what we all considered to be a department of poorly qualified misfits. He had been hired to turn the department into a professional security force, but he had had little to work with. As the need for a zoo security force had become evident, word had circulated that a line of new security positions would soon open. True to form, zoo personnel administrators had felt that the members of the zoo plumbing shop would be best qualified to fill the role of zoo security guards. In short order, a cadre of plumbers had traded their mud-soaked dungarees, plaid shirts, hole-riddled sneakers, and daily beard stubble for spiffy uniforms and equipment, and tried to look like security guards. The head plumber had hired all of his friends from the plumbing shop, along with a few relatives, and as his first order of police business, he had purchased gray police shirts, black pants, leather garrison belts, cowboy hats, and badges for everyone, ordered out of a police supply catalog. Their glory days were short-lived, however, for Mike was placed in charge of the new department on his arrival. Mike's men resented him and immediately set about to make him look as bad as possible. They filed union grievance after grievance to make Mike's life miserable, and created situations to show how efficient they were in fighting crime, or at least in harassing small children who threw popcorn to the giant tortoises.

In this atmosphere, our own security staff seemed like prime suspects for the break-in. Keys to all of the buildings, including those for the Reptile House, were kept in the security office. It would be easy for someone from security to use his key to gain entry to the Reptile House during the night shift. One man was a knowledgeable reptile enthusiast with connections to the pet trade; he had once even worked at the Reptile House. It would not be difficult for such a person to handle and dispose of the snakes that had been stolen.

Besides, Reptile House staff members were not particularly well liked by the security staff. When "the plumbers" had moved to get formal peace-officer status and be allowed to carry loaded guns, the Reptile House staff had signed a petition against the idea. When one particularly large and simple security person had run for election as president of the local zoo union, he had used as his election platform that if he were elected, he would see to it that the zoo restore the annual bonus Christmas turkey, which had been discontinued as a holiday gift to all employees the previous year. This was a sore spot among the employees. One year, a curator, trying to show how fiscally conscientious he was, had tried to save money on the Christmas turkeys by purchasing frozen birds with disabilities. That is, when the employees had gotten them home and thawed them, most of the birds had turned out to have a missing drumstick, one wing instead of two, or some other unappetizing deformity. We had countered Alvin's "Get Back the Turkeys" campaign by posting signs throughout the zoo work areas saying, A VOTE FOR ALVIN IS A VOTE FOR A TURKEY. He had lost the election and had turned a bit mean toward us.

A few days passed before it happened again. This time, the thefts included three Australian green tree pythons. In the interim between the first and the second break-ins, Bob's keys had mysteriously reappeared, on top of his locker. Had they accidentally been put there by Bob as he had changed his clothes, or had the intruders moved them?

The stolen green pythons were special animals. They were being held as evidence as part of a U.S. Customs seizure in a smuggling investigation involving a reptile dealer. As such, they now became stolen U.S. government property, and U.S. Customs agents had to be notified by the zoo. More humorless men in topcoats arrived the next day and questioned all of us. Unlike the New York City detectives, who looked as if they worked long and hard in their crumpled clothes and acted uncomfortable in their plaid woolen sports jackets and tasteless ties, the customs agents were relatively young and clean shaven and wore white shirts with pants and jackets that had clearly been purchased as coordinated suits. They didn't look tired, and they mumbled to each other a lot. Our detectives had seemed to think of themselves as real street cops, where the action was, as opposed to the cleaner "feds." The customs agents assured us that they would conduct their own investigations—in secret. I did not get the impression that the New York City cops were going to go out of their way to cooperate with the feds, nor the other way around. What was difficult to explain to everyone was that, although the green tree pythons were now missing, the African rock python that had been stolen several nights before had been returned to its original tub and carefully locked inside, along with its carrying case. The thieves had broken in to return snakes as well as to steal them. We were now even more convinced that there was someone within the zoo taking part in the thefts.

Our detective friends, not wishing to overlook the possibility, devised a plan. Whenever they could—they were working on several unrelated cases simultaneously—they would spend time overnight in the Reptile House. The catch was that one of us had to stay overnight with the detective, as "no cop in his right mind, armed or not, would spend the night alone, in the dark, in a building full of snakes."

The plan included placing wireless intercom units, with open speakers, around the building. Any unusual noise, such as someone breaking in, moving, or talking, could then be heard on our own receiver as the detective and I sat sequestered in one of the offices in the rear of the Reptile House. But what was an unusual sound in the

Reptile House at night? Throughout the night, we would periodically hear coughing and hissing as tokay geckos threatened one another over invaded territory, or found and fought each other over succulent cockroaches or a sexy female gecko.

We had deliberately introduced these ten-inch-long, pugnacious lizards to the Reptile House, allowing them to roam at will around the building at night to catch and kill mice and any other vermin they could find. They served as expert living pest-control officers, as they had the ability to race in any direction, even across walls or ceilings. Geckos possess a series of soft skin flaps on the underside of their wide flattened toes, which are lined with numerous extremely fine hairlike hooks. These are so fine that they are able to grasp the smoothest surfaces, even a glass plate that is covered with the minutest film of dirt. The tiny, hooklike appendages allow the lizard to hold on as it runs upside down across a ceiling, unhooking the appendages with each step by curling its toes upward. One had taken up residency behind the clock that hung on the office wall, racing out to catch a mouse on the floor below or loudly call Uh-oh as it spied another male to fight over territorial rights or a female.

Giant marine toads, as big as a nine-inch dinner plate—also loose in the Reptile House—made flopping and croaking sounds as they also hunted pests. Occasionally, a high-pitched squeal could be heard from somewhere in the darkness, as either a gecko or a toad dispatched another unsuspecting mouse. Other frogs, in their own cages, chirped and trilled during the quiet of the night, as did the hundreds of escaped crickets, which called from dozens of dark recesses.

I don't think the detective ever enjoyed his full measure of sleep. I relieved him sometime during the night. At about 3:00 A.M., we both jumped with a start as a great crashing sound of water came from the area of the crocodile pools. Complete silence followed from every quarter as we sat and listened. Then the crocodiles could be heard making their muffled growls, and more water swished and splashed as they lashed their tails from side to side. Two of the larger crocodiles were settling a minor dispute over which one would occupy a choice spot on the heated concrete slab that made up the basking area in their exhibit. By morning, we had achieved nothing; no one had shown up, and the day's work began as usual.

The next day, we decided that no one would stay that night. The following morning, more snakes were missing; the intruders seemed to have freely toured the building. They had not only stolen more snakes, but this time they had also stolen rats and mice to feed them. The detectives vowed that they would solve this case if it was the last case they ever worked on.

"Was there anyone who had recently been fired or was a disgruntled employee?" the detectives now asked. There was one kid, a part-time worker, who had not done well; I had had to let him go, I recalled, retrieving his first name and an address from my files. He was only sixteen or seventeen, I told the lead detective, and lived in a South Bronx tenement not far from the zoo. He was tall and skinny, with a wide assortment of pus-laden pimples covering his cheeks and forehead, and a nose that hung like an enormous pickle from his face, complete with warts. His face was shaped liked that of a horse—long, drawn, and narrow.

The detective did not believe my description. No, we did not have a picture to offer, but we could do the next best thing: our staff artist could draw a picture of the kid if we described him well. As the artist drew, we kept telling him, "Make the pickle bigger." An hour later, the artist produced an image of a kid with a face like a horse and a nose like a pickle covered with pimples. The detective carefully folded the picture and put it in his inside coat pocket—more, I think, to satisfy us than as a tool by which he could identify a possible suspect. He then left us to ponder our next move.

Now certain that the perpetrators were from the ranks of our own security staff, who could certainly know when we were waiting in the Reptile House and when we weren't, we decided to be devious. In the late afternoon, reptile keeper Joel Dobbin and I made our way unobtrusively to the far end of the zoo, where we kept our large tortoises in an old farm building. In case we were being observed, no one would construe this as anything but a usual part of our afternoon feeding schedule. There we waited. At the end of the day, the other keepers loaded a large coffinlike pine box on the back of the electric cart and drove to meet us, making a great show of transporting the box back to the Reptile House, and making sure our security staff saw what was said to be a shipping box we were preparing for the following day, so we could send a tortoise to the airport and on to another zoo.

In reality, the box contained Joel and me, secretly being smuggled to the Reptile House for the night's surveillance. This time, however, the curator had decided that whoever stayed should be armed, and had provided us with a .410 shotgun for good measure. The night wore on as Joel and I took turns sleeping and listening to the sounds that reached us over the open microphone. Then, at around 1:00 A.M., a tinkling of glass could barely be heard over the system. I woke Joel, and we listened. Nothing followed. We decided to search the building in the semidarkness, aided only by the incidental glow that emanated from the dozens of heat lamps and aquaria. We moved slowly and cautiously, staying within the shadows, and pausing for long periods of time to listen—at least, they seemed like long periods.

The main exhibit floor showed nothing. Diurnal Chinese dragon lizards slept with their eyes closed and their legs folded neatly against their sides, on a branch in their cages. Tiny, brilliantly colored dart poison frogs sat alertly, as if waiting for an insect meal to crawl by. Vipers and rattlesnakes, energized by the darkness, which heralded their time to hunt, prowled their cages, freezing in place when we approached their cage glass. Roaches scurried everywhere as they fed on pieces of popcorn that had escaped the nightly sweeping. They hung in legions in corners, swarmed over exhibit branches, and crunched underfoot. A surprised king cobra, startled by our presence in front of his exhibit glass, flattened his neck in a halfhearted threatening hood, gave us an evil stare, then dropped his head back down to continue his open-eyed slumber. Nothing seemed to indicate that anything was other than normal.

We next made our way through the darkness to the gray steel stairway leading to the second floor. Despite the cold outside, I sweated in the warm, humid air, which lay like a soaking blanket throughout the building. Why, I asked myself, did I feel more like prey than the hunter with a gun? Joel and I paused on a landing halfway up the stairs, to watch and listen. We were just able to peer over the edge of the top step and see the four rooms that had been built as box-like wooden chambers on the second floor, flat-roofed and topped with ventilation ducts and fans. Some of the snakes had been taken from cages within these rooms, which served as holding and quarantine facilities. During more research-oriented times, these rooms had served as experimental chambers for the study of python metabolism and the snake's unique ability to raise its body temperature to incubate its eggs. It seemed as though we stood there for a very long time, poised, brandishing our shotgun, and straining to see or hear an intruder before we were detected.

There was nothing—no movement, and no sound other than the chirping of undisturbed crickets and running water as it coursed through a dozen or so filters on its way back to its origin. We quietly moved on to the top step and strained to see into the shadows. Nothing. Could the momentary sound of tinkling glass in some distant place have been only imaginary, a trick a sleepy mind played in the middle of a week of nearly sleepless nights? Somewhat emboldened at having found nothing, we quickly searched the rest of the second floor, around the corners of the rooms, between open tubs of wide-eyed crocodiles, who seemed to view us with suspicion, and sleeping turtles with their heads tucked inside their shells. Daylight was just beginning to seep through the covered windows of the seminar room we used as a base for our surveillance as I allowed my head to rest on my arms on the oaken conference table. The keepers would soon arrive, and Joel and I would have to report another wasted and sleepless night.

The next day, the detectives called to say that they had a report of snakes in an apartment in a public housing project not far from the zoo. Could I meet them at the zoo and go with them in an hour? "Sure," I said, recalling that the area and housing project they were talking about was in a very tough neighborhood, rife with drug dealers, prostitutes, and guns.

There was no chance of blending obscurely into the surroundings or the local population as our unmarked police car pulled up to the curb and parked in a clearly marked no-parking zone. Several days before, on a previous trip to the precinct house, we had driven the wrong way up a one-way street, with some degree of speed, to avoid a traffic delay. A rather young-looking uniformed police officer had jumped out from between two parked cars, waving his arms in an effort to stop us. The detective had simply swerved around him, leaving the young officer to chase frantically on foot as we sped off. "Stupid kids they train today," one detective had said. "They don't know anything. Stepping out in front of a police car like that." The other detective had added, "Yeah, he should know an unmarked car."

We did not have the same recognition problem at the housing project as the three of us stepped out of the car and approached the graffiti-decorated entrance to the lobby. A number of young men stood here and there. Cigarettes dangled from their lips, and they half-glanced in our direction from under hooded sweatshirts, then turned and slunk off with hands in their pockets. It seemed they were more concerned with recognition than we were. Besides, everyone seemed to know, instinctively or by personal experience, that the pile of junk we had left at the curb was a highly misused, unmarked, secondhand, throw-away police car, and that the two men in open topcoats with belts dangling, wearing well-worn shoes, were police detectives.

Glancing at a small piece of paper for a number, the detective led us directly to an apartment door in a bleak green-tiled corridor on an upper floor. Pounding with his fist on the designated door, the detective shouted, "Police. Open up. We only want to talk to you. You got snakes in there?" "Why?" was the response that came from behind the door. "C'mon, open up," repeated the detective. The door opened a crack, the most space allowed by the short security chain, and the person who now peeked out asked, "Snakes, what snakes? We got no snakes here." In the meantime, a chorus of "Snakes?" "What snakes?" "Who said snakes?" "Where's a snake?" came from behind the doors of adjoining apartments, as people began to gather in the hallway. "We got no snakes here," one tenant offered. Another said, "I hate snakes. We had them down in Georgia when I was a kid." A third chimed in, "If they be snakes here, they be in the other building. Not this building." This was an apparently fruitless quest, we silently agreed, and we looked at one another, turned, and left. Amazingly, the police car was still where we had left it at the curb, and even remained unburned.

The detectives had been working on the case every moment they could. As the animals were of pet value, it was reasonable to presume that some attempt would be made to sell them to a pet shop. The detectives began to canvass pet shops throughout the Bronx, including a shop on Fordham Road, not far from the zoo, owned by a New York City fireman. By chance, and unknown to the detectives, they were on the right track and actually walked past one of the robbers leaving the shop as they were going in.

They also found the kid with the pickle nose. The detectives had located the neighborhood the boy frequented and learned that he lived in a nearby apartment with his mother and sister. When they knocked on the apartment door and identified themselves, the young girl who answered said he was asleep in the next room. Without hesitation, the detectives went to the room and awakened the sleeping boy. As he turned over, the lead detective looked at him and compared his face to the face our artist had drawn from our description. They matched perfectly. Later, the detective would tell us that he could not believe anyone could look the way we had described the boy. However, the boy had been out of town visiting a relative at the time the burglaries had taken place, and so was no longer a suspect.

Night after night went by as our nocturnal surveillance continued without incident. A detective and one of the Reptile House staff remained on some nights, two Reptile House keepers on others, and the head of security with a keeper on others. The robberies had begun on Christmas Eve, and it was now February. Then, as soon as we discontinued the surveillance, there was another robbery, and a number of baby boa constrictors were gone. At this point, forty snakes and lizards had been stolen in just over a month.

Early in April, the detectives called me at home to say they had apprehended one of the thieves and recovered some of the missing snakes. Could I come to the precinct and identify the snakes? There, handcuffed to a wooden office chair by one wrist, was a fifteen-year-old boy. The detectives were searching for at least two additional boys. They had already arrested the owner of the Fordham Road pet shop, whom they had questioned earlier, on charges of receiving stolen property. At that store, they had recovered some of the snakes, including the green tree pythons. Indeed, I could verify that the snakes were the ones stolen, as each bore distinctive markings that correlated with the identification markings that were drawn on each snake's feeding records.

We then went to the boy's home, where he said he had kept some of the snakes for a while. However, his grandmother hated snakes and wanted none living in her house, so she had flushed the baby boa constrictors down the toilet when the boy wasn't home. Another of the larger boas had escaped and had been run over by a New York City bus as it had tried to cross Fordham Road. A number of other snakes, traded to the Fordham Road pet shop, had been sold to customers and were never recovered. In all, fewer than half of the stolen snakes were returned.

The boy's story of how he had successfully entered the Reptile House over and over without being found out was equally astounding. His motive was simple: he liked snakes and was too poor to buy them. He said that, unlike some friends of his, he would never hurt anyone, so he never robbed people and he would never steal from anyone. Therefore, he reasoned, he should not steal snakes from a pet shop, because they belonged to someone—the pet shop owner. But the snakes at the zoo belonged to the zoo and, thus, to his way of thinking, had no owners.

The first night, Christmas Eve, he had entered the building through a window, he said, and had spent the night with a flashlight he had taken from my desk drawer. Using a book about snakes he had purchased from the pet shop, he had looked at the snakes in their cages, read the labels and identification cards, and studied quietly in the semidarkness. The next morning, Bob had found the flashlight left out of place on his locker.

The next night, the boy had commandeered a friend, another boy, and together they had returned to the Reptile House. They had climbed over the ten-foot-high, barbed-wire perimeter fence that surrounded the zoo, walked the quarter mile in the dark to the Reptile House, and entered the building. Taking Bob's keys from his belt on the uniform that hung in his wall locker, they had carefully and selectively taken the snakes they wanted. Included was the nasty-tempered African rock python and a number of rats to feed it. Before leaving, they had returned the keys to Bob's belt, considerately thinking he would need them the following day to take care of the snakes. This was repeated each time the boy returned for more snakes, carrying the cloth bags filled with snakes back through the zoo, over the fence, and home in the dead of night. He had used Bob's keys at night, while Bob had used them during the day.

The African rock python had been carefully returned to its cage on one of the boy's adventurous nights because it wasn't as friendly as they had expected it to be. It had chased the fifteen-year-old around his kitchen one evening, and had eaten all of the rats he had offered it. It had to go back, so the boy had broken in and returned it. To care for the snakes, he had realized, he would have to sell or trade some snakes for mice, and so he had broken in for the baby boas and had been planning to give them to the Fordham Road pet shop—until his grandmother had flushed them down the toilet. He said he had felt bad when the boa that escaped had been run over by the bus, but no one had noticed, or thought it strange that there was a dead boa, killed by a city bus, on a busy street in the Bronx.

The nights he had chosen to return to the Reptile House had had nothing to do with knowledge or planning and everything to do with chance. He had simply looked for a friend who was available and willing, and when he found one, they had gone to the Reptile House. Carrying the heavy bags of snakes alone, over such long distances, was just too difficult. One night, at around 10:00 P.M., the boy and a friend he had inducted into the operation climbed over the perimeter fence only to come face-to-face with one of the zoo security guards on patrol. The guard had asked them what they were doing. They had replied that they were just taking a shortcut to the train station on the other side of the zoo. Obligingly, the guard had given them a ride through the zoo in the zoo patrol truck. No snakes had been stolen that night.

Luck had watched over the boys each time they had made their forays for snakes. On one occasion, the boy said, he had opened a glass front of a small red snake's cage. The snake had reared up, spread a hood, faced him, and "spit juice" on the glass. He had quickly closed the cage as he "didn't like the look" of that particular snake. In fact, it was a juvenile African red spitting cobra he had disturbed, and he had narrowly missed receiving a blinding spray of venom in his eyes.

The night Joel and I had been awakened by the tinkling of glass and had stalked an unseen intruder had not resulted from our over-active imaginations. The boy had entered the building alone that night. He had been hiding on the roof of the experimental room on the second floor when we had appeared on the gray steel stairway, brandishing the shotgun. In absolute fear, the boy had fainted. When he had awakened, we were gone, and he had left as quickly as possi-ble. He had come close to losing his life in the darkness that night, and Joel and I had come close to changing our lives forever.

How he had gotten onto the roof of the room, and in and out of the building each time, was unclear until several months later, when a pigeon flew into the Reptile House. As we were chasing it, the bird flew up to the second floor, reached the peak of the inside of the roof between the steel rafters, and vanished in front of our eyes. It had ac-tually flown through a twelve-by-fourteen-inch opening that, at one time, had held a small pane of glass. It was next to the whirling blades of a thirty-six-inch exhaust fan. The fan operated on a ther-mostat, going on and off automatically according to the temperature.

Our small thief had also benefited from luck in another way. After entering the zoo by climbing the barbed-wire fence and making it to the Reptile House in the dark, the fifteen-year-old, being the smaller of the two boys, would climb the sloped sheet metal roof of the Rep-tile House to the peak, fully thirty feet above the ground. There, he would remove one of the small panes of glass, inches from the steel blades of the exhaust fan. By chance, it was never in operation when he was working his way through the opening. A sort of bologna-slicing version of Russian roulette, I thought. After squeezing through the hole, he would find himself on a catwalk—fully fifty feet above the floor below—which he would follow, climbing down the steel girders supporting the Reptile House roof, to the roof of the wooden experiment rooms, and then to the floor. Once in the building, he would go to the exit doors and open them from the inside to admit his accomplice; later they'd use the doors to exit with the snakes.

Of the three boys who were most involved at one time or another, the youngest, the fifteen-year-old mastermind, and a sixteen-year-old boy who had helped once were charged as minors. Although the zoo pressed charges, it agreed to allow the boys to perform public service. They could work at the Reptile House they knew so intimately. The fifteen-year-old disappeared without completing his probation, only to show up one day at the Reptile House with several rather dirty but expensive cameras for sale. Ostensibly, the cameras had been given to him, by a friend, in Jamaica, Queens, a neighborhood in one of New York City's outer boroughs. By coincidence, an Eastern Airlines jetliner had crashed in the marshy swamps near Kennedy International Airport—just south of Jamaica—the day before, spewing luggage and killing over 110 passengers.

We never saw the boy again. The other adventurer completed his public service and was offered a job at the children's zoo, with glowing recommendations for all of his hard work. He eventually left to join the military, and came by once years later with his family in tow. As for me, the experience taught me a lot about people and the hazards of jumping to conclusions. I will always recall the detective's wise proclamation the first day of his investigation: "Kids. It was kids that done this."

19

POLICE BUSINESS AND ODD JOBS

My introduction to the inner workings of police business came in the form of a dapper, highly amusing old-time officer. Jack Soldier, a New York City police detective, was assigned to the zoo nearly every Sunday afternoon. His job was to catch pickpockets and perverts. Jack was a real fount of knowledge, and very good at what he did. During the week, his job was to watch the men's toilets at certain subway stations. Even to this day, through Jack's tutelage, I can spot a potential pervert or pickpocket in a crowd. Jack was a specialist, and it was fun to watch him work the crowd.

The perverts Jack apprehended were often older men, dressed in a raincoat, with their trousers pinned open so they'd have ready access to their exposed genitalia. We called them "touchers" or "feelers." They often carried a folded-up newspaper under one arm, a trait sometimes shared by pickpockets. The trick to spotting perverts and pickpockets was to look for lone men who were focusing on the visitors rather than on the exhibits or the animals. The real giveaway was when they were seen entering and leaving the building several times. They would usually come into the building the first time and make a circuit in and out rather quickly, followed by a second visit to "do business." This first pass around the building was to see if there were any security guards or plainclothes police officers on hand.

Jack assumed a different identity each week to avoid being recognized. We were instructed never to acknowledge or greet Jack while he was on the job, to avoid any possibility of alerting someone he might have been following from one dimly lit building to another. The Reptile House, the Great Apes House, and the World of Darkness buildings were favorite hunting grounds. Jack was great fun to watch. While Jack was assigned to the Reptile House every Sunday, the same perverts might be there "working," as well, having been released by a judge, on their own recognizance, after their last encounter with Jack. He even knew some of them by their first names.

You never could anticipate how Jack would arrive for work. One Sunday, he would arrive impeccably dressed in a black topcoat with a velvet collar, wearing a camera around his neck, a black homburg, and purple sunglasses. This was his version of a British tourist. Another day, he might wear a plaid sports jacket, a sports shirt with a pointed collar, and a gold necklace and wristwatch. He would tantalizingly expose the jewelry, as if it were so much bait. He was "fishing," and he loved every minute of it. Jack preyed on the predators. He had to be invisible, camouflaged, moving unnoticed through the crowd, patiently waiting and watching for his particular form of prey to make its move. Jack was not racist, and he had no prejudices; he simply cataloged people by their behavior patterns. Besides, Jack did not have all day, and he did not want to waste his time on "lookers," as opposed to actual molesters. I always felt that Jack would have made a great snake.

Once the potential offender felt confident that he was unobserved and free to operate, he would follow a likely person, usually an attractive young woman or a child, deep into the crowd. Shoulder-to-shoulder with the other visitors and intent on the exhibits, few people knew who or what was pressing against them. This is where the newspaper would come into play. Used as a distraction, to prod or touch the person harmlessly, it diverted their attention from the perpetrator himself, who might be pressing his organ or a hand against the victim's buttocks or breast.

Pickpockets, in contrast, often worked with one or two accomplices. One accomplice opened the handbag and made it ready. The second lifted the wallet from the handbag, then quickly passed it to a third accomplice, who removed the cash and discarded the billfold in the bushes in front of the building or behind a door. In this way, there was a broken trail between the person taking the wallet and possession of any possible evidence.

Jack often worked with another detective, as well. Sometimes, while the pervert or pickpocket was moving in on a potential victim, Jack would be a single step behind, and Jack's backup would be behind him. The moment the act of touching or taking the billfold was done, Jack would seize the person, his backup would grab the second thief, and, in a flash, the perpetrators would be thrust inside the keepers' hallway. Many times, the victim never even knew she was being targeted until she was asked to identify her possessions and handed back her wallet.

A police van waited behind the Reptile House most of Sunday afternoon. It was the unlucky "perp" who got caught at noon on a hot day. Handcuffed, he would have to wait in the van until 4:00 P.M., as Jack continued to fill it, before being taken away for booking and a possible weekend in jail. Strangely enough, some of these characters had come to the zoo with their own families; once arrested for molestation, a man might weep and plead, then, embarrassingly, have to ask for someone to find his wife and tell her what had happened. More than one perpetrator had to be protected from a beating from his outraged wife, once she had learned what her spouse had been up to.

It was not unusual for the New York City Police Department or other law enforcement agencies to call on the reptile department for assistance. All too frequently, as my reputation as a forensic specialist—

who worked free of charge a good part of the time—spread, I would be called at home, often at ungodly hours.

Contrary to the desires of the press, no one has ever actually seen anything close to an adult alligator in the sewers of New York, although I am sure that many unwanted baby South American caiman (a cousin of the alligator that was found in the pet trade by the thousands over the years) have been flushed down toilets. Alligators and, especially, caiman cannot tolerate New York's cold climate and would die as soon as winter rolled in.

Nevertheless, Myrna foolishly wrote a letter to the New York City Department of Environmental Protection (DEP) offering our services to pick up any alligators that found their way into the city's sewers. We never expected to hear from them. Several weeks later, we received a call from the DEP, which is responsible for the city's water supply. The caller said that an officer had seen an alligator in the Kensico Reservoir in Westchester County. Myrna and I packed our long aluminum pole, alligator nooses, and headlamps and headed north for a New York alligator hunt. The DEP's director of public relations met us at the reservoir, which, if you didn't know what it was, would look like a lake in the woods. He was inappropriately dressed in a suit and tie. His boss, a rather large woman, accompanied him. She wore an elegant skirt and blouse and high-heeled shoes. It was curious to watch how she managed to navigate through the woods and over rocks and fallen branches as we walked along the edge of the bank to the waiting rowboat.

We need not have bothered with a boat. Not more than a few feet from where the boat was tied sat a young alligator in the water, emaciated and cold. I easily reached down and scooped it up. We brought it over to the nearby pumping station, where the young man on duty asked us to take a photo of him with the alligator. We then packed the alligator in a pillowcase, for safekeeping, and took it to the zoo.

At the office the next morning, I had barely poured my first cup of coffee when the phone began to ring. First it was the press, clamoring to know what had happened to Kensie, the Kensico Reservoir alligator, as the DEP people had named her. Then I got calls from our own public relations people, irate that they had not been notified. I finally hid under my desk. Kensie became a hit, and she resided for many years in the Bronx Zoo's education department, where she grew to be almost six feet long and remained tame enough to be petted and to delight children and grown-ups alike.

Years later, we met a man who told us that Kensie had been his pet. When his girlfriend left him, he said, she took the alligator and threw it into the reservoir. We have no reason not to believe him.

Another New York alligator-hunting experience was even a bigger deal. After days of watching the TV news show various police agencies using helicopters to try to locate and capture some alligators in a small lake on Long Island, I finally received a call from the U.S. Fish and Wildlife Service. It was Special Agent Sam LiBrandi. "Peter," he said, "can you help us out? Someone has been releasing alligators into a Massapequa lake. The police tell us that whomever it is says he will turn loose another alligator each week until the county lowers the property taxes." At that rate, I thought, the lake will soon be knee-deep in alligators.

Over the years, I have worked with many top-notch special agents and wildlife inspectors. Sam was one I particularly liked and respected. "Sure," I said. "Meet us at the lake with a rowboat at one A.M." We wanted to finish a pleasant seafood dinner with friends first. But we also wanted to minimize interference by local residents, as the media coverage had made the whole area into a circus grounds.

Our guests were hardly surprised. Helen, who lived next door, was used to seeing an army of police cars and emergency rescue trucks with their lights flashing blocking the street below, in front of our apartment house on Columbia Heights, on the Brooklyn waterfront. The police, having been called in the middle of the night to investigate a loose boa constrictor or python in a New York apartment, would then bring it to me for identification. Our guests casually kept dipping their mussels in the butter sauce as Myrna began taking her tattered—and much beloved—tan field shirt out of the closet.

Myrna and I had kept abreast of the newspaper and TV news over the past week, so the call from Sam was not really surprising. The newspapers had chronicled how, each day, scores of police officers in boats, aided by helicopters flying overhead, had been scouring the lake for three American alligators, originally reported by an angler to be three to four feet long. Since the alligators weren't going to make it through the fall and winter, they had to be removed. One alligator had been caught early on, but two remained. At first, the local police had tried their hand, chasing the animals during the day, but never getting close. With the press looking over their shoulders, amused at everyone's failure to capture the alligators, the local police and the state Department of Environmental Conservation (DEC) had come to the conclusion that alligators were an endangered species, which made these alligators a federal problem. In turn, Sam had called us. We wondered what had taken him so long.

The press was having a field day, with more than a few pundits appearing on the nightly news joking about how the alligators were eluding the police. Some local residents had taken to wearing T-shirts that said, *Anti-Gator Squad* and *Gator Busters*. The alligators were winning the contest.

We arrived at the appointed time to find Sam, a DEC officer, and a rowboat waiting. I had brought with me a long aluminum pole fitted with a steel wire noose. Our plan was simple. We would row out and use the beam of our headlamps to scan the surface of the water, as I had done hundreds of times before while catching caiman in Brazil, and Myrna had done while studying alligators in Georgia and Louisiana. Any alligators that were on the surface, where they should be at that time of night, would easily be seen by the reflection of the light from their eyes.

As in most nocturnal creatures, light is reflected straight back to the light source by the tapetum lucidum, a reflective structure in the rear of the alligator's eye, behind the retina. The trick to seeing the reflection is to have your eyes directly behind the beam of light. Alligator eyes will then light up like brilliant diamonds in the darkness.

Mist rose from the water as we paddled out onto the lake. I swept the beam of my headlamp across the surface of the water. Two floating Coke cans gave us some false starts, as the bottoms of the cans caught the light. We had been on the lake less than half an hour when a bright glowing coal appeared in the distance in the beam of my headlamp. The blinding light would cause the animal to stay immobilized long enough for us to get close and slip the noose over its head—that is, if we didn't make any loud noise or bang the bottom of the boat.

A minute later, the alligator was thrashing to free itself from the noose. It was too late. I held his jaws closed in my hand, as Myrna shone the light and Sam taped the jaws safely shut. The animal was already thin from lack of food, starving in the cool temperatures of the lake. Pretty soon, the second animal was spotted near the shore, and was also captured. We all left for home, smug in the knowledge that the next morning, the press would arrive once again for a feast of news, but there would be none. Eventually, the alligators would be returned to the marshes of Louisiana.

Police calls were always interesting. Workers in a building being demolished in the South Bronx found a twelve-foot-long reticulated python. Several of the Reptile House keepers arrived in a police car to find a throng of people, many of whom had emigrated from the West Indian nations of Haiti and the Dominican Republic, in the street, waiting for the large python to appear. Excitement ran high. At one time, the snake had been someone's pet, and after it had escaped it had miraculously survived on rats, cats, and probably an occasional feral dog, in the rubble of the old collapsed buildings and their buried basements. A workman who had pet snakes of his own had already captured the snake, and he was carrying it to his truck when we arrived with the police and took possession of it. With the snake safely locked in a plastic barrel, we loaded it into the police car for the trip back to the zoo. The onlookers now surged around the police car, touching us through the windows, kissing their hands and touching them to the car, and making religious signs as we drove off. Perhaps the snake had been seen many times before as it prowled the neighborhood on warm summer nights. I wonder what unbelievable report the people who had seen it—perhaps while walking their dogs—had made to their neighbors in such a superstitious community.

On another occasion, I received a call from the police in a New Jersey town. "Would you identify a snake found by a woman when she cracked open an egg to make an omelette for her husband?" the officer asked. The detective was soon at my office door, holding a bottle that contained an eggshell and a dead snake. The reptile was easily recognizable as a harmless Dekay's snake, a native species of small ground snake that feeds on earthworms and slugs and is quite common in rural gardens and brush piles. The woman had called the police and told them that the snake had plopped out of the egg as she had broken it open at the edge of a bowl. Police officers had rushed to the scene and, on the spot, bludgeoned the poor six-inch-long creature to death.

The woman and her husband were suing the supermarket where she had purchased the eggs, the farm where the egg had originated, and, I'd bet, the chicken that had laid the egg. Their position was that she had been so traumatized by the experience that she could no longer accept her husband's sexual advances; therefore, he, too, was traumatized and under a doctor's care. The story was not credible. There was no way an adult Dekay's snake could have gotten into a chicken's oviduct.

Several weeks later, I received a call from a social service worker who said that the woman and her husband were his clients. He was irate. "How could you have told the police officer that you did not believe a word of the story and that having a live snake in an unbroken chicken egg was not believable?" he screamed. "The chicken could have eaten the snake and passed it on inside the egg the chicken laid." "That's impossible," I countered. "A chicken's digestive system is entirely separate from its reproductive system." He retorted, "How do you know? We learn new things in science every day." He slammed the phone down as I nearly fell on the floor laughing.

Several months later, I received another call from the police about a snake found inside a chicken egg, and the woman who found it suing the supermarket, et cetera. The story was familiar, except that the woman's name was different. Oddly, the address was the same as the first woman's, and they shared the same attorney, who also lived at that same address. The detective was very interested.

Sometimes the calls were much more sinister. One day, another New Jersey detective came to the Reptile House with a dead snake that I identified as a baby timber rattlesnake. The snake was evidence in the prosecution of an attempted murder case. The snake had bitten a woman's cat on the head. What was unusual was that the bite had occurred when the cat had gone under the couch in the woman's second-floor apartment. The cat had emerged from under the couch in great distress, and when the woman had looked underneath the couch, she had found the snake. She had called the police. A search of the apartment had then turned up several other eight-inch-long baby timber rattlesnakes. The woman hadn't a clue about where they had come from.

It seems that the defendant, a well-known local snake fancier, had been in trouble many times before with wildlife authorities in several states for poaching and interstate trade in endangered species, including timber rattlesnakes. He was accused—and later convicted—of conspiring with the woman's landlord in a plot to force her to vacate the apartment so a higher rent could be charged. The two had pushed a number of baby rattlesnakes, which the fancier had collected at a nearby rattlesnake den he frequently hunted, under her apartment door. They had hoped to scare her into believing the apartment was infested with dangerous snakes. It was, but not under the snakes' own volition.

Oddly, Warren Wetzel knew the defendant, who had been one of his early cobra-bite cases. The defendant asked Warren to testify at the trial as a character witness. I didn't consider it a smart idea . . . and Warren never told me if he did it.

20

STRANGE DEATHS

It was 3:30 P.M. on a New Year's Eve that would soon become like no other. Only Juan Soto and I were on duty at the Reptile House. I had let the other keepers take the day off to prepare for their evening holiday celebrations. Some had a long way to travel, and no one really likes to work a full day, travel home, and then get ready for guests or go out on the town. Besides, Myrna and I were just having the usual clique of close friends over for a casual dinner. All of them lived either in the same building as us or only a few streets away.

The day had followed the usual pattern for visitors on such days. Most people worked, school was not in session, and the weather was cold and gray. The animals had been serviced for the day, and all that was left was to wait through the final hour before closing, locking up, and leaving. Juan and I talked about nothing special as we sat in the office. We would make one last round of the building, checking cage doors to be sure they were locked tight, turning off lights where they were not needed, and turning on lights where they were needed for extra warmth, or where some diurnal species, like tortoises, might require a few extra hours of daylight to finish eating their trays of mixed salads and canned dog food.

Then the phone rang. The holidays could be bad. People got depressed, drank too much, and did stupid things. The New York City Police Department's Emergency Services Unit and the New York and national poison-control centers listed the reptile department as an emergency contact for snakebite information and antivenin. Besides, whom else would you call with an animal-related problem, if not your local zoo? We all knew that a disproportionately greater number of venomous snakebites happen on or around holidays. Most bites occur when the victim drinks too much or gets high on drugs, then tries to handle or show off his venomous snake to prove his masculinity or impress friends.

This phone call would bring together the worst combination of nightmares I could imagine. It was a sergeant with the NYPD's Emergency Services Unit. They had two dead bodies and an apartment full of snakes and spiders in a building in the Bronx. Would we come to help secure the apartment before the police put their men at risk processing the scene?

I said no. We were beginning to get frequent snake-related calls from city agencies and the public, and this was not a service we were equipped to undertake or a responsibility we really wanted to assume. Eventually, we would help train emergency-services personnel in how to capture snakes. For the moment, however, we were going home to our respective New Year's Eve celebrations. The last thing I wanted to do was to devote my holiday evening to the problems some morons had visited upon themselves.

It was a harsh position to take, but a practical one. All too often, what starts out as simple help to the police often mushrooms into problems of property rights, liability for damages if an animal dies under the zoo's care while it is being held as evidence, lost time in testifying in court if a prosecution results from an investigation of a crime, and so on. More than one zoo has helped with a confiscation of animals from a private individual by police only to have the facility broken into at a later date and the animals stolen.

The phone rang again; this time it was a captain requesting assistance. I said I could not help without the administrative approval of the director, although by now, Juan and I could anticipate that we would not be joining our families and their respective celebrations any time soon. The phone rang a third time. It was Dr. Conway, the director of the zoo. He had gotten a call from the captain and said he guessed we should give assistance if we could. Happy New Year. Juan was already collecting our equipment: long-handled grasping tongs to capture venomous snakes; thirty-gallon plastic trash barrels with locking lids and elastic tie-down cords to transport them; twelve-inch surgical forceps, for small venomous animals; and two sets of protective goggles in case there were spitting cobras involved.

When irritated, these African snakes can spit their venom for six to eight feet as a first line of defense. They aim for the eyes of any intruder and are incredibly accurate, being able to deliver several streams or bursts of venom in quick succession. The snake's objective is to blind the attacker so it can escape.

We had several species of spitting cobras in the collection; they always spit during routine cage cleanings. The keeper wears a full-face, clear plastic mask to service them. If the venom lands on undamaged skin, it is relatively harmless unless you are particularly allergic to snake-venom proteins; if it lands in your mouth, it is horribly puckering and bitter, but also without effect if there are no mouth abrasions. It's a chilling effect, being spit at by a cobra; one anticipates the worst but expects the least. One simply washes the venom away with soap and water, and goes on with the animal-care duties. However, should the venom find access to the bloodstream through an open abrasion, the effect could be as traumatic as an actual snakebite. If it gets into the eyes, the venom is immediately absorbed and the pain is excruciating. The venom needs to be washed away as soon as possible, and even then, pain, blurred vision, and sensitivity to light last for hours afterward. If left untreated, permanent blindness can result. Should someone trekking in the bush come upon a spitting cobra and receive a spray of venom in the eyes, an extreme treatment is said to be to urinate into the eyes, to wash the venom away with the natural salty liquid. Ordinary water would be my first choice. Our eyewash of choice was a little more advanced: a bottle of normal medical saline solution.

Juan continued packing, selecting several ampoules of antivenin from the drug refrigerator: North American polyvalent for treating snakebites from North American species, South African polyvalent for those species, and Australian polyvalent just for luck. He added syringes, an elastic tourniquet, and cloth pillowcases for snake-carrying bags. We had no idea what we would encounter. We could guess, but if one of us were to be bitten during the process, we would pretty much be on our own. Have you ever tried to get hold of a doctor on New Year's Eve, especially one who knows how to treat a cobra bite in a hospital that stocks antiserum manufactured and imported from South Africa, specifically for the treatment of African cobra bites?

By now, a red light flashing through the Reptile House office window told us that our police escort had arrived. We would follow in our van. It wasn't that we were antisocial; it was just that if we had to bring snakes back, it had been our experience that no one from the police department would want to let us and the snakes ride in their vehicle with them, in case a snake got loose.

The apartment was located in a large complex. It didn't take long to get there. Juan and I had already begun to speculate on who might be involved. After all, how many apartments in the Bronx could be filled with live snakes and spiders? In reality, we knew there are many—too many, in fact.

Police cars and emergency-services vehicles with their lights flashing filled the street. Dozens of curious neighborhood residents peered from their windows, asking what was going on. Juan and I followed the officers to the apartment, which the police had by now entered. It was a tragic scene. Detectives had just finished examining a man's and a woman's bodies, while a mortuary team from the medical examiner's office prepared to carry out the second body bag. The initial call had been received by the police at about 1:00 P.M. from someone in the building. The police had entered the apartment and immediately found not only the bodies but numerous tanks and jars filled with live snakes and spiders. The rooms were in total disarray, with clothing and household objects strewn about. Some of the clothing indicated that a female child also lived in the apartment. Her whereabouts were as yet unknown.

Both of the dead were preliminarily thought by police to have committed a planned suicide, possibly from a drug overdose, as there were no signs of the violence that might suggest a homicide. Someone had supposedly found a scrawled suicide note. The man lay on a couch, while the woman was found on a mattress on the floor nearby. Nonetheless, we were informed that the police were treating the apartment as a possible crime scene and we were to disturb the surroundings as little as possible. Our job would be to search the apartment carefully for venomous snakes and spiders that might pose a danger to the police officers conducting the investigation. We were to look in every closet and corner. We were also told that we might find the child, as well. I hoped we would not, and I secretly prayed that she was safe. Thankfully, we later learned that the couple had sent the woman's five-year-old daughter to a neighbor's apartment down the hall. Sadly, it was the child who had gone back to the apartment and discovered the bodies of her mother and the woman's boyfriend.

I immediately found out that the dead man was someone I knew: Arthur Bordes. Arthur had been a night watchman at the New York Botanical Garden, across the street from the Bronx Zoo. He was known there as an odd but gentle man, renowned for his entertaining ways and his outgoing but bizarre tastes. Arthur's facial features resembled those of Count Dracula, an attribute he capitalized on by dressing up as the evil, blood-slurping, but formally attired horror. Dressed in a black cape and tuxedo, Arthur would entertain Garden visitors and children on Halloween with live spiders he carried to work in jars in a suitcase. His demonstrations and talks about spiders were legend, filled with facts and fascinating information, and he did them for free. Some said that he often brought his suitcase to work with him as he made his night-watchman rounds during the warm summer months and would capture live insects to feed to his arachnid colleagues.

Barney Merlo had introduced me to Arthur a year before. Barney, one of the foremen at the Garden, and I commuted to work from our respective homes seventy-five miles away in Dover Plains, New York. Barney had often spoken about the "weird duck" he worked with at the Garden. He wanted me to meet the fellow who liked snakes and spiders, figuring that as I was superintendent of reptiles at the zoo, we would have a lot in common.

I'd finally met Arthur at lunchtime one day. He was busy creating one of the art pieces for which he was famous. Arthur explained that it was destined to hang on the field office wall. Instead of using a canvas, Arthur had painted an eight-by-four-foot plywood sheet white, as the backdrop for his work. It was slightly more than half completed, but the form and scope of his creation were both incredible in their detail and horrific in their content. His painting showed hundreds of tiny slave humans being herded to their doom by ants and insects, driven in marching death columns to castles and sites of torture. Here were scenes seemingly taken from the annals of Vlad the Impaler and the torturers of medieval times. The ants were impaling humans on spikes, disemboweling some, beheading others. Some were being thrown from castle parapets onto curved spikes protruding from the walls, then left to drip blood on those below. The miniature marchers were driven by whipping guards, had their limbs severed, and were feasted upon. Every inch of the panel held a new scene of torment. If you looked closely, in nearly microscopic detail, Arthur had meticulously, and with great accuracy, drawn the faces of his bosses and coworkers on the most anguished figures. I wondered if the work would ever hang on a public wall.

But there was another side of Arthur that I would learn about, as more of his life unfolded in the weeks after his death. Arthur was deceptively "only a night watchman"; he was also well known and respected as an amateur scientist and a recognized expert on arachnids. He regularly used his vacations to travel to the tropics of Costa Rica and Venezuela to collect specimens, which he added to the entomological collections of the American Museum of Natural History and used for educational demonstrations and displays at the museum. In fact, Arthur had a small circle of colleagues and friends who shared his scientific and collecting interests in spiders and other arachnids, well beyond the level of simple curiosity seekers.

My next encounter with Arthur had come as a surprise to me.

Jane, a young keeper at the Reptile House, told me that she had met a man at a party who was interested in spiders; he was going to give her a large tarantula to keep as a pet. He had invited her to come to his apartment in the Bronx at lunchtime to pick it up and receive instructions on its care. She was reluctant to go alone, however, not knowing anything about the individual, and asked if some of her coworkers would join her.

Several of us walked to the red-brick apartment house, in a rather secluded area on a secondary street not far from the zoo. Inside, we encountered a strange scene with a strange person; I did not immediately realize he was Arthur until he reminded me of my earlier introduction by Barney Merlo. The apartment could have come straight out of a gothic horror film. Black and purple draperies darkened the living room. A painted zodiac fluoresced under an ultraviolet black ceiling light. The couch was draped in black velveteen. Aquaria containing spiders and snakes were everywhere—on the floor, on shelves, and tucked into corners. Dust and spider webs covered everything: the walls, the spaces between aquaria and the bookcases, suggesting that not all of the inhabitants of the apartment were confined to cages. I was definitely not comfortable.

Arthur, on the other hand, was upbeat and delighted to have us. He had already selected a fairly large, dark-haired tarantula to give to Jane, explaining it was a good starter species, as it was both gentle and easy to care for. All spiders are venomous, and while some tarantula species are nervous, rearing up on their legs and extending their long fangs in a defensive posture when alarmed, others allow themselves to be gently handled without much response. The venom varies in potency and effect, but by and large, a bite from most of the tarantula species results in swelling and discomfort, perhaps nausea and cramps, but is not fatal. The hairs that cover a tarantula's body and legs are, however, extremely antigenic. In some people, any contact with the hairs causes an allergic reaction, including itching and hives. Even the slightest touch to some species can make their hairs break off; these are easily inhaled, and may cause an immediate and severe asthmalike reaction.

Sometime during the year, Arthur had been bitten by a Mitchell's rattlesnake, a relatively small, rare species of rattlesnake from the southwestern U.S. As with many species of rattlesnakes, the venom destroys cells and tissue, acting like a potent digestive enzyme, and produces an instant gangrene. Arthur lost a finger to the bite, and he now wore the incident like a badge of honor, along with his abbreviated finger.

At some point, Arthur had left the botanical garden to become a morgue attendant at Bronx Municipal Hospital, mostly because, as his friend once said, "It gave him more time to devote to collecting specimens." He spoke of enjoying the worst jobs, of picking up the cadavers, bloated remains, and long-unfound bodies. Arthur's paintings, which hung on the walls of the living room, spoke even more of death and decay. One picture creatively showed the decaying stages of a human head, another a color version of a diseased heart. He had also found a new circle of friends, who seemed to share his interest in spiders and venomous snakes. Arthur told us that a colleague of his at the morgue had gone to pick up the body of an old lady who had died; her son had kept the corpse secret to keep her Social Security checks coming each month. The body had been covered with spiders, undoubtedly attracted by the insects and maggots. On hearing the "good news," Arthur had hurried to the scene to look for the spiders for his own collections.

Now, both Arthur and his girlfriend were being taken for autopsy to the same Bronx Municipal Hospital morgue. Juan and I began our searches, reluctantly opening each drawer and closet, then peering inside with a flashlight. Here and again we would find a jar or bottle containing a live spider. An African ball python lived in one aquarium, and a baby boa constrictor and a Florida garter snake in another. No venomous snakes, I was happy to report to the police officers who followed behind us. For a moment, I let myself anticipate joining the New Year's Eve party that was waiting at home. But the worst of the night was yet to come. This was only the woman's apartment. The police had also gone to Arthur's apartment, on Barnes Avenue, and found more. Juan and I had a long, painful evening ahead of us.

We arrived at the small red-brick apartment house and were greeted by the now familiar sight of red flashing police lights, two emergency trucks, a number of police squad cars, and a number of curious neighbors wondering what had happened. Several children sipped soft drinks on the steps into the building, forcing the police to walk around them. More police officers in black SWAT team outfits and bulletproof vests, carrying shotguns, waited outside an apartment door in the darkened hallway of the second floor. As we followed the police inside, a tallish, dark, curly-haired, rather disheveled man spoke to me. He said he had been Arthur's roommate, and asked if I had called some person at the American Museum of Natural History. I could not understand what he was talking about. He stuffed a phone number in my hand. The police quickly intervened and cut me off from any conversation. There was a dark car parked in front of the house with a bumper sticker that included the word *Tarantula,* which the police noticed as well.

Juan and I entered the partially open door of the apartment. I led, followed by a serious-looking SWAT officer with a shotgun. As we got inside the doorway, one of the other officers reached down to touch the leg of the officer with the gun and went, *"Sssssssss."* The cop behind me yelled out and jumped high in the air, coming down cursing and shaking. I was sure I would be shot dead if, out of sheer reflex, he pulled the trigger of his shotgun.

We continued on into the living room. It was as I remembered it: black and purple draperies, fluorescing zodiac, spider webs, and dust covering everything—tanks, jars, and cages. But now I took in everything in detail. Stacked cages held a huge eastern diamondback rattlesnake, a cottonmouth water moccasin, and a deadly Russell's viper from Asia. A blue-and-yellow banded rear-fanged mangrove snake pushed its six-foot-long body against the top of its tank in an effort to escape its confinement. At the entrance to the bedroom, an aquarium held a salmon-pink snake with a black neck band, as well as a slice of pizza. It was a red spitting cobra. I warned the police officer not to go near the tank, as the top of the tank was made only of screen, and would not stop a spray of venom from reaching the eyes of someone who tried to look through it. I draped a nearby towel over the tank, just to be safe. Dirt, cobwebs, and jars of live spiders, scorpions, and centipedes were everywhere. One tank contained a huge tarantula, at least five inches across, and a silver occult ring with a large black stone, all covered in webs. A crystal ball enveloped and magnified a large dead black scorpion. Under the bed lay old torn clothing and shoes, and a jar containing a live spider. Each closet was filled to overflowing with used and filthy clothing, behind and under which were more jars of spiders. A sound came from the bedroom closet. I opened the door slowly, and with my long-handled tongs parted the hanging clothes and began to search the floor underneath with my flashlight. There was a white porcelain autopsy pan filled with water, and in it was a four-foot-long African dwarf crocodile. The crocodile lunged in a hissing defense as the light interrupted the darkness. No problem, I thought to myself; there is a lot worse here than a runty crocodile. We would come back to him later.

Under the stereo in the living room was an aquarium housing a colony of dermestid beetles. These beetles are the adult stage of a hairy maggot that feeds on dead flesh, and are used by museum workers to clean the dry flesh from delicate bones so that they can make skeletal materials for study. We could see the larvae congregated, feeding on the remains of some small body, but we couldn't tell what it had been when it lived.

On the top shelf in one closet, among the jars of live spiders that had been tucked into every inch of space that could possibly hold a jar, were the cast-off shed skins of generations of tarantulas and scorpions. Why were they being saved, except, perhaps, as a testimonial to the growth of the animals that had emerged from them? Spiders shed their skins as they grow, and each shed skin is an exact copy of the body of its originator, down to each leg and even each hair. When a tarantula prepares to shed its skin, it becomes lethargic and soon makes a silken pallet of webbing on which to lie. As the time to shed its skin arrives, the spider turns on its back. Its underside splits open, and the spider struggles to free each leg, its fangs, and its body. The spider then leaves the shed skin behind.

The allergenic spider body hairs combined easily with the dust, so it wasn't long before Juan, the police officers who followed us, and I were itching and scratching. Our necks and arms were turning red from the constant irritations. It was inconceivable to me that anyone could have lived there. The stench of rotting insect bodies, killed by spiders and left covered with webs for future meals, emanated from hundreds of tanks and jars, permeating the air with a sickly, musty, sweetish odor. The police officers could hardly bear being with us.

Just before we turned to bagging the snakes, a stout woman with short black hair, wearing a black coat, came in. Through intermittent tears, she told us that she was Arthur's first wife. She said she had left Arthur four years before, after he had begun living with so many dangerous things, and it had been over a year since she had been in the apartment. She said she had an eight-foot-long boa constrictor herself, and that Arthur had given the crocodile in the closet to her. However, as he had fallen in love with it, she had given it back to him when she had moved out. She wanted to see the crocodile he loved so much, and she felt better when we told her we would give it a good home at the zoo. She asked that, if possible, we donate the spiders to Arthur's friend Alice Gray, at the American Museum of Natural History. I promised to do what I could as she said her tearful good-byes to the crocodile and left.

One by one, Juan and I then prepared to place the most dangerous venomous snakes in cloth bags for transport to the zoo. We started with the four-foot-long Russell's viper, lifting it slowly out of its tank with a long-handled pair of aluminum tongs, specially designed for safely handling dangerous snakes. We had brought a long-handled net, which we had then lined with a cloth bag. Juan held the bag in the net safely at arm's length while I lowered the snake into it. By quickly turning the net over, Juan then secured the snake in the bag before it could try to escape. He quickly placed the net on the floor, I placed the tongs across the neck of the bag tight and held it in place with my foot, and then I drew the neck of the bag and knotted it shut, with the snake inside it.

We repeated this process with each venomous snake in turn. Next came a large hissing African puff adder. This is a short, stout snake with an overly fat body for its three-foot length. The venom of this species is particularly destructive to tissue. When it bites, the snake injects a large quantity of venom deep into the wound with its long fangs. Most people bitten by a snake this size die. Those who do survive often lose the use of the body part that was bitten, usually their fingers, hand, or arm. The danger of having any of these snakes living in a private collection in a private house, where they can escape and pose a lethal danger to innocent people, is incomprehensible.

An African-American police officer who had been rather jovial until now, in an effort to calm his own nerves, called me to look at a strangely streamlined shiny steel hunting knife with a long blade. Next, we found a World War II bayonet. Hanging on the walls were color photographs arranged in collages. There were close-up pictures of bloated human bodies being taken from the water, dismembered bodies removed from under trains, and cadavers in various stages of decomposition.

At one point, as we were just preparing to bag the spitting cobra, an Emergency Services Unit police lieutenant came in to check on the progress of his men. The lieutenant looked at the snake, mumbled something about everything seeming to be under control, and left. This simple act broke the tension, and we found ourselves laughing to the point of tears. We still, however, had to bag the red spitter, and Juan and I needed help. The snake was aggressive, lunging violently whenever we tried to restrain it with the tongs. It would take three people, we determined: two with tongs grasping the snake in two places on its body, and a third holding the net and bag the snake had to go in. The jovial officer, not quite so at ease as he had been, volunteered to hold the bag for us. As I gave him a pair of goggles to wear to protect his eyes from the venom, the snake began spitting repeatedly with every movement in front of it. He said, "I am doing my best, but if I drop this thing and run, please don't tell anyone. I am doing my best." I assured him that if anything happened, we would take care of him, and then the snake was bagged. I loved that man.

The three of us then continued our search. We entered the kitchen and looked in horror at the kitchen sink and a nearby cupboard. Hanging over the sink was a human leg and pelvis. Not a skeleton, but a whole leg, taken and dried, from a human body. I looked inside the cupboard. There, at each end of the row of canisters labeled COF-FEE, TEA, FLOUR, and SUGAR, were two dried, dark-skinned human heads. Sparse hair hung down onto the withered necks. Each was decorated with a baseball cap; one wore an earring, and the other had a cigarette dangling from its drawn and parted lips. I braced myself as I opened the door to the refrigerator. There was no food inside, only more spiders and jars; the refrigerator had apparently not been working for some time. More pictures of a human head, with an eye hanging out and face torn away, hung on the wall. Another photograph showed severed hands and the top of a sheet covering a purple, bloated body.

In the next room was a crucifix, hung upside down. The now-somber police officer gently picked it up and apologized to Arthur in absentia, saying he respected Arthur's beliefs, no matter what they were. He then stood the crucifix properly upright against the wall on top of a cabinet. It toppled over, and together we set it in place again. The cop said that in his belief, God was to be respected, even in this house of horrors. I agreed.

It didn't take us long to load the tanks of animals into our van. We were exhausted from the stress of the night and the physical exertion. It was close to midnight as our procession of police vehicles, their lights flashing, with us sandwiched in between, proceeded down Pelham Parkway on our way back to the zoo. Now and again a squad car sped ahead to block the intersection for our passage.

Inside the Reptile House, we unloaded the animals, and the police soon left. Juan and I pondered, in our fatigue, leaving the bags containing the venomous snakes locked up on the office floor. We would be glad that we had indeed taken the extra time to place the bags inside locked holding cages, for on our arrival the next morning, we would find that the bag that had held the red spitting cobra was empty. The snake broke through the cloth during the night, and hid underneath it. We could have walked into the office that morning and received a deadly spray of venom in the eyes before we could protect ourselves.

As we parted that night, Juan and I wished each other a Happy

New Year, knowing full well that we would never forget what we had seen and done that night. An hour later, I was home with Myrna and our friends. But the party was a mute celebration for me. I ached for the little five-year-old girl, for like Myrna and me, she had lost her mother forever.

There is an epilogue to the story. Arthur's roommate and coworker in the morgue had helped him collect many of the spiders in Venezuela, and he came to the zoo and helped us identify each species for our records, care for them, and find homes for the collection. Arthur's stepfather mounted an effort to have the spiders and snakes turned over to him as valuable assets in Arthur's estate. He lost those legal appeals. The New York City Department of Health took legal possession of the collection and allowed us to distribute the specimens to other institutions. Most of the spiders and scorpions went to Alice Gray at the American Museum of Natural History, where Arthur would have wanted them to go, in his name. Arthur's mother did not seem to recover from the loss of her son, as she sadly blamed Juan, me, and the zoo, in rambling letters and phone calls, for not recognizing her son's scientific achievements and virtually stealing her son's collection of animals from the two apartments that sorrowful night. In all, we had removed one African dwarf crocodile; a turtle; thirteen assorted snakes, including those already mentioned plus two copperheads, a timber rattlesnake, the Mitchell's rattlesnake that had cost Arthur his finger, and a deadly saw-scaled viper native to the Middle East and Africa; and more than thirty-nine spiders, centipedes, and scorpions.

We never knew what we might have left behind, undetected.

21

DRUGS, COBRAS, AND FOOLS

Once I started making my expertise available to federal law enforcement authorities, the word soon went out through the various agencies that they had this guy who would come out and help open just about any shipment for inspection, even those that might contain venomous reptiles or spiders. While I had been assisting the U.S. Fish and Wildlife Service for some time, the U.S. Customs Service soon wanted to use me as well, as did agents of the Drug Enforcement Administration (DEA). I soon had a contract to provide government services at the seemingly exorbitant rate of fifty dollars a trip. There was, at the time, an expectation that illicit drugs were being shipped into the United States inside boxes containing venomous animals, perhaps even inside the animals themselves, often destined for private individuals. Shipments of snakes and other small animals for the pet trade often flowed in from private exporters and collectors in Southeast Asia, Africa, Colombia, Ecuador, and Panama. Air cargo was becoming cheap and fast, with new air routes to remote regions opening up every day.

It is relatively easy to stuff a significant volume of drugs, packed in plastic bags or latex condoms, down a snake's throat, particularly in larger or thick-bodied species. While U.S. Customs inspectors were always loath to open a box of snakes, venomous snakes were even a better choice for concealment, since they elicited a greater degree of avoidance behavior from the inspectors. To be sure, the boxes would often be clearly marked VENOMOUS SNAKES, sometimes in large red letters. The snakes could be bought very cheaply from dealers in Third World countries. Once the snakes arrived at their destination, they could be killed to recover the drugs, or a fat-bodied snake could be manipulated until the packets of drugs were expressed from the animal's stomach, back out through its mouth. One could also remove the packets by putting a long pair of surgical forceps down the snake's throat. If the snake survived the ordeal, fine—it could be sold again. If not, there was not much value lost. While the snakes could be seen inside shipping boxes by using X rays, trying to find soft packets concealed inside the snakes, which were tied inside cloth bags, then placed inside the boxes, among packing materials, was too difficult and imprecise. Besides, if something suspicious was evident, you still needed someone to open the box and handle the snakes.

So it wasn't unusual for me to come home from a day's work of taking care of venomous snakes and other reptiles, and receive a call from customs or DEA agents who wanted me to go to a particular air-cargo building to meet with an agent. It seemed they always knew in advance which shipment on which plane they wanted to look at. I would collect my equipment and trudge to the airport. Often, the flight might not be due to arrive until late into the night, particularly on weekends. It was a game between smugglers and the agents, each trying to outfox the other. The bad guys tried to figure out what flights would arrive at times when inspectors would most likely be hurried, working with minimal skeleton crews, or least likely to have time to make thorough inspections. The inspectors, on the other hand, could opt to simply have the shipments wait for their convenience, but this had its drawback; the importers could then counter that the shipments contained live animals and any delay would cost the animals their lives—at the expense of the airline or agency. Often, a complaint would be made to the importer's elected representative, indicating they were poor simple businesspeople and big government was picking on them, hampering free trade, and so on.

While political pressure sometimes worked with the U.S. Fish and Wildlife Service in Washington, D.C., it rarely had any effect that I could see with U.S. Customs or the DEA. The time-sensitivity ploy did work for shipments of live tropical fish, which would quickly die if delayed, and many were then conditionally released. That is, the shipment was released to the importer, but it could still be subject to later inspection. In short order, the shipment would then be broken down into smaller shipments and reshipped to a multitude of other destinations or distributed to other dealers. Any follow-up inspection would really become a moot point. The importers knew it.

On this night, I received a call to meet a DEA officer at the "Animal Port" building at John F. Kennedy International Airport at 9:00 P.M. I arrived a few minutes early. No one at the Animal Port seemed to know anything. There was one other visitor in the waiting room, an early middle-aged man dressed casually in an open shirt and brown leather jacket. He sat there somewhat interested all the time I was asking if anyone knew about someone I was supposed to meet there. Giving up, I decided to sit down and wait. A full twenty minutes later, I began to get impatient, as I was tired from a long day of work. Finally, I said to the fellow who was waiting with me, "Well, I guess the person I am supposed to meet here isn't going to show up." He said, "Are you Peter?" I said, "Yes." He simply said, "Let's go."

There was no further conversation until we got to the KLM aircargo building. Going in through a restricted accessway, we arrived in the customs officer's office, where the inspector in charge explained what flight the shipment was coming in on. It was supposed to be a shipment of snakes from a reptile dealer in Kenya. The individual to whom the shipment was consigned had already been notified of the shipment's intended arrival, and would undoubtedly be in the KLM waiting area to receive it after he had provided the appropriate documentation and the shipment had been cleared by customs. What was going to happen, I was told, was that DEA and customs agents would meet the shipment at the plane and bring it into the cargo building. I was to open the box and examine it and its live contents for any possible contraband, in the presence of the agents. Afterward, I was to reassemble the shipment, and it would then go to the waiting importer as if it had just come off the plane.

It never sat well with me that in providing this service, I had to work alone, contrary to all of my teachings at the zoo. Safe practice dictated that no one work alone when handling dangerous snakes. Alone meant that I would not have at my side another person trained in handling dangerously venomous snakes if I needed help, or familiar with emergency snakebite procedures, should I be bitten in the process. To this day, I have no idea why I was willing to perform this service. It certainly was not the money. I think I was motivated by a feeling that I had a skill that was needed at the time, a sense of public service, and a deep hatred for the drug trade. I had also rarely met an animal trader who cared as much about the well-being of the animal as he did about the profit margin inherent in the shipment.

At about 11:00 P.M., the plane arrived and the three large boxes that made up the shipment were brought to a small room where they were to be opened. It was the worst possible sort of place to perform such a job, with no table and in close quarters. The lighting was good, but the room was cluttered with stacks of leftover wooden pallets from previous cargos. Furthermore, there was only one door, and it was small. In short, with all the pallets, there was no place to go if I had to avoid an angry venomous snake. Apparently, the airline, citing security and safety rules, would allow us to use only this particular room for this purpose. Besides, it was out of the way and out of sight and sound from where the importer would be waiting; the DEA people did not want to draw attention to this preinspection inspection, even by KLM workers. One might make some casual comment to the importer that the shipment was already undergoing inspection, alerting him to the possibility that all might not be well. It was good for everyone, except the importer and me.

Each box was clearly marked LIVE ANIMALS, NO DELAY, THIS SIDE UP, and VENOMOUS. One thing always worked in my favor: shippers usually marked the boxes appropriately, as they did not wish a potential customer to be lost from encountering an unexpected venomous snake in the shipment. The exception was an individual or reptile collector in a foreign country, sending animals to a friend or U.S. contact on a one-to-one basis. Normally, reptile shipments came from established reptile dealers or exporters to a "customer," which most often was an established business, and were handled through a formal customs broker. Individuals would have considerable difficulties at best, in compiling shipping documents. Besides, obtaining export documents and veterinary certificates, avoiding exorbitant export tariffs, and conforming to other rules of export in a Third World country often meant bribing various officials. This process could not easily be navigated by private individuals. Besides, there was no easier way to lose a customer than to have them bitten, or even die, by an "extra" or unanticipated venomous snake, before they paid for the shipment. For me, it meant that I could read the invoice and be prepared for what might be in the box. I could never be entirely sure, but it would provide me with a heads up.

The invoice, in this case, indicated that contained in the boxes were numerous reptiles, starting with ball pythons, a small, harmless species of African python that rolls itself into a tight ball with its head hidden tightly in the center. Once the snake is in a ball, it is virtually impossible to unravel it without causing it injury. Next came Nile monitor lizards, baby African rock pythons, forest hinge-back tortoises, nearly fifty black-lipped forest cobras, and a dozen African puff adders. While the puff adders were dangerous, they would be only about two feet long. They could strike savagely, but only within a few inches. Their venom, however, was potent and highly destructive to tissue. A bite on the hand from this species often results in a lost digit or hand, due to gangrene. At worst, there may be death from the overwhelming effect the toxins produced: uncontrolled bleeding and shock.

Most people who work with venomous snakes group them into

one of several, albeit subjective, categories, based on their defensive behaviors and the degree of danger working with them presents. In captivity, most of the short, fat Old World vipers are sedentary creatures. If left alone, they move only when necessary. Although they may possess highly toxic venom, they do not pose a particularly hazardous threat. They just sit there, as though confounded, while trying to figure out what is going on around them. If you don't put yourself within striking distance—usually less than the snake's body length—you have little risk of being bitten.

A subgroup of vipers, the pit vipers, including rattlesnakes and the pit vipers of the New World tropics and Southeast Asia, are relatively active and irritable animals but generally are not aggressive either. Like the true vipers, they also seem to sit there as if they were assembling data, waiting for the intruder to come within close proximity before striking at the danger.

Then there are the elapids. These are the species whose venom is relatively fast acting. Besides destroying tissue, the venom may also quickly attack the central nervous system of a victim, causing cardiac arrest, suffocation, and death. Elapids comprise the cobras and mambas of Africa; the cobras of Asia and the Middle East, including the eighteen-foot-long king cobra; and many of the venomous snakes of Australia. These snakes are active animals; they move often and quickly throughout the day. In captivity, cobras seem particularly alert to their environment. They often display curiosity about what is happening around them, as if trying to assess what is going on and then decide whether the actions of an intruder warrant ignoring, defense, attack, or simply avoidance and flight. Our fourteen-foot-long king cobra would glide to the front of its cage and quite calmly place its head against the glass to try to catch a glimpse of whoever was moving about in front of the adjoining cages. These behaviors make cobras difficult to work with.

Black-lipped cobras inhabit forests and wet habitats throughout tropical Africa; they are the largest of the African cobras, reaching lengths of more than ten feet. Black-lipped cobras seem to be rather smart, as snakes go; are completely aware of what is going on around them; are calculating; and will deliberately and fearlessly press home an attack against an intruder. They are sometimes called forest cobras or white-lipped cobras, for their yellow-white lower jaw and lip scales, which are edged with a black line. The anterior body of the snake is often pure glossy black. Most adult black-lipped cobras average five to seven feet in length. In the wild, these cobras are said to be rather shy and reluctant to bite. Consequently, few bites are reported.

However, in my experience this species is far from shy in captivity. An aroused, angry black-lipped cobra will stand upright, fully a third to a half of its body length, with its neck gradually widening to a hood, and fearlessly face its tormentor. The snake seems highly focused in its own defense. The tongue flicks quickly in and out, testing the environment. At any perceived threatening movement, the snake will rush toward the agitator, still reared upright with its mouth already open. Understandably, a captive snake in a closed environment that feels attacked has no place to go but toward an intruder or keeper, to bite or to escape. At the end of the rush, the snake strikes downward to bite, often finding a target high on the victim's body, face, or upper arms, where a bite can be most serious. Although its fangs are relatively short and rigidly fixed at the front of its upper jaw, the viciousness of the attack and the strong, open jaws nearly always ensure that a bite will be successful. The venom is extremely toxic, and even a portion of the amount usually delivered in a bite can be fatal in humans.

The black-lipped cobra was decidedly not among the species I liked to work with. Our collections had three black-lipped forest cobras in one exhibit. The snakes ranged in size from four to seven feet. At the slightest touch of spray from the cleaning hose, one would dash to the top of its cage along a branch, the second would hide its head under a coil of its body, and the third, the largest, would stand upright in a hood, face me squarely with its mouth open, and rush the open door. On one occasion, as I opened the cage door, there was no hesitation on the part of the snake. It charged the open door and was in the corridor with me before I had had any opportunity to do anything except step back out of striking range. My general feeling was that it was better to let the rushing animal out onto the unobstructed tile floor, where there was room to deal with it, rather than try to fight it half in and half out of its cage. At least there was no place for it to escape to, I thought. Besides, once out of its cage, a snake usually takes a few minutes to try to figure out the unfamiliar surroundings before it tries to escape further. This snake was different. The moment it cleared the door and fell to the floor, it continued its flight down the corridor. I prayed that no one would enter the corridor from the other end, a blind corner leading to an entry door from the public spaces.

Suddenly, the snake turned into the entrance to the keepers' room. It lunged upward onto the oak seminar room table, in one sleek motion, and headed straight for a window at the end of the table, left open a few inches by an unthinking worker to allow ventilation in the hot lunchroom. I lunged after it with a long-handled pole fitted with a blunt hook at the end, which was routinely used to move snakes. As the snake's head disappeared out through the slit in the window, I caught up with its body and, with the snake hook, picked up a coil and threw the snake back into the room. By now, the snake was frightened—at least as much, I hoped, as it had terrified me. A few more maneuvers with the snake hook and the snake was guided, in its flight, back toward the cage door from which it had escaped.

In the meantime, I had automatically closed the door and locked it to prevent the snake's two cagemates from escaping, as well, while I chased the larger animal. We were both tired as I fumbled for my keys to open the door, and the cobra seemed willing to calm down and wait, a few feet away. As I opened the door, the snake, at blurred speed, again lunged upward, this time to get back into its cage and the security of its familiar home.

Drenched in sweat, I went back to the lunchroom. My lips and mouth were uncomfortably dry as, trembling from the close encounter, I poured myself a glass of water, closed the lunchroom window, and sat down. At that point, one of the other keepers came into the room from the now quiet corridor. Seeing me sitting at the table sipping a drink, the keeper, a young woman new to the department, asked, "Taking an early coffee break, Peter?"

In preparation for responding to calls for assistance from federal agencies, I had assembled an assortment of tools that would allow me to work alone and minimize the opportunity for direct contact with venomous animals. These included snake tongs, which had been invented by a professional snake catcher years before and were standard equipment for handling dangerous snakes. The main part of the tongs consisted of a three-foot-long hollow aluminum shaft about an inch in diameter. A handle shaped like a pistol's grip with a hand-sized trigger was mounted at one end. When the trigger was squeezed, it pulled a metal rod that, in turn, closed a six-inch-long grasping jaw with an interlocking clasp at the end. Thus, when the grip was released and the jaw at the other end opened fully, it could encircle the body of an animal several inches in diameter. By compressing the handle, the operator could close the jaw with whatever pressure he wished to exert; he could securely hold the snake's body at whatever point he wished, with the head of the animal held at a safe distance.

The second important tool was a twelve-inch-long pair of stainless steel surgical forceps. These could be used to pick up or move a cloth sack with a venomous snake inside it—which is the way most snakes are packed and transported—without actually touching the bag. Venomous snakes have bitten people through a cloth or plastic bag; the snake inside feels a touch on its body and reflexively strikes at the point of contact. The snake's fangs easily pierce the fabric or plastic, and the act is so quick that the person doesn't have time to move their hand. Along with the tongs and the forceps, a flashlight, a small, flat "jimmy bar," a hammer, masking tape, a thirty-gallon plastic barrel and lid, and a pair of leather gloves made up the rest of my box of tools of the trade.

I began by carefully and slowly prying up the corner of one of the wooden boxes, so I could keep the top of the box closed but still see inside with my flashlight. One could never be sure that a snake had not escaped its cloth bag during transit and was loose in the box.

Also, a snake could give birth to live young while in transit. The babies are born with toxic venom and are just as capable of biting as an adult snake.

Once I had determined that no snakes were free in the box, I continued to pry away the top. The bulging bags inside were, as usual, nestled in a bed of crumpled newspaper for insulation and cushioning against the buffeting the box might take during transport. I reached in and, one by one, lifted each bag, knotted at the top, with my long forceps. Each bag was labeled as to the species it contained, although I had learned never to trust any labeling and to treat every bag as potentially containing a venomous snake.

Luckily, all of the bags labeled as holding a venomous snake were confined to a single box. I decided that the safest and best way to go about my examinations was to first inspect all of the boxes and bags containing harmless tortoises, monitor lizards, and pythons, putting the venomous-snake bags aside for last. They would take the most caution and time, and I did not want to accidentally mix them with the harmless animals and touch the bags by mistake.

Each bag was first placed on the floor, with the tongs held in place with my foot across the neck of the bag, between the knot and the bulge of the animal inside. In that way, using the tongs as a separator between my hand and the animal inside, I could draw the bag against the tongs and open the knot. I could then simply grasp the harmless pythons and lizards behind the neck with one hand, to prevent them from biting me, and palpate their abdomens with the other hand, searching for any unusually large, firm lumps that could be packets of drugs. Most shipping boxes for snakes coming from tropical countries are intricately made from thin veneers of hardwood over an inner frame. These hollow walls and floors are very flimsily fastened together. I am always amazed that they make the journey intact. (Some don't, but that's another story.) While I was palpating each animal, the DEA people were examining the hollow walls of the box for whatever they might contain.

Next came the bags of venomous snakes. These I would handle a little differently, opening each bag and pouring its contents into the plastic barrel I had brought with me. That way, I could grasp the snake near the base of its head with the long tongs, lift it from the barrel, and, with the other hand, feel and palpate the snake's body with my free hand. I began with the bags of puff adders. Puff adders hiss like the sound of a broken steam pipe when aroused, and they thrash, spraying vile-smelling musk and yellow urine and fecal material all over the surrounding area, which in this case included me. As the first snake was pulled from the barrel and began its display, every agent and inspector instantly disappeared. I hoped they were just outside the open doorway, but one could never be sure. Actually, I mused that the added strange odor I was smelling might well have come from the exiting agents, who had just executed their own form of display.

I continued on to the cobras. Here, the danger was that a snake could be so large that when dumped from the bag into the barrel, it could easily turn and race back out over the open top. Therefore, rather than dump out the bag, I would gently lower it to the bottom before opening it, allowing the bag to open on its own and the animal inside to crawl out with as little agitation as possible. One after another, I picked up the bags and went through this process. As each snake, once examined, had to be replaced in its bag before another bag could be opened, the whole procedure took some time. When I reached for the twentieth cobra bag with my forceps, it seemed too light. In fact, it was empty. It had contained a large, bulging body when I had taken it from the shipping box and laid it on the floor with the others, about an hour before. My heart began beating faster as I realized that the cobra had escaped through a hole it had created by forcing its snout against a faulty seam. Most snake bags are really old grain sacks or pillowcases that are used over and over again, and they are rarely checked for integrity.

It took several minutes for the severity of the situation to sink in. Not only was the snake at large in the room, but I didn't know how long it had been out of its bag. The doorway opened onto the main cargo area, where dozens of workers moved about amid thousands of boxes, crates, and parcels in bins stacked at least fifty feet high. I could already see the headlines in the morning newspapers: "KLM Closes New York Cargo Operations Indefinitely as Snake Handler Looks for Escaped Cobra." I was also afraid to move, not knowing how close the snake might be to me; yet I was infinitely glad the DEA and customs people had vacated the room earlier, although I still wished they were just outside the door.

I began to visually scan the nearby stacks of wooden pallets that littered the room. Would the snake, on emerging from the bag, do what most frightened snakes would in a strange place? That is, would it head straight for the first dark retreat it could find—in this case, the stacks of wooden pallets? As I scanned the stacks, a long, glossy, black shape came into focus among the wooden slats, not more than a few feet away from where I knelt amid the bags on the floor. My eyes followed the form of the snake's body, trying to find its head. The body, nearly seven feet long, weaved in and out of the wood, then upward. The snake was raised in a defensive upright posture, and had simply been watching my every move, testing its surroundings periodically and calmly with an occasional flick of its tongue. I had been working all the time only with the snake's permission, well within its striking distance.

I backed slowly out of range, increasing the distance between us, in case the snake suddenly decided to change its mind and attack. It continued to watch me intently. Its mouth opened abruptly, just a little, each time I moved a little too quickly to suit it. It was as afraid as I was, I thought. Once at a safe distance, I reached over and then gently grasped the snake with the aluminum tongs, lifted it free of the pallets, and placed it safely back in another bag that I had brought with me. It did not take me long to finish inspecting the other bags of snakes, and I was repacking the boxes as the DEA and customs people returned. I felt physically and emotionally drained.

No drugs were found that night, and the box was routinely handed over to the importer to continue its journey after a cursory mock inspection. The importer's shipments had been under surveillance for some time, and there would, according to the DEA people, "be a next time for sure." Under my breath I quietly replied, "Perhaps for him, but not for me, if I can help it." The importer never suspected how close KLM and I had come to disaster. I packed up my belongings and returned home. It was nearly 5:00 A.M., and I was thankful I was not scheduled to work the next day. As I began to doze off in bed, the phone rang. It was another U.S. Customs officer at JFK asking that I come to the airport to open a shipment arriving from Thailand, containing Asiatic cobras. I said, "Call me tomorrow."

22

THE BALD-HEADED SNAKE KEEPER IN THE BRONX

The bald-headed snake keeper in the Bronx" is a title that was dubiously bestowed on me by the reptile-leather industry, and I continue to wear it with considerable pride. I didn't inherit it easily. It came by word of mouth, coined by defendants in cases in which I assisted federal prosecutors dealing with violations of wildlife laws. Members of the reptile-leather industry, especially those who had been the target of prosecutions, felt they would not have had so many problems with importing reptile products, forfeited hundreds of thousands of dollars in reptile goods, and paid penalties and huge attorneys' fees, if that "bald-headed snake keeper in the Bronx" had minded his own business. I was helping federal and state wildlife authorities identify species that were contained in manufactured products. Since I certainly was not getting rich working as an occasional consultant or expert witness for the government, it was incomprehensible to the trade why I would do such a thing. To me, it was simple. I had the skills, the feds needed the expertise, the animals needed protection, and I couldn't care less if there was one less $10,000 crocodile handbag on the market.

One European tanner, having just had a large shipment of tanned skins seized based on my identification that the species of crocodilian represented did not agree with the documents he had presented, decided he could stop law enforcement cold. He could buy me. And if he couldn't buy me, he could buy my wife. After paying the penalty and forfeiting the skins, he asked me if my wife and I would like to have a month or two of vacation in a major European capital, at his expense. In return, while I was there, I could sort out those skins that had been prohibited from importation into the United States. He could send them elsewhere. It never occurred to him that the problem was that the skins were from an endangered species, and he was part of their demise. His interest was only in figuring out which skins he could get past the authorities, which was a typical position for commercial skin traders. I declined. He went on to court some of my colleagues who were more pragmatic than I. My interest was in the animals, not the profits of the trade. My irksome reputation had it that I was stupid because, against logic, I could not be bought.

It all started between 1971 and 1973, when a convention was held in Washington, under the auspices of the United Nations, to address the international problem of increasing commercial trade in endangered and threatened species and declining wild populations. It was called the Convention on International Trade in Endangered Species of Wild Fauna and Flora, or CITES for short. At the same time, the United States also put into effect the Endangered Species and the Lacey Acts, which brought protection to U.S. endangered and threatened species and enforcement power to CITES under U.S. law. Individual states passed their own laws, adding local species to those under national and international protections.

Suddenly, everyone from law enforcement authorities to importers and local department stores had to use scientific names and deal with mountains of permits and documents. Not only did live animals and certain plants and insects fall under these regulations, but so did skins, feathers, claws, teeth, ivory, organs, tissues, and, eventually, even DNA, in whole and in part, either in a raw state or after being processed into products. Wildlife authorities were now expected to be able to distinguish rare species, some of which were scarcely even represented in zoological or museum collections, and not just as live, whole animals but any part of one, whether it had been cut up into small pieces, dyed unnatural colors, tanned, or pressed into leather and sewn into handbags, small belts and bill-folds, or even smaller watchbands. This change happened overnight. No one was ready.

It never occurred to me that my special interest in identifying crocodilians from their scalation, and the mountain of data I had collected since my first days as a keeper, would take on new importance nearly twenty years later. Besides, my taxidermist origins had taught me about tanning processes and techniques.

I knew I wanted to learn something about the reptile-skin trade and how the fashion industry worked. A New York attorney friend of mine, Sam Slaff, who kept a pet boa constrictor in his Fifth Avenue office to frighten away unwanted clients, suggested that I consult for his relative who owned a prominent New York fashion house that featured reptile skins. It was the perfect opportunity to see inside a fashion and reptile-leather business. For several hours a week I would care for an exhibit of reptiles in the lobby. Sometimes I would bring live animals to trade shows and awards dinners. In the mean-time, I freely roamed around their cutting rooms, design department, and tanneries and factories, absorbing everything I could. However, the more I saw and learned, the more I was convinced that the exotic-leather business, even though it was on Fifth Avenue and related to celebrities and glitz, was basically devoted to killing wildlife with-out concern for its future, for the indulgence of a wealthy few.

My adventures in the fashion world came to an end after an aquarium containing a Java wart snake collapsed the poorly designed shelf it was sitting on and crashed to the floor, sending fifty gallons of water cascading across the lobby and down the elevator shaft, to short out the electrical circuits on the twenty-eighth floor. Or per-haps the fashion dinner in Gloversville, New York, may also have had something to do with it. Instead of carrying a six-foot-long alli-gator from my room on an upper floor of the hotel to the dining room,

I walked the animal down the hall to the elevator and pushed the call button. When the elevator arrived and the doors opened, the alligator walked in on its own volition. How was I to know that there was an elevator operator inside who wouldn't relish having an alligator join him?

Flying home was not easy either. Although the plane stopped rumbling and moving after takeoff, my handbag on the floor did not, as it contained a three-foot-long tegu lizard. The flight attendant noticed the bag bouncing along on its own and asked what it was I had in it. I produced the tegu, which the flight attendant then spent the remainder of the flight kissing and petting. When the plane landed, she asked me to wait. Moments later, the captain and two security guards marched me off the plane to a security room, where they read me the FAA regulations that could send me to prison for a long time, told me never to do that again, and threw me out of the airport. I felt I knew quite enough about the fashion trade by then.

Soon after the new regulations came into effect, two U.S. Fish and Wildlife Service agents, Warren Dieffendal and Ed Baker, dressed in their brown uniforms, came calling at the zoo. Based at Kennedy International Airport, back then they were the government's entire wildlife law enforcement staff in the Port of New York, where thousands of shipments came and went by air, sea, truck, and mail each day. "Could we look at some reptiles?" they asked. How could they enforce the new laws if they didn't know what they were looking at? We showed them the entire collection of lizards, snakes, crocodilians, and turtles, along with books and pictures. It was daunting. Their task was all but impossible.

A few weeks later, they made the first seizure under the new regulations in the Port of New York, confiscating a baby crocodile—which I later identified as a New Guinea crocodile—from an importer. After five years, a federal judge would vacate the seizure because the authority under which the seizure had been made was, at that time, vague. He ordered the crocodile returned to the owner. However, by now the animal had grown from barely a foot long to more than five feet. There was also the cost of veterinary care, housing, and food for the past five years to consider. Faced with the bill, the importer no longer wanted the animal and gave it up to the zoo. It was, in the end, a victory of sorts.

Warren and Ed learned quickly. The next seizure, shortly after the first, came about when they were walking through an airlines cargo building and tapped on some wooden boxes. Soft *yonk* sounds returned. Boxes of trade goods normally do not call back. They opened the crates to find over a dozen baby Siamese crocodiles, a species thought to be almost exterminated in the wild. These animals, seized in 1974, became the core breeding population for the species in captivity. This bloodline continues today in populations in zoos around the world.

While the trade in skins and products was my special focus, the trade in live animals was not far behind. I recall one of the early shipments that wildlife inspectors brought to the Bronx Zoo for me to open. The unlabeled box was destined for a local wholesale animal dealer. It was a good guess that it contained something or -things living. As I cautiously pried away the top of the box and light flooded into the dark recesses, an army of hundreds of five-inch-long black African scorpions raced out over the walls of the box in all directions. The two assisting keepers, the wildlife inspectors, and I soon found ourselves standing in a sink full of running water as the scorpions took over the floor below. A quick radio call to another keeper, asking him to bring the bug spray, saved us.

We once were visited by agents of the U.S. Customs Service who were interested in live reptiles that were allegedly being smuggled illegally out of Australia into the States. John Behler and I had no idea what we were getting into when we showed the agents price lists of Australian species. Several subsequent meetings later, when they asked us to examine documents and invoices they had seized from an animal dealer, the agents gave us a little additional information on what was taking place. They had ascertained that a particular dealer had engaged innocent businesspeople and ordinary members of the community to provide investment money so he could buy reptiles in Australia. When the animals were shipped, these innocent victims were expected to pick them up at the airport and await the dealer's return.

An observant security guard noted the license plate of a vehicle belonging to one individual who was picking up one of these shipments. This led customs agents to the person's home. Armed with a search warrant, the agents literally took the home apart, as we waited to identify any reptiles they might uncover. There was nothing. Finally, the case broke when the son of one of the families that had innocently become involved told the authorities of how the boxes of snakes, lizards, and crocodiles had been there just prior to the search, but they had been warned to dispose of the animals. In fear, they had buried the animals alive in a remote area of southern New Jersey. The case was far-reaching and eventually included nearly a dozen zoos around the country, as well. These zoos had unthinkingly housed contraband animals on behalf of the dealer, in return for the opportunity to acquire rare reptiles for their collections.

But these were live animals. What about the leather trade? What were the leather goods manufacturers doing? To answer the question, we began a tour of companies listed in the phone book as working with reptile skins. The first stop was the office of a small company in the Bronx that made watchbands for export. There, a little old man, probably seventy or more years of age, sat before a small mountain of crocodile-skin scraps. In his right hand was a huge pair of scissors, the thumb ring wrapped with a rag to protect his withered hand. He would pick up a piece of skin, look at it carefully, then trim off a narrow piece of leather, which he would carefully add to a bundle of similar strips of leather. At that rate, we felt, he could not possibly cut up one whole alligator in his remaining lifetime. He was the endangered species, in fact, because in the ten years following the enforcement of the new wildlife regulations, many such small tanning and manufacturing operations in the country would close.

Although tanning was traditionally a family operation, with the business and formula secrets handed down from parent to child, succeeding generations left the business for other pursuits. It was also a very labor-intensive business, sensitive to the lower labor costs in Third World countries. Because of new antipollution laws, it would soon become difficult for tanneries, which produce polluting effluents, to remain profitable in most parts of the country. Manufacturing leather products from crocodilian and other reptile skins was also a highly specialized art. U.S. artisans were disappearing, and the industry relied most heavily on France and Italy as the centers for manufacturing. The United States would eventually become largely importers of reptile products, rather than producers.

Soon I had produced a number of publications that were being used by wildlife law enforcement officials as forensic tools, and I started regularly testifying as an expert witness in federal and state court. My credibility came under nearly constant attack, not only from defendants' attorneys but also from my own colleagues who had learned to benefit from industry support. The stakes were high: since laws limited the number of legally available skins, sometimes to fewer than the consumer market would like, the illegal skin trade flourished. Confiscated reptile-skin shipments often represented tens of thousands of dollars in lost profits. At one point, the new head of the U.S. Fish and Wildlife Forensic Laboratory sent samples of crocodilian skins of known identities to all of the biologists being used to identify species, including my colleagues. He discovered that I was singularly consistent in making correct identifications. I was in the hot seat.

By now, the New York office of the U.S. Fish and Wildlife Service had grown with the increased traffic in wildlife and prosecutions. Sometimes two thousand wildlife shipments a month, both dead products and living animals, would need inspection. Special Agent in Charge Bill Donato headed the office, which included his colleagues Special Agent John Meehan and Wildlife Inspector Paul Cerniglia. I now found myself working closely with the New York office in the entirely new and interesting field of forensic sciences, with a group of honest, dedicated people whom I liked and respected.

The more cases that were made, the more the leather industry complained that free trade was being hampered. It was. But only if you were improperly dealing in protected species. At one time, the industry demanded to be educated in how law enforcement authorities were making identifications. The service agreed and set up a meeting at the Florida Museum of Natural History, at the University of Florida. Industry members, tanners, and people who traded in skins from around the world came from all over the Americas, including some who themselves had been subjects of prosecutions. As my colleague and I began our presentation and I described the techniques I used, the whispers and knowing looks began to circulate around the room. Myrna, who was unknown to the participants, was seated between two rows of dealers. As they passed her notes to pass on to other members, she read them. The notes, curiously, advised their recipients to keep secrets and "not tell everything you know."

At lunch, as we sat collectively in a local restaurant, the conversation was casual. "How's your family?" an importer would ask. "Fine," we would reply. "And yours?" It was as though we were old friends. At the end of lunch, one gentleman turned to us and said, "This was very pleasant. We must do this again." We all agreed. As we walked back to the office to reconstruct the torn-up notes they had left in several ashtrays, Myrna asked, "Do you know those people from someplace?" "Yes, as a matter of fact, we do," I replied. "We helped put one of them in prison a few years ago."

Each case was different. One case called for the identification of fourteen thousand scraps of skin, which I would have to testify that I had personally examined in an unreasonably short period of time. Gathering together a half dozen assistants, I had each handle the scraps and hold them up for my inspection, which I did standing directly behind them, one hand on their shoulder. There was always a way.

In one landmark case, some entrepreneurs had thought to evade U.S. regulations by having a large number of skins from endangered black caiman shipped directly from their origin in Bolivia to manufacturers in Hong Kong. Hong Kong authorities seized the shipment and notified U.S. Fish and Wildlife Service authorities, which, in turn, extradited the skins to the United States, "arrested" them, and prosecuted the U.S. citizens involved. During the trial, while I was on the witness stand, the defense attorney produced a number of large photographs of crocodilians for me to identify. The judge and jury looked on as I examined each photograph. The first showed a Nile crocodile, the second an American alligator, and the third a pair of Nile crocodiles. The fourth filled me with disbelief; not only could I identify the crocodilian as another American alligator, but I identified the plant behind it as a southern species of palmetto and the meal it was eating as an eastern diamondback rattlesnake. The defense attorney looked at me with his jaw slack as the jury giggled. He had failed to heed the first rule a lawyer learns: Never ask a question you don't know the answer to. One defendant pleaded guilty and received a prison term, while the other paid a stiff penalty.

The worst case and the longest involved dozens of bales of raw skins. I was at the Florida Museum of Natural History when I got a call from a special agent asking if I would look at some tanned skins he had picked up in an Atlanta tannery. The skins turned out to be those of the Yacare caiman, a then-banned endangered species. They had somehow escaped seizure as they had passed through New York. A second shipment had since arrived in New York and was being detained. It consisted of dozens of bales of not only the endangered caiman but a second endangered species as well. Within days, a third shipment arrived, destined for the same importer. There were thousands of skins, representing as many illegally killed animals. The importer abandoned the shipment, paid the penalty, and cited the dealer in Singapore as at fault in supplying illegal skins. The Singapore dealer, in turn, filed a civil lawsuit against his supplier, a Singapore tannery. Years later, I would find myself in Singapore testifying before a judge. Opposing me, representing the tanner, would be a professional colleague and old friend.

The case was settled out of court. However, the judge thought it would be great sport to hold a mock trial for some law school students. We both declined, for scheduled soon after was another trial, when he and I would once again face each other as opponents in the forensic arena. When it was over, the dealer told me that the skins had, in fact, illegally originated in Brazil and had then been shipped to Paraguay, where they had been packed as cattle skins and shipped to Singapore. Export documents having nothing to do with the skins had been received from accomplices in Colombia, citing a species that could be legally exported from Colombia. The bogus documents then accompanied the illegal skins and were shipped to the U.S. importer. The trade in reptile skins is a circuitous affair, and involves many of the same countries known for traffic in other contraband.

These were not nice people to be dealing with. There were times when pressure was brought to bear to have me removed from my job as a zoo curator because of my work with the U.S. Fish and Wildlife Service. Fortunately, I was on the right side of caring about what happened to wildlife, even if my charges were only lowly reptiles. Rather than censor me, the zoo management encouraged me to continue my work. However, to this day, any criticism I may make about the reptile-leather trade always results in a backlash of condemnation from a handful of my peers.

One day, as I testified in a trial against an importer, the defense attorney tried to paint a picture of me as someone who loved crocodilians so much, I would say anything to protect them. "Mr. Brazaitis," he began, "isn't it true that you love crocodiles and have devoted your life to studying crocodiles? Isn't it true," he pressed, "that you love crocodiles so much you would say anything, do anything to protect them?" Feigning naïveté, I asked, "Would you like me to put my feelings into perspective?" "By all means," he replied, before the prosecuting attorney could object. I said simply, "I love my wife. I like crocodiles." The judge and jury burst into laughter as the attorney turned scarlet. He lost the case.

There may well have been more than just professional risk involved, although I shudder to think so. While I was working on another smuggling case, early one Sunday morning a man entered the lobby of my apartment building and began studying the names on the mailboxes. The superintendent, who was out early sweeping the sidewalk, came in and asked the man who he was looking for. "Peter Brazaitis," he responded, saying he had "a package to deliver." The super, being very sharp, said, "Give me the package and I'll deliver it to him. It's Sunday morning, and you can't disturb him." The man fled, and no package was ever delivered. After that, Myrna contacted the authorities whenever strange parcels arrived. This included an unannounced package with no return address that contained batteries; it turned out to be my new E-ZPass toll transponder.

Working with the New York State Department of Environmental Conservation was perhaps the most fun. Periodically, the enforcement officer for New York City would call the Reptile House and say, "Peter, we have to destroy some evidence. Can you and your staff help?" "Sure," I would reply, knowing what he meant. A few hours later, we would have a large vat of water boiling in the kitchen, waiting for the most recent seizure of undersized Long Island oysters or clams to arrive, whereupon we would join in a feast, destroying the evidence by eating it. It was our duty as good citizens to help in any way we could.

One night, as I prepared to give a speech to members of the Wild-life Conservation Society on my work involving the illegal skin trade, Bill Conway, for many years the general director of the society, said to me, "Only a reptile needs a reptile skin." That's a fairly profound statement, if an obvious one. I never saw a reptile that didn't need its own skin, and certainly no reptile would willingly give it up for the gratification of a wealthy few.

Commercial trading in wildlife, live or dead, is an ugly, often dirty business, where living creatures translate only into dollars and cents, profit and loss. Today, wildlife conservation is too often convoluted by the sanitizing philosophy that wild animals have to be killed so they may be utilized, and thus inherit a value that makes them important enough to protect. Thus, to make a crocodile valuable to local humans, we use a certain number in commerce. Somehow, I keep wondering what that philosophy holds for those millions of species and their habitats that as yet have no known commercial use, and play a role we may not yet have considered in the makeup of the world around us.

23

CENTRAL PARK: IT'S NOT OVER YET

It was March 1988, and my second job interview in thirty-four years was about to begin. I wasn't leaving the Wildlife Conservation Society; I had spent too many years in one place to do that. Besides, I liked who I was and what I did for a living.

I had gotten a call the previous week from Jim Murtaugh, the curator of the new Central Park Zoo, which was just nearing completion. Some years before, the Wildlife Conservation Society had agreed to assume the role of managing all of the New York City zoos. For years, these zoos had been beset by problems of poor animal care, substandard animal housing, lack of funds, and several incidences in which members of the public had been eaten by animals. This is not a good reputation for a zoo to develop.

One by one, the Central Park Zoo, the Prospect Park Zoo, and the Queens Zoo would be torn down, then rebuilt as world-class zoos.

Jim had casually asked if I would have lunch with him a few days later. I had guessed what it was about: he wanted my body. Jim was the recently appointed curator of an almost-built zoo that had no animals, and a deadline only a few months away new facility to the public. It did not take

out that he was going to ask if I would leave my secure position, achieved over many years of hard work, and take a job as assistant curator at the new zoo. What he didn't know was that I had already been thinking of requesting such a transfer. He confirmed my hunch over a pasta lunch at a nearby Italian restaurant. Yes, I said, I would go to the Central Park Zoo, contingent on my wife agreeing; there was also the formality of an interview with the department of human resources.

Myrna was elated. She had been worried that with my advancing years, I was pushing the limits of my physical abilities to work with fast, dangerous snakes and large crocodiles. Often, upon leaving for work in the morning, I would announce that I was going to have a busy day handling venomous snakes for medical treatments or capturing crocodiles to ship to another zoo. She would fret, saying she didn't like it very much, and of course, I would disagree. No self-respecting, fifty-two-year-old, virile, bald-headed Adonis, such as I considered myself, would accept that he was slowing down. But she was right, and there was young Peter to think of. I called Jim and said, "Yes."

There were other good reasons for the move. I had risen through the keeper ranks to a supervisory and management position, which was as far as I could go within the reptile department. Also, I was now overqualified for my supervisory role, and it was time that I begin to think seriously about the not-so-distant future when I would retire. I had a young son; his future was paramount, and his education would benefit from whatever monies could be amassed in my pension savings. Also, in crossing the barrier between the uniformed-keeper ranks to curator, I would be able to do more research and have funds available for my crocodilian conservation work. It really was time for me to move on.

I was a logical choice for the job. I had many years of experience managing animal collections and personnel, and I knew the work-like when it ~~~~~~~~ ~~~vation Society. I had carved out a special ~~~~~~ to date. I was well respected and rocke ~~~~~ hroughout my field—especially ~~~~~ ~~rensic scientist. (Although

I must admit that I was hated by some colleagues and wished dead by others because of my strong convictions on wildlife conservation and my work with wildlife law enforcement agencies.) I had published close to a hundred papers and articles in scientific journals and popular magazines, had traveled throughout a good part of the world chasing crocodilians and giant frogs, and was just about to complete my Master of Science degree. Best of all, I had learned to live with, accept, and like people for their honesty, humanity, and what they were, regardless of what they looked like, their culture, or their status. Not bad, I thought, for a kid who had barely made it out of high school and who most of my early schoolteachers had believed was too dumb to accomplish much of anything. I had, so far, accomplished a great deal. For better or worse, the coming interview would be a major step in my life.

The interview was quickly scheduled in the office of the director of human resources, Angelo Monaco, whom I never saw wearing socks. He was a tough man, and I liked him immensely for his straightforward manner. Before long the deputy director of the zoo, John McKew, joined him. John was tall, lean, and seriously good-natured. He and I shared many years during our tenure with the zoo, and he freely offered both legal and personal advice many times—although I am not entirely sure that he ever forgave me for obliviously passing him on my way to work one morning, during a snowstorm, as he stood on the side of the road by his disabled car.

Angelo and John spoke together, as though sharing the same thoughts: "We're glad you decided to accept the position. The promotion was long overdue." Each then took credit for thinking to ask me. "I kept telling Jim to ask you," Angelo claimed, "but he kept saying you would never leave the Reptile House. Congratulations." "There are benefits to being a curator that you don't now enjoy as a manager," John added. "First off, your wife is now entitled to psychiatric coverage on your medical plan."

"Should I be concerned about that?" I asked. "Does that mean that the wife of a curator may need psychiatric help?" I had the feeling this was not going to be an easy interview.

"Your son will be entitled to a college tuition grant to help him through college—as long as you are working here, of course," they added. I calculated out loud: "I'm fifty-two, and he is a little kid. By the time he's ready for college, I may be dead." "Don't think that way," Angelo said. "Time goes by fast." "Like the blink of an eye," John quipped. I continued: "Why should I want what may be the last days of my life to pass by quickly? How about funds for his nursery school or day care?"

"Congratulations, and get the hell out of here" was the reply. I was now starting a new phase of my career.

It was difficult to keep the news of my impending transfer a secret from my staff at the Reptile House, even for the few days until the paperwork was formalized. A few days later, Bruce Foster, who had worked with me for nearly twenty years, entered my office and reluctantly announced that, at last, he would be free of me, after years of helping me catch ornery crocodiles and sticking fingers in places fingers were never meant to go. He confided that he had accepted a position as supervisor at the new Central Park Zoo. "Guess what?" I asked with a smile. "You're not leaving anything. I'm going to be right there with you as your boss. I'm going, too." His face froze in a cracked smile. A few days later I got a visit from Joe Martinez, another keeper, who equally penitently said he was going to be sad to leave me, but he had accepted a job as a keeper at the new Central Park Zoo. His only reply to the news that Bruce and I would still be with him was "Oh, God."

The old Central Park Zoo had been completely razed. The new zoo copied the original architecture, replacing the barren, barred, concrete cages with large, new, natural-looking moated exhibits with deep, filtered pools. There would be no lions or tigers, elephants or hippopotamuses in small, cramped exhibits made of steel and institutional concrete. Fewer animals in open, natural spaces was the overriding theme. The zoo grounds covered only three and a half acres, and would contain only animals that could live well in appropriate-sized spaces. All of the animals would come from captive-breeding programs in other zoos, not from wild populations. The zoo would become the fund-raising and development center for the zoological society, a jewel in the very heart of Manhattan.

My office was located in the old Arsenal Building on Fifth Avenue. It took me three days to find the unmarked door to the men's room on the main floor. Getting to the zoo in the first place was a challenge. Daily, I would negotiate the heart of New York City's infamous traffic, dodging turbaned taxi drivers, smoking buses, and wild-riding bicycle delivery boys. I had thought I was prepared for anything. I was wrong. One day, as I waited at a traffic light to cross through Central Park at the Sixty-fifth Street transverse, a man without legs, strapped into a wheelchair, maneuvered out into the street in front of me, behind a truck. As the light turned green, he reached up and grasped the back of the truck with his gloved hand, and proceeded to hitch a free ride cross-town, flying along behind the truck at more than twenty miles per hour.

The offices of the commissioner of parks for the City of New York were located on the second floor. It soon became apparent that upper-level Parks Department staff and their aides considered themselves of a higher class than us zoo folk, and rarely interacted with their downstairs neighbors. My first year there, I found it was rather ludicrous that each morning the signboard listing the names of the Parks Department staff would be personally checked for accuracy by a high-ranking supervisor, accompanied by the commissioner himself. It was as though the signboard reaffirmed importance of the listees. And it may well have been an emotional necessity, given that the entire staff sat at the pleasure of the current mayor. Over the years, I was always amused to see that commissioners' dogs enjoyed privileges, as well. Some commissioners would bring their dogs to work each day, and have them "dog-sat" by a department employee. One commissioner left the zoo for an evening function, dressed quite elegantly, and got into her official chauffeured limousine. Her dog followed, in a second car, driven by a staff member. I guess we differed in one way; I always showed up at parties covered with animal hair.

I sat next to a commissioner once at a zoo fund-raiser; I was impressed by his ability to snatch food from everyone's plate. I was glad that the zoo was completely autonomous of the Parks Department operations—especially when this commissioner bestowed silly nicknames on the small army of young aides who followed him about.

Their vocabulary seemed to be limited to "Yes, Commissioner," and their gold-colored name tags read, EAGLE, SPORT, or TIGER.

The new exhibits were spacious and luxurious by zoo standards. Our snow monkey exhibit consisted of a well-planted island that included rock columns, trees, fallen logs, and stepping stones to smaller islands, all of this surrounded by a luxurious 260,000-gallon moat. The macaques could jump from rock to rock and use the branches and logs to springboard into the moat for a summer swim. Our first job in the new exhibit was to install motorized fans underwater to keep the moat water circulating during the winter, preventing it from freezing. Such meticulous care was taken to enhance the visitors' experience that a harmless black vegetable-based textile dye was used to color the water, to hide these fans and the unsightly coins visitors threw into the pool.

Duckweed grew profusely on the pool's surface during the summer months, and soon blanketed the water with a thick green carpet. One day we noticed a young boy who was conspicuous among a line of students leaving the zoo. He was covered to the chest with a thick green substance. It seems that he had climbed over the glass wall of the moat, thinking he could walk on the carpet of green over to the monkey island. He had soon found that it was not green plastic outdoor carpeting, immediately plunging chest deep into four feet of black water. Before his classmates could help him out of the pool, he had been covered with duckweed.

In contrast, the snow monkeys always seemed to know exactly what they were doing. Snow monkeys are wonderfully intelligent animals; they're the ones who figured out how to lock the keepers out of the exhibit so they could continue to enjoy the warm summer evenings, rather than being returned to their dark underground holding cages. The two swans that inhabited the moat with them were no match for their antics. One monkey would make threatening faces and motions at the edge of the water, knowing that the dumb bird could not possibly resist the threat and would come closer to defend its imaginary territory. There was no swan territory. There was only the monkeys' territory, and the monkeys knew it. As soon as the swan was close enough to one monkey, another would quickly rush in to pluck a feather from the swan's rump or wing, and together they would run off, screaming in delight over the prize.

It was even difficult for the keeper staff to outsmart them. I never ceased to enjoy watching them. There was a grand male I'll call Ollie, who was the titular head of the troop. However, the real boss was the dominant old matriarch. She let nothing escape her attention, and she wasn't shy about imposing her will on everyone and keeping the troop in line. Next came an assortment of young females, their buttocks reddening as they reached maturity. These were the troop breeders and the delight of the old male, who would mount them one by one whenever the mood struck him.

I received two letters from members of the public who were concerned about the monkeys' well-being—or, perhaps, their own emotions. One letter complained that the monkeys were doing "bad" things in public, in front of schoolchildren, and that we should station a keeper with an electric prod to shock the monkeys whenever they engaged in sexual behavior. The second letter complained that the monkeys should be dressed in diapers so that the females' alluring red buttocks would not be visible.

A few young upstart males joined one another in a bachelor group, much like a group of teenaged boys strutting on a street corner to work off their increasing levels of testosterone. Any effort by a member of the bachelor group to mate with a young female usually brought down the wrath of Ollie, who considered all the females his and his alone. However, he couldn't be everywhere all the time. Thus, we usually had several baby macaques suckling, being carried, or running around and getting into monkey mischief.

Anyone who wants to learn about family interactions or behavior needs to watch a troop of monkeys. Although we may not like to admit it, we are all just primates, and all of our interactions with one another have a basis in primate behavior. Ollie would sit in the choicest spot, in the warm sun, next to the water's edge, doing nothing important whatsoever. Along would come a mischievous baby macaque, who would curiously tug at his stumpy tail or pluck at his hair. Ollie would stop what he wasn't doing and glare at the baby for a moment, then return to his own thoughts. Back would come the upstart, who would tug again. This time, Ollie would grunt his annoyance and make a threatening face as the youngster raced off, out of reach. The youngster would repeat the fun, each time annoying Ollie even more. Finally, when Ollie could take the little pain in the butt no longer, he would jump up and begin chasing the young guy to teach him a lesson. The young monkey would run to his mother, screaming in fear at the prospect of being beaten. By then, the whole troop would be looking over and racing around in agitation. The old matriarch, like a grandmother, would put an end to all the to-do by yelling at everyone. The same scene could be played out in any human household in the world. I wonder if my son will ever realize that his upbringing had been influenced by a troop of Japanese macaques.

Everybody wanted to come to see the new zoo and either complain or rave about the new exhibits. One visitor wrote that the new zoo did not smell anything like the old zoo. Couldn't we make the new zoo smell more of dung? Most complaints involved having to pay for a visit that, for over eighty years, had been free, reminiscent of the fears generated by the turn-of-the-century politicos that the new zoo would be a zoo for the rich. Actually, in a way it was. A number of our trustees and patrons lived in the penthouses and exclusive apartments overlooking Central Park and the zoo, and would call to say that the barking sea lions were interrupting their sleep at night. The public loved the new zoo. It was beautiful and tranquil, a postage-stamp-sized oasis in the heart of Manhattan.

Without officially counting anyone as they came and left through the open gates, before the renovation the Parks Department had boasted that 2 million people visited the Central Park Zoo each year. The true figure turned out to be somewhere around 800,000, as we found out once we began to collect admissions fees. These fees went entirely to the Parks Department and not at all to the zoological society.

Of course, not everyone was counted. One day I was looking out my office window, toward the side gate and the fence that separated the animal area from the free public walkway. Two young, well-dressed men in suits, probably in their late twenties, accompanied by an impeccably dressed, lovely, gray-haired grandmother-type woman, paused to look over the four-foot-high iron fence at the sea lions, cavorting and barking as they swam around their pool. I thought it was a lovely scene—that is, until the two young men grasped the elderly woman by her arms and buttocks and gently lifted her over the fence into the zoo. Then they hopped over the fence themselves to escape the few dollars' admission fee. Security was in disbelief when I called them by radio and directed them to the three well-to-do-looking people.

There were many corrections to be made before the zoo was to open to the public. It had to go through what amounted to a shakedown period, when each and every weakness, possible escape route for animals, and other problem was detected and corrected. We knew that once the animals were introduced into their new homes, they would test and prod every corner and crevice to find a way out. Any problem we might miss, they would find. My nightmare was that a snow monkey or other large, potentially dangerous animal might escape. While the Bronx Zoo was enclosed in over 250 acres of forest and miles of high fencing, insulating it from the surrounding neighborhood, an escaped animal from the Central Park Zoo would instantly find itself at the corner of Sixty-third Street and Fifth Avenue, and on the national evening television news.

The original barren, concrete-walled sea lion pool in the central garden was replaced with a beautiful, clear pool of glass surrounded by a moat and a second glass wall, through which visitors could watch the four young sea lions as they raced like torpedoes around their new enclosure. Periodically, the sea lions would pause at the pool's glass wall, hang over it, and tease people into paying attention to them by allowing curious visitors to reach out to only a few inches from their noses.

However, the sea lions did not fully learn the limits of the glass pool wall for several weeks after they were introduced into the exhibit, as evidenced by their nocturnal behavior. It was not unusual for me to receive a call from security, in the middle of the night, saying that a sea lion had jumped over the glass and was now chasing his friends around the perimeter of the pool, watching them through the glass. On those nights, I traveled back to the zoo and met the curator at the sea lion pool. Armed with a cargo net, we would spend the next several hours joining the sea lion in a chase around the pool. Finally exhausted—us, not it—we would manage to interrupt the chase when the sea lion ran over the net, and we could quickly hoist it up and back over the glass wall and into the pool to rejoin its cohorts. Eventually, they learned the glass was the limit of their environment.

One day, not long after the zoo was opened to the public, a terrible summer rainstorm suddenly dropped inches of water on Central Park. The nearby lake swelled, overflowing its banks. As the water rose, it rushed back through the underground storm drains to burst from the floor drains that surrounded the sea lion pool. In minutes, the low-lying basin in which the sea lion pool was built filled with water. First it rose halfway up the glass wall of the pool, and then, more quickly, it rose to the top and spilled over the glass.

The sea lions could not believe their good fortune. Here was an opportunity to see the world on their own. Like schoolchildren on a trip to the zoo, the sea lions followed their curious leader and swam over the glass and into the surrounding garden, now six feet deep in water. After swimming a few laps around their new world, playing with a piece of floating bark or a broken branch on the way, they decided that a rest might be in order. A series of wooden benches were conveniently located not far from the rocks where they would be fed their next meal. Before long, each sea lion had staked out a bench of its own to rest on. Thinking quickly, Bruce Foster, the animal supervisor, put the pool's filters into high gear and began pumping the water back out through the filter system. As the water once again began to drop, the sea lions followed the flow and simply swam back over the glass wall, into their pool—and to a reward of fresh herring.

While the first flood of the sea lion pool and the escapades in the garden went virtually unnoticed by the press, they were not forgotten by the park commissioner's office, always hungry for publicity. The opportunity came during the next tropical-storm downpour—by coincidence, when Gus the polar bear was undergoing a vasectomy.

There were many details to coordinate in preparation for the scheduled surgery. Downpour or not, the surgery would take place within the confines of the holding building. For humans, the patient usually checks in at the hospital on the appointed day, hands over his medical insurance card, and waits patiently. Polar bears have no patience, or medical insurance for that matter. Polar bears are one of the smartest, strongest, and most dangerous of the world's carnivores. Even though Gus would initially be immobilized with drugs and unable to move, it would be far too dangerous to take him completely out of the security of his barred holding area. The surgical team would come to him.

The plan was simple. Gus would be shot in the rump with a carbon dioxide–powered dart gun. The dart would contain an immobilizing drug. When the drug took effect, in about twenty minutes, and Gus was lying quietly, we would enter his cage, and carry all six hundred pounds of him out and down a flight of stairs to the waiting surgical table. There he would receive a second injection of anesthetic, be placed on life support—a breathing apparatus—and hooked up to an anesthesia machine. After the surgery was over, the process would be reversed. Once Gus was back in his holding cage, he would be given an injection of a third drug, which would reverse the effects of the first immobilizing drug, and we would all get the hell out of his cage before he was able to get up.

Immobilizing drugs prevent an animal from activating its muscles, although mentally the animal is very aware of everything that is going on around it; it simply can't move. However, an anesthetic blocks pain and renders the animal unconscious. Throughout the process, one of us would stand by with a loaded shotgun. Tensions always run high during such times. It is always entirely possible that the immobilizing drug will wear off prematurely or unexpectedly, and the bear will become alert while he is outside of his cage. The standard joke was "If the bear has me, shoot me instead of the bear, as the bear won't leave much that works."

There are four holding cages, or dens, constructed of reinforced flat steel bars, in the holding area where Gus and the two female polar bears spend their nights. During the day, the bears leave the dens through connecting doors with a triple-locking security mechanism, and go into the main exhibit. This allows the keepers to enter the bears' sleeping quarters through a second set of access doors along a keepers' service passageway, so they can clean. Once the bears are outside, they cannot reenter the den, so the keeper will not be interrupted by an ill-tempered polar bear. A second barred steel door further isolates the access to the service passage and the bears' dens. If a bear did manage to get out of its den during the night, it would still be confined in the service passageway within the building.

Concern for safety was one of the reasons why New York City had asked the zoological society to take over the city zoo operations. Over the years, there had been several instances in the city-run zoos in which members of the public had been injured or killed by a polar bear. Since the zoological society is a private organization, its level of animal care is not answerable to political appointees or dictated by hand-me-down budgets. Our staff was well trained, and no expense was spared to maintain a safe, healthy environment for animals and staff alike.

The preparations began with the arrival of six bales of hay at the underground polar bear holding area. Covered with a fresh, clean sheet of canvas, these would serve as the operating table. Gus paced in his den, knowing from the extra activity and people that nothing good was going to happen. One of the vets slid the barrel of the dart gun through the bars and waited until Gus turned, exposing a good spot on his rump. *Poof.* The dart landed squarely in the seat of Gus's furry rear end. Gus jumped, more surprised at the sudden noise than the prick of the dart. *Poof.* A second dose of drug hit home. Now all we could do was watch and wait.

At first, Gus went back to pacing as though nothing had happened.

The empty darts fell out as he moved. One minute, then five, then seven passed. Gus began to wobble a little, unsure of his steps. Within fifteen minutes, Gus lay on the floor with his tongue hanging out of his mouth and his eyes open. One poke through the bars with a broom handle brought no response from Gus. Nothing with a second and third poke, either. It was time.

The steel door was unlocked and slid open a few inches. Another poke. Still there was no response. The door was slid open farther, but still ready to be slammed shut if Gus so much as twitched. Just on the other side of the access door to the exhibit, the two female polar bears, Ida and Germany, sniffled and snorted. One of them occasionally scraped a claw against the metal frame of the door that separated them from us, just to remind us where we were. It was time to take the plunge and commit to being inside the cage, unprotected, with a mean-tempered, six-hundred-pound polar bear.

Those first few moments when you find yourself in a place that every emotion and all logic tell you that you should not be in make your heart pound. Right next to me, Gus's head seemed many times bigger than it had ever looked through the bars of the cage. I could see rage in his eyes as the vet coated them with ophthalmic ointment to keep them moist. I knew he could see, smell, and, I imagined, taste me, without being able to move. I picked up a paw; it was as big and wide as a serving tray, let alone a dinner plate. His white fur was coarse and thick, and the inside of his mouth black, in contrast to his great white teeth. Gus was yet a teenager. What would he be like at seventeen hundred pounds and ten feet tall? I felt dwarfed next to him now. Six of us rolled Gus onto a canvas, and together we carried him out of the den and down to the waiting operating table.

The two vets were gowned and ready. The security man with the shotgun was at our side every step of the way. Within minutes, Gus was intubated and receiving anesthesia. Gus was a young male, and although he was willing and able to breed, we had no wish to have baby polar bears. We could not keep a second male, nor did we have a place to hold a pregnant female, separated from the other bears, until she gave birth. Gus was about to receive a reversible type of vasectomy. If all went well, he would be back in his cage in an hour and a half. All, however, was not going to go well.

I was tired and drained as the call came over the radio. "Animal One. There's a fire truck and a truck with a boat on the roof coming into the zoo. You had better take a look outside." As I stepped outside the great wooden door that separated the public from the bears' holding area, it seemed as though the rain had just ended. The flashing red and white strobe lights snapped through the last falling drops of water from behind the fence that formed the perimeter of the zoo, facing Fifth Avenue. "Oh shit. What the hell are fire trucks doing in the zoo?" I muttered to myself. There, lined up along the fence, was a string of flashing red fire engines, police emergency-services vehicles, a fire chief's car, and, just arriving, the New York City river rescue squad, complete with a Zodiac boat lashed to the roof of the truck. Firefighters and police officers rushed into the zoo and began to run toward me, past the sea lion pool, led by a fire chief in his yellow-striped raincoat. "Where are they?" he shouted, nearly out of breath. "We got a call from the park commissioner's office saying that the zoo was flooding and the animals were escaping. What do you want us to do?"

"I don't know," I replied, taken completely by surprise. "No animals escaping here."

"We have pumps," he yelled.

"Good, go suck out the basement over there," I said, wanting to divert any attention as far away as possible. There was always some water in that basement after a rain, I was sure. "And don't leave the basement until the rain's over," I added, "just in case."

Not seeing any exciting floods or animals to catch, some firefighters began to wander off to look at the animals. "Let's go, men," the chief called. "Get the pumps out." "Can we see the birds?" someone called back. "Look at the monkey with the fire-red butt!" another added, catching sight of a female Japanese macaque in the nearby exhibit. I could see a row of white faces in the second-floor windows of the commissioner's offices.

Next to arrive were trucks with TV news logos painted on their sides. One truck barely came to a halt before the mast of its antenna rose upward. Men with headsets, carrying video cameras on their shoulders, sprinted toward the sea lion pool. Reporters with hand-held microphones and coils of cable looked for someone to inter-view. The sea lions barked from their ringside seats on rocks in their pool, entertained by the human circus. "We heard the zoo was flood-ing and animals were escaping. Where are they?"

I knew that the last thing I wanted was for anyone, especially the press, bored for a story on a rainy day, to even guess that just a few feet away, behind the door, was a polar bear out cold, getting a va-sectomy, while a guy with a shotgun looked on. More rain began to pour down. I ducked back into the polar bear den.

With nothing to report, but not wanting to leave empty-handed, the news reporters stood at the sea lion pool and interviewed one an-other.

A half hour later, Gus was back in his cage. The last danger was nearly over as one of the vets gave Gus the antidote to the immobi-lizing drug, adjusted the bear's feet under him, and quickly exited the cage. Within a couple of minutes, Gus was up, wobbling and un-steady, but mad. The process had taken most of the early morning. By then, the fire trucks and the river rescue squad were reloading their gear and leaving.

Gus, now fully revived, got a meal of frozen mackerel as his re-ward for bravery. I peeked through a crack in the door to see what was happening, then stuck my head outside. It was safe. The re-porters, tired of talking to one another in the rain, began to disap-pear. Everyone, including the commissioner's office, had missed the real story that had taken place that day, behind a door only a few feet away. I knew Gus would never tell.

The new zoo was beautiful, but it was poorly designed from the point of view of animal care. An exhibit initially designed for hous-ing a pair of mountain lions called for a keeper to enter the holding cage with the lions in order to move them. The keeper would have to walk through the cage in the lions' presence to the opposite side of the enclosure and politely open an access door by turning the door-knob, allowing the lions to pass into their exhibit. The exhibit was immediately transformed into a bat cave for four hundred fruit bats.

The Tropical Building included a forest of life-sized rain-forest trees, rock ledges, and jungle streams made from fiberglass and rub-ber. These were accurate to life in every detail and enhanced by live plantings of bromeliads, ferns, and other tropical plants. People tapped "stones" and "tree trunks," felt live palm fronds, and still came away not sure of what was real and what was artificial. One woman, trying to get a particular angle for a picture, left a designated path at the far end of the zoo and climbed on a large "boulder" set among a planting of flowers along a streambed. Before she knew what was happening, the top of the "boulder" had opened, plunging her into a dark, underground room with a humming filtration sys-tem.

The Tropical Building held exhibits of tropical forest–dwelling black-and-white colobus monkeys, pythons, small reptiles, and rare, endangered species of tamarins, some of the world's smallest pri-mates. Freely flying throughout the main part of the building was a wide variety of nearly one hundred colorful tropical birds. The birds nested in the vines and mosses that covered the walls, presenting a unique problem: How does one monitor the daily health of a hun-dred free-flying birds in a tropical rain forest?

The keepers' ingenuity soon solved the problem. Instead of trying to find each bird each morning, which is impossible, why not have each bird present itself for daily inspection? Every morning, the bird keeper would prepare a rolling cart of food dishes that contained prepared diets and a tray of succulent, wriggling mealworms and juicy white grubs and maggots. However, before the various dishes were set out in their designated places throughout the forest, the keeper would pause on a wooden walkway overlooking the treetops. There, he would sit on the floor with his inventory list of birds and the color codes corresponding to the tiny plastic bands that each bird wore around one leg. The hungry birds soon learned that the best part of the meal would be the wriggling grubs and worms, which they could get if they arrived at the feeding station where the keeper sat. As each bird arrived, the keeper would toss a succulent wriggling morsel on the ground for the bird to eat, which would give him a few moments to note its color, identification bands, and health.

At one point we thought, What is a tropical rain forest without a tropical fruit bat? We had to try some, which surely would enhance the visitors' experience as the terrier-sized bats swooped through the treetops. Flying foxes, as they are also called, inhabit the world's tropical regions by the thousands, living in the treetops during the day and flying in great clouds of bodies at dusk to feed on fruit. Their three-foot-wide wingspreads blacken the sky as they whoosh through the air.

The U.S. Department of Agriculture has stringent regulations concerning the housing of fruit bats of any type, for fear that any escaping bats could—improbably—reproduce in sufficient numbers to threaten the domestic fruit industry. Besides, wild bats are notorious carriers of rabies, and a rabid bat can infect a human through direct contact or even—but rarely—by droplet infection. Our fruit bats would be captive-bred and raised under the most stringent health conditions, would never come in contact with wild bats, and would be vaccinated against rabies as well as a host of other diseases.

Five bats were obtained from a colony at the Bronx Zoo and prepared for introduction into the aviary. We knew the bats would have no interest in the birds, as neither would compete with the other for food or space. At first, the bats were held in large, screened cages, slightly away from the main area but within sight and sound of the aviary and the birds in it. The object was to teach the bats that food was available only in the screened cages, and that they had to return to these cages each night to be fed. It took Supervisor Tony Brownie several weeks to accomplish this task.

Finally, the day arrived and the bats soared out into the aviary to roost in the tropical treetops. They flew day and night, to the astonishment of the visitors, who saw the great bodies fly silently through the trees. Soon the Tropical Building was scheduled for numerous night fund-raising events. It was during one of these evening events that we learned just how well acclimated the bats had become. As one evening-gowned woman strolled through the aviary sipping a drink, a huge fruit bat swooped down, landed on her arm, and with its long tongue began lapping up her sweet drink. She was startled at first, but the good-natured woman immediately appreciated the uniqueness of the moment. It was a wonderful experience, and no one else would ever top that story at her exclusive women's club. The bat, however, soon found itself back in its original colony at the Bronx Zoo, where cocktails were never served.

Animal escapes should not happen on Fifth Avenue, but they did. Despite every effort to keep the zoo escape-proof, the animals continually tested their enclosures for possible routes out. On the first New Year's Eve the zoo was in operation, security called me. They told me that one of the officers had seen a muntjac, a species of tiny, brown Asiatic deer not much bigger than the average mutt dog, walking along a back path of the zoo.

We had several muntjacs in an exhibit, held in by an inwardly curving wall. But the deer were particularly agile and nervous. While they could not jump over the wall under normal circumstances, we did not know what their capabilities might be if they were frightened into flight. That night, a series of fire engines, their sirens wailing, had passed close to the muntjac exhibit on the road through Central Park. Frightened by the noise and the flashing lights, the deer had bounded around their enclosure and gained enough speed to breach the wall. Once outside their exhibit, they had settled down to munch grass and hide in the nearby underbrush, still within the fenced confines of the zoo. It was then that they had been spotted.

I would need a number of keepers armed with large, round, long-handled nets to quietly stalk the deer in the dark with flashlights. Recapturing the deer would be neither fun nor easy. The deer could hurt themselves if they crashed into a fence or tree as they fled. Or the muntjacs' short horns or razor-sharp hooves could hurt someone, especially if anyone not wearing leather gloves tried to hold them.

I called the senior keepers first, had them call their keeper staff, and instructed them to meet me at the zoo. I had no idea who would show up, given that it was New Year's Eve and most of the keepers were at parties. I arrived at the zoo within an hour to meet security at the gate. While a security guard was telling me that all three of the muntjacs had escaped, to my amazement, other cars began to arrive. The keepers were not only responding, they were bringing their party guests and bottles of champagne with them, ready to celebrate the coming of the New Year and, hopefully, the capture of the muntjacs. The experienced keepers would wield the capture nets, while their guests would simply follow instructions.

There were enough people to quietly encapsulate the muntjacs in a tightening human circle. Two of the three muntjacs were netted when they tried to run past a zookeeper. The third, and last, muntjac decided it had had enough. It jumped into a net on its own volition as a keeper walked past it in the dark. The great muntjac New Year's Eve party ended with hugs, kisses, and well wishes, as the New Year rang in, beneath the glowing lights of New York's finest hotels and to a chorus of barks from the raucous sea lions. Who, partying in the apartments overlooking the zoo, could know of the party they had just missed?

Several weeks later, on the night of my wedding anniversary, the muntjacs escaped again. Myrna and I had rented a movie—on her favorite topic, China—and bought a bottle of champagne. We were getting ready for a quiet celebration when zoo security called. I asked Myrna to stop the movie and tore out of the house, promising that I'd be home soon. Hours later, I returned home exhausted from chasing those little deer. Myrna had given up and put the champagne in the fridge, watched the movie, and fallen fast asleep. The next day, after almost no sleep, I shipped the muntjacs out to another zoo.

The American Zoo and Aquarium Association (AZA) accredits every professionally run zoo. The Central Park Zoo is no exception. However, despite the stringent inspections conducted every three years by the AZA, the USDA has a team of veterinarians that visits zoos unannounced and performs site inspections. John, the USDA veterinarian assigned to New York, was a dedicated young man who had served in the Gulf War and took his job very seriously. Since he refused to allow me to even buy him a cup of coffee, lest it be construed as a gratuity, I would always remind him that he could buy me a cup of coffee instead. John would arrive at 8:00 A.M. on Sunday morning, at 4:30 P.M. on Friday night, or any time in between, shooting for when he was least expected. You could not prepare for John's inspection. He was a man after my own heart; I was also fond of showing up in a keeper's section, unannounced, yellow pad in hand, searching for problems. He would check every corner, looking to see if lightbulbs were burned out, if food was allowed to sit in crates on the floor of the kitchen instead of being elevated on wooden pallets, if the roach and rodent populations were under control, if primates were picking paint chips from walls in their cages, and if inventory records, medical reports, and water-quality-analysis records for the marine-mammal pools were being maintained properly, on a daily basis. He would walk the perimeter fencing to ensure that it was intact—no matter how long the fence was or how long it took him, or you. He knew exactly where to look to find deficiencies—and he did. Everything went into his report, and any violation, from simple housekeeping problems to serious lapses in dealing with an important issue, had to be addressed within a stipulated number of days.

His inspections always included a request for me to open the gun safe, which held the weaponry and ammunition that would be used to dispatch a dangerous animal that had escaped, as well as the tranquilizer gun, darts, and drugs that would be used to immobilize an animal for medical reasons or, again, in case of escape. Each of the key members of the staff, myself included, received special training in using the tranquilizing equipment. However, we all knew that no animal succumbs to the effects of a tranquilizer dart immediately; rather, it may take ten or twenty minutes, or even longer. In the meantime, a darted animal could leave the grounds or attack and kill someone. Our only dangerous animals were the three polar bears— Gus, Ida, and Germany—and perhaps the largest male Japanese macaque. To deal with such an event, we were also trained in the use of high-powered rifles and shotguns, which were kept secure in the locked gun safe.

On one particular inspection, John arrived at the secure gun safe and asked me to open it for his inspection. As I arrived at the last digit of the combination, the lock clicked open, and I swung the door wide. There, nestled comfortably on the floor of the safe among the stored rifles, was a family of mice in a well-made nest of shredded cloth cleaning rags. I was shocked. How could a mouse, not to mention a whole family of mice, have gotten into the most secure place one could imagine? A locked safe? John pushed aside the guns for the answer. When our maintenance people had bolted the safe to the concrete floor, they had taken a bit of a shortcut. They had used only two bolts instead of four. The mice had entered the safe from underneath, through the vacant bolt holes, and had found the best warm and secure place possible—my locked safe. John could hardly contain his laughter at my embarrassment as he recorded and had me sign the violation: "Housekeeping: vermin in safe."

Animal enrichment became the focus of the zoological community in the 1990s. Full of public relations potential, a balm to the animal-rights movement, and perceivably beneficial to captive animals, the movement to improve the emotional and social well-being of captive animals grew exponentially. Federal regulations already recognized the social needs of nonhuman primates by requiring that they not be housed in isolation, deprived of the company of other primates. By federal law, marine mammals, including whales, dolphins, sea lions, seals, and polar bears, had to be given adequate space according to a specific dimensional formula for land, water, and shade. My own conviction is that animals such as polar bears and social, intelligent whales, dolphins, and porpoises, which normally range thousands of miles across the open Arctic Ocean or ice and swim the open seas of the world, can never be adequately and humanely kept in captivity, regardless of the size of the exhibit or the amount and type of care they receive.

Early on, we embarked on a program of providing social enrichments for our nonhuman primates. Our exhibits were huge and replete with natural settings, waterfalls, trees, swings, ropes, and things for the animals in them to do. The Japanese macaques had peanuts and kibble spread throughout the exhibit, so they could entertain themselves by foraging through the area for tiny treats, much as they would forage for food in the wild. The tamarins were given crickets to hunt, while the polar bears had balls, floats, and toys to entertain them.

But it was no surprise when the director called me into his office to tell me that a director of a zoo in California had called him to say that a New York writer had just left his office. The writer was asking about stereotypic behavior in his polar bears, and what was being done about it. The writer said he had just visited the Central Park Zoo, and one of the polar bears there was badly neurotic. A pox on us. Gus had been seen swimming in repetitive patterns in his pool.

This could be a public relations nightmare, particularly if bad press from any article the writer might produce resulted in an attack by animal-rights groups. Because of who we were and where the zoo was located, good public relations seemed to be the overriding focus of the Central Park Wildlife Center (the zoo's official name). We were in a fishbowl, and the world in the heart of New York was watching us.

Suddenly, unlimited amounts of money seemed to fly in every direction. A California-based so-called therapist-analyst-trainer was summoned immediately to the Central Park scene, and the media feeding frenzy was on. This "therapist" was no more a therapist than my pet cat; he was an experienced animal trainer who had realized that "animal therapy" was good business. The zoo paid him accordingly.

Gus did indeed swim in a repetitive pattern in his pool, when he chose to swim. He would push off a rock with one foot, throw his head back, and do the backstroke until he reached the glass on the opposite side of the pool, then turn by flipping over and pushing off with another foot. There were times during the year when he swam more often than others, and other times when he never swam at all. But it was too late; poor Gus had inherited the bogus title of being a neurotic New Yorker in need of psychoanalysis. Newspaper and magazine articles appeared by the score. A cartoon book depicting a neurotic polar bear who came to New York soon followed. New

Yorkers fully understood the need for an analyst. At last, neurotic New Yorkers could identify with something else neurotic, and everyone could be happy on Prozac. I wanted to vomit. However, attendance at the zoo to see Gus, the neurotic polar bear, surged.

Keepers were thrown into the breach, to the last man or woman. Gus had to be stopped from swimming. "Why?" I asked. Polar bears are predators, usually solitary except during the breeding season, and roam constantly over hundreds of miles of open ice in search of seals or even whales to eat. Groups of bears, even polar bears, sometimes raid garbage dumps for a feast of junk food and tasty leftovers. With their webbed feet, polar bears can, and often do, swim sixty miles a day in the wild, more than ten hours a day; they can dive fifteen feet deep and stay under water for at least two minutes. They are superb hunters, aggressive and keen-sighted, with an excellent sense of smell. They roam the ice floes, using their wide, fur-padded feet to support their weight—up to 1,760 pounds—as they traverse the snow packs. They can find seals—their primary source of food—under the polar ice, and they will wait for hours until a seal comes to a breathing hole for air. Instantly, the bear will seize the seal in its jaws and haul it through the ice. During the Arctic summer, polar bears wander at the edge of the receding ice, occasionally feeding on berries, until the winter ice again brings them seals.

So why, when we put a polar bear in a bathtub, are we surprised to see it swim in a small, repetitive pattern? What do people do when they go to a pool to swim? They can't sit on the bottom to drown. They can't float, motionless, in one spot forever. So people swim repetitive laps, back and forth, traversing the length of the pool, then turning by flipping over and pushing off the pool's wall with their feet, contacting the same spot on each lap. Why are we surprised when Gus does the same thing for the same reasons? Wild polar bears have been seen swinging their heads and pacing, just like captive bears. In comparison to some bears that paced and swung their heads incessantly, Gus rated a possible two out of ten.

Polar bears simply should not be in zoos. One visitor called the general director of the Wildlife Conservation Society, Dr. William

Conway, and suggested that Gus should be returned to where he came from—presumably, the wild. Bill Conway is reported to have replied, "Toledo? Why should anyone be forced to go back to Toledo?" That's where Gus was born, in a zoo. It was no use. The press was racing uncontrollably away with another juicy New York story.

The therapist prescribed training to perform an act, to divert Gus from swimming. It seemed to me that performing on command was a lot more unnatural for Gus than swimming. Calming drugs were considered. Contracts were contemplated for the development of mechanical trees that would spew out berries or honey at irregular intervals, spring-loaded rocks that would test Gus's muscle strength and his ability to look under ice for food, and so on. One fact became clear: it was not the elaborate and expensive mechanisms that were most effective in amusing Gus, but simple things that were new to him, or presented to him in a new way. Used Christmas trees, discarded after the holidays, were great fun for him to drag around his exhibit and demolish. Apples or mackerel fish, frozen in a pail of ice, would provide hours of pleasure as the bears tried to extract the food from the ice. Ida figured out in a wink that if you dragged the frozen pail of ice into the flowing stream, the water would melt the ice quickly and the frozen fish or apples would fall out in a block that was easy to break open. A bear could then wear the pail on her head for sport. Gus never figured out how to melt the food out of the ice, being rather dumb even as polar bears go. He would often sit and cry as he sat in front of the pail, trying to think of what to do.

Once, after a special event that had left gallons of orange sherbet and Italian ices uneaten, Gus and the "girls" were offered these unusual treats. They ate them with gusto. Well infused with sugars and a full stomach, the bears immediately fell asleep. The answer to satisfying Gus could well be Italian ices. Gus and the two girls also enjoyed the new regimen that the keepers developed of hiding treats, which allowed the bears to hunt for food throughout the exhibit all day. Roy Riffe, the senior keeper, became a master at entertaining Gus.

People constantly asked whether the polar bears suffer during the heat of a summer day. Actually, they don't, and they can often be seen sleeping in the hot sun on a ninety-degree day. Their hair is hollow and filled with trapped air; the white color results from the refraction of light through the hair. Actually, the hair is an amazing organ. Like a fiber-optic tube, the hollow hair transmits light and probably infrared rays from the sun to the skin at the base of the hair. The skin underneath is coal black and absorbs heat readily. However, the layers of underlying fat are what insulate the bear from the extreme Arctic cold during the winter and, equally, the heat of the sun during the summer. The summer heat does not bother polar bears— unless they are stressed or become overactive, and as long as there is adequate ventilation and a cooler place to retreat to.

While our underground bear holding dens were air-conditioned, I felt we could do more in the outside exhibit. One day, as we emptied a restaurant ice cube–making machine we had on hand, packing the ice around a penguin that needed to be transported to the animal health center, I wondered if we couldn't do something similar for Gus and the girls. I called the manufacturer. "What would it take to produce a mountain of ice cubes all summer long, all day long, in the open air?" "Why?" he asked. "To give our polar bears ice to enjoy," I replied. "I'm a member of the Wildlife Conservation Society," he answered. "I'll be over with my people to look at the job on Monday." A few weeks and $30,000 later, three ice cube–making machines were tumbling six thousand pounds of ice cubes onto a pile in the bear exhibit each day. Gus and the girls could now dig for berries and fresh fruit in the mountain of ice throughout the summer. Otherwise, they ignored it. After all, polar bears do not necessarily like to do what we think they like to do.

I still miss the cold, snowy nights and the lights of Manhattan as seen from the polar bear balcony overlooking the snow monkey pool at the Central Park Zoo, the place I called home for ten years. I miss the diving and jumping penguins racing from one end of their exhibit pool to the other before the public arrives. I miss the smiling ticket takers readying their cash registers for the day's visitors, the supervisors assessing the problems of the day over a cup of coffee. I miss the overstuffed sandwiches from the cheap deli tucked away behind the most expensive hotel in New York, and a thousand other small things and dozens of people that made the zoo "happen" each and every day. I still feel sorry for Gus, who never was a neurotic New Yorker. He was just a polar bear who had to live in a bathtub.

24

I REALLY DO
LIKE BIRDS

My new job as assistant curator of animals at Central Park now included birds as well as mammals, fish, invertebrates, and my beloved reptiles. I had to adjust. Although I'd always had a keen interest in mammals, and actually knew a lot about them, birds had so far mostly represented food that I might feed to reptiles.

Not only did I have a knowledge hurdle to overcome as a new curator, needing to learn nearly as much about birds as I knew about reptiles, but there was also the problem of the animosity between some very intense "bird people" and "reptile people." In short, some of the principal bird people in the department hated me. One young senior bird keeper, whom I'll call Ames, was particularly passionate in his desire to see me dead. Ames was indeed an excellent bird person; his gentleness, great knowledge, infinite patience, and close attention to detail made him a master of his work. The root of the problem was that I was a "reptile man" and he was a "bird man." Reptiles meant snakes, snakes eat birds, and since I liked snakes, I was therefore the enemy of any and all bird people. It was the equivalent of a bird man's holy war against reptiles.

As a lifelong reptile man, of course, I couldn't help but find it amusing to hear bird curators describe what had happened to one bird or another in their collections, in terms a reptile curator would never entertain. A bird was never simply killed by another bird or animal, it was "murdered." When one bird stupidly stuck its head in a drain and got sucked in and drowned, it had "committed suicide," and the implication was that the facilities the organization had provided for the bird were so inferior that the bird had chosen death rather than live in such indignity.

Despite our good-natured differences, however, reptile and bird keepers do share great similarities in their somewhat obsessive feelings about their respective animals. In fact, the two are all too similar. Both amass great libraries of books, spend their free time watching birds or collecting reptiles, belong to professional organizations, and may have private collections of animals. On the other hand, each insists that *their* animals appeared first in the evolutionary scheme. Each time some new scientific evidence appears to suggest that birds came before reptiles, or vice versa, the opposing camp is sure to be told about it at the very next morning coffee break. Bird people would chide, "You can tell a herpetologist in a crowd by the missing fingers"—presumably the result of their equally low reptilian mentality, and being bitten by one of those "sneaky" venomous snakes. On the other hand, reptile people quip, "Why are bird people most apt to get bitten by venomous snakes?" The answer: "Because they spend their time looking up in the air instead of watching where they are going." The plain truth is that reptiles eat birds, and bird people never can forgive reptile people for that sin, even though many birds feed on reptiles, as well. The mammal keepers, by the way, were for the most part ignored.

My earliest introduction to birds had come when, as a young boy visiting my grandparents in the small coal-mining town of Coaldale, Pennsylvania, I had been sent by my grandmother to bring in the large brown-backed goose she was fattening for Sunday dinner. The goose, more than twenty pounds in weight, was temporarily living under the pigeon coop. As I stooped to enter the goose's domain, unable to stand upright without banging my head on the beams of the floor above, the goose made its move. It immediately attacked, flailing me with its wings, and beating me to a pulp with well-placed blows to my shins and arms. For all of their beauty, swans and large geese can be quite formidable, even breaking a person's arm or leg with a blow from one of their strongly boned wings. I managed to grab the bird by its neck, but not before I was black and blue all over and had gained a new feeling of respect for birds. I was not all that saddened when Grandmother turned the beast into blood soup and a roast.

This early training would come in handy when, as a new keeper, I had to feed several swans on a small pond as part of my daily chores. One particular swan would watch me intently as I approached the gate surrounding its pond. As soon as I got near the feeder at the water's edge, the dumb bird immediately attacked, forgetting that I was the one carrying its daily ration of grain in my pail. Each and every day the ritual was repeated. The swan attacked; I held the pail of grain between the enraged swan and me; it flailed the pail with its wings and spilled the grain. I then reached around the pail and grabbed the bird by one wing, spun it around me for several revolutions, like a shot-putter, finally releasing it to sail off in a white feathered arc and land dizzy and dazed back in the center of the pond. It never learned.

Although the majority of birds really can't cause a fatal human injury, as many venomous or large reptiles can (unless they get stuck in your throat as you eat them), bird people sometimes tend to exaggerate the danger birds pose to them. Ames was no exception. He never knew much about my background, my years of working with really dangerous snakes and crocodiles; to him, I was simply one of those distasteful reptile people. One day, when I approached him on a path as he was returning from helping capture several black-necked swans for the veterinarian to examine, his wry comment was, "Don't worry, Mr. Brazaitis. It's safe for you to go down to the bird holding room now. We have already caught the swan." I smiled and thanked him for his concern.

It took me several years to even partially atone for my sinful reptilian associates. An opportunity came my way one day when a pygmy duck, employing the great wisdom of its duck brain, managed to force its way past a protective screen and enter the labyrinth of ventilation-system ducts encircling the Tropical Building. Eventually, the duck, following the air currents, would no doubt find its way to the blades of the circulating fan and become another "suicide."

When I said I would rescue the duck, Ames was prepared for the worst. Entering the ductwork was fairly easy, requiring no more belly-crawling effort than I had exercised many times before as an amateur spelunker, exploring caves for salamanders in Virginia and for fun in New York. However, before long I had impaled my scalp on a sheet-metal screw protruding through the ductwork, and blood dripped from my nose. I also found the duck, quite oblivious to the fact that it was imminently close to being sliced into sandwich meat by the whirling blades of the fan. My accident report reflected my true feelings about the matter: "A dumb duck entered a duct," I wrote. "I entered the duct to save the dumb duck. However, I failed to duck and stuck my head on a screw in the duct, but I did save the duck. In the future I will be sure to duck if it ever happens that I am again required to enter a duct to save a stupid duck." The personnel department was not amused.

Whatever gains I made by my heroic rescue were soon lost when several bird-eating tree boas escaped their cage through a poorly fastened cage top and found their way into the aviary. Tree boas are not venomous snakes, but they have extremely long teeth, specially designed for piercing through the dense layers of feathers of the birds they prey on. These long, thin, tree-dwelling, nocturnal snakes have prehensile tails and strong muscular bodies for constricting their prey. They are also armed with special heat-sensing pits, located along the edges of their lips, for detecting the warm body of any nearby bird in the darkness; furthermore, they have an extremely long strike. Thus, a tree boa is incredibly well suited for finding, catching, and killing birds in treetops, or even in flight. No bird is safe when a tree boa is hunting. Certainly, a bird sleeping in a nest or roost at night in the dark, in tree boa habitat, would be wise to keep one eye open.

Each morning, I would anxiously ask Ames if any birds had turned up missing during his daily inventory. His reply was always a sarcastic "No, not yet." I knew that any ordinary bird death was officially forgivable, even if the bird had killed itself. However, any bird killed by a snake was invariably looked upon by my superiors as a martyr, and the snake subject to such quick retribution as a permanent trip to another zoo.

After work each day, I would wait until dark, when the snakes would be actively hunting, then search the Tropical Building with a flashlight, looking for the reflection of eyes in the treetops and the tangles of tropical plants. I managed to recapture two of the three escapees without any loss of birds. Finally, on the fourth night, I spotted a pair of glowing eyes in the top of a palm tree. Alone in the dark, I climbed the adjacent railing and, wrapping my legs around the trunk of the palm, shimmied some twenty feet up the tree to where I could reach the resting snake with my long-handled pair of snake grabbers. I did this while wearing the curatorial uniform of a dress shirt and tie. Stretching as far as I could, I seized the snake at midbody and climbed back down the tree. I soon had the snake safely contained in a large plastic trash barrel.

That night, I mused at how delighted Ames would be at having the marauding "snake devil" safely "behind bars," no longer a threat to his beloved birds. The next morning when I arrived at the zoo, I went straight to the barrel containing the snake I had captured the night before. There was the snake, as I had left it. However, along with the snake were three slime-covered, freshly killed tropical birds the snake had eaten moments before I had captured it, then vomited back up after I had left. The snake had not even had the nutritional benefit of its recent valuable, and as yet unreported, meal.

I would often marvel at the work and dedication of the penguin keepers, which was certainly beyond anything I could ever have mustered. Our penguin collection consisted of about thirty gentoo and chinstrap penguins from the Falkland Islands. Prior to the zoo's reopening in 1988, a joint zoo expedition had been sent to the Falklands to collect penguin eggs. The timing had to be perfect, for press releases and a deadline had been set for the zoo grand opening. Besides, the mayor of New York and the commissioner of parks were scheduled to give the usual bureaucratic opening speeches. The Penguin Building was a major component in the opening-day festivities, and there had to be penguins on exhibit.

Two of our keepers had traveled across the country to spend four months hand-feeding and rearing the young chicks until they were big enough to transport, under special refrigeration, back to New York in time for the grand opening. It came very close to not happening quite as planned. The refrigerated truck carrying the penguins and the keepers to the airport got stuck in a traffic jam on their first attempt, and had to return without catching the plane to New York. This was no little problem, as the entire trip called for the birds to be kept at no greater temperature than fifty degrees Fahrenheit, under constant refrigeration. Coordinated planning with the airline was equally essential, as the keepers had to attend to thirty-two boisterous, fishy-smelling birds throughout the five-hour flight. The date and time for the opening of the Central Park Zoo and the new penguin house were set in stone, so we now had less than twenty-four hours to get our penguins into the exhibit.

Phone calls between zoos frantically relayed the course of events. "Yes, the birds are on the way." "No, they have not reached the airport." "Yes, the birds are fine." "No, the traffic has not abated." "Yes, the plane is on schedule." Keepers had been sent in a rented refrigerated truck to Kennedy International Airport to meet them. Finally, word came over the two-way radio: the truck, keepers, and penguins were crossing the Triborough Bridge, either a few minutes from the zoo or two hours, depending on traffic. Should the refrigeration fail at any time, the August heat would kill the birds. We stood by with blocks of ice, just in case.

As the mayor of New York took his turn to speak, the refrigerated truck appeared on the pathway to the Penguin Building. Keepers and administrative staff quickly formed a chain, like a fire-bucket brigade of old, and began passing bewildered penguins from hand to hand, from the truck to the exhibit. Just as the last bird splashed down in the exhibit, the speeches ended, the Penguin Building's doors opened to the enthusiastic public, and there were thirty-two penguins to be seen, content in their new "Antarctic" home.

Keeping them content would not be easy. Huge refrigeration and filtration systems had been built to maintain the water temperature of their pool at precisely forty-two degrees; another system kept the air temperature at thirty-four degrees. Artificial rocks ringed the perimeter of their land area, simulating the black, barren, rocky landscape of their Falkland home. The pool, more than fifty feet long and six feet deep, allowed the penguins to seemingly "fly" through the water. Visitors would watch, entranced, as the birds accelerated at high speed, porpoising and leaping together in black-and-white waves, then effortlessly propelling themselves upright onto the rocky shore. Not only was the exhibit illuminated, but special astronomical electric timers created an artificial sunrise of increasingly pink-hued light in the "sky," then raised the intensity of the lighting to mimic full daylight. The process was repeated in reverse at the end of the day, ending in a spectacular sunset. The length of day also changed, to match the seasonal changes in daylight the penguins experienced in the latitude of their natural habitat. These were essential elements of the exhibit, as the birds were extremely dependent on natural light cycles for developing healthy feathers, proper molting, and reproduction.

The next important element is the keeper staff. No matter how aesthetically pleasing the exterior of the Penguin Building is, or how homey the exhibit is for the birds, the inside work areas are a dungeon for the keepers. There are no windows in the concrete building. The keepers see daylight only when the clock tells them it's time for break, lunch, or to go home. In the winter months, they may arrive in daylight, but they leave in the dark. Mornings are spent in the nearly freezing exhibit, hosing the penguin living area clean with cold water.

Penguins eat fish. Tons of it. Deep-frozen fish, small mackerel, and capelin, are stored at 20 degrees below zero Fahrenheit in walk-in freezers. The building is unheated, except for overhead infrared heaters strategically placed over certain work areas, so the keepers will have warm spots to stand under as they place several multivitamin tablets inside the gills of each of hundreds of freezing-cold, half-thawed fish. Two or three times a day, two keepers enter the exhibit for bird feeding. While one keeper hand-feeds each bird, the second keeper records the number of fish each bird eats, noting each individual by the identifying colored plastic tag bracelets affixed to the bird's wing. The keepers must wear winter coats and life jackets. Should they accidentally slip on the rocky ledges and fall into the icy water, their survival time would not be appreciably more than if they had fallen into the North Atlantic Ocean. These are the jobs the keepers perform seven days a week, year in and year out, to keep the birds happy and healthy, under conditions most people would find physically intolerable.

I personally prefer the warm climates of the Reptile House or the Tropical Building, and reptiles that may require feeding as little as once a week. It was amusing to see the penguin and polar bear keepers lunching with the Tropical Building keepers, one group in short-sleeved shirts and shorts, summer and winter, the other in winter jackets, sweaters, and neck wraps. One senior penguin keeper, Rob, stalwartly refused to give up the symbolic warmth that wearing shorts suggests, and wore them all summer despite the perpetual winter that pervaded the Penguin Building.

A bird keeper once came to me with a problem involving one of his birds. He explained the situation in detail: a drain cover had come loose and one of the ducks had voluntarily stuck its head in the open pipe, had gotten sucked farther into the pipe along with the rushing water, and had almost drowned. Another "suicide," I imagined, mentally attributing the incident to simple, plain, birdbrain stupidity. Tears came to the keeper's eyes as he described the bird's trauma. Seeing my distant look, he paused and said, "You really don't give a shit, do you?" I defended myself, sure that reptilian specters were visible behind my shoulder, and pleaded, "Really, I really do like birds. I really do."

Years later, I would be vindicated. The moment came unexpectedly, and without warning. On a bright, cool spring day, my family and I were planting bulbs in the yard of our Connecticut home. I had almost forgotten that I had spent most of my adult life living under a cloud of accusations that I hated birds, having long since resigned myself to the stigma associated with being a herpetologist, a "bird hater." How could I know that this was the day that all would change? As I knelt to dig in the moist soil, I could feel the wet creeping through my trouser knees. Then, almost imperceptibly, I heard it behind me: *Gblle-gblle, gblle-gblle, gblle-gblle.* I turned. Coming toward me, from the driveway, was a handsome tom turkey. The red and blue warts of his neck and head shone beneath the sparse feathers that adorned his naked features. A crimson red, fleshy nasal tube hung limply across his beak, while the thick "beard" of hairlike feathers that hung from his inflated chest clearly announced who and what he was. His brown and black feathers glistened with green and yellow iridescence in the afternoon sunlight. His wings hung at his side, while the fan of his tail spread halfheartedly, but ready to spring into full display should the need arise to assert his true masculinity.

At his side, respectfully, strode a hen, not too close and a little to the rear. She was trim but not thin; pretty but not vain; stately but with little bearing; and obviously the product of no special breeding. I immediately thought, He could do better. They had most likely come from the farm down the road, a long, dangerous journey along the blacktop, threatened by speeding cars and past a number of houses with bothersome, untethered dogs.

I rose to welcome them. "Good afternoon, sir and madam," I greeted them. *"Gblle-gblle, gblle,"* came the reply. I could see him tilt his head to one side to get a better view of me. I think I felt a little naked under his gaze. Myrna, our son, Peter, and I gathered around our guests. Reaching down, I began to pet the tom's wart-covered neck and head, stroking him, intoxicated by the petal-soft feel of each lump and dimple as they slid past my hand. "What a nice turkey," I remarked. The hen pensively stood alone, apart from us. Each time I stroked "Tom," he moved closer to me, now rubbing against my leg, now pushing me—seemingly in the direction from which he had come, toward his home. This was most peculiar behavior, I thought, as Tom the turkey raised and lowered his fantail, puffed his chest, and *gblle*'d. He was smitten—with me.

As I returned to my digging, he became more and more insistent on my attentions, pushing and displaying his hardest to gain my favor. He ruffled and puffed out his feathers, hung his wings as low as he could, nearly dragging them along the ground, and inflated his prodigious nasal tube. This turkey was becoming a nuisance to my digging, blocking my every move. I pushed him away time and time again, but his advances only became more determined. Finally, I pulled my tools together and we went inside, leaving Tom and his female companion alone to sort things out. After all, I was a married man with a family, a house, a car, and tuition payments to make; I had two dogs and four cats, and I had a reputation for not liking birds to uphold. Peeking through the window, I could see Tom and his companion walking slowly, somewhat forlornly, down the driveway and out of sight as they turned the corner toward home.

What happened after that I will never know, nor what transpired between him and his companion. However, several hours later, as I was changing clothes after a shower, I heard a now familiar call coming from the beneath my bedroom window: *Gblle-gblle, gblle-gblle, gblle, gblle.* It was Tom calling to me. He had returned alone, without his female companion. "Myrna, Peter," I called. "Tom the turkey is back and without his girlfriend. He's calling for me to come out and play." Myrna did not seem thrilled with this. Tom immediately came to me when we all went outside to greet him, completely ignoring Myrna and Peter. He was soon deeply involved in displaying his finery, rattling his feathers, and dragging his wings, as vigorously as he had done before.

"I wonder, what would he do if I were to lie down on the ground?" I asked Myrna. After all, she had a degree in animal behavior and had studied bird mating and maternal behavior as a prelude to studying crocodilian maternal care. "Try it," she said, with a hint of amusement in her voice. I was no sooner on the ground than Tom climbed onto my back and began to display in a rather sensual mating dance. "Enough," I said, as Peter and Myrna erupted into uproarious laughter. I was not to be solicited by a turkey, no matter how handsome he was.

It was already too late; Myrna was taking photos. I retreated back into the house, followed by more laughter and the now plaintive calls of Tom, the rejected turkey. For the next several hours, Tom called from beneath my window—*gblle-gblle, gblle*—hoping I would reconsider. I would not. By then, Myrna had found out that Tom's owner lived several houses away. She called them up, and minutes later the owner unceremoniously threw Tom into the back of his pickup truck and drove away. I never saw Tom again.

As I thought about Tom over the following months, I realized that what had happened held genuine meaning for both of us. Tom, I hope, had learned that courting a herpetologist, a person who eats turkey and feeds turkeys to pythons, posed truly insurmountable barriers to any long-term relationship. I had learned not only that I could truly like birds, turkeys in particular, but also, and more important, that birds liked me.

EPILOGUE

Few people can look back over a forty-four-year career that combined making a living, pursuing their lifelong interests, encountering adventure, enjoying travel, and achieving professional and personal successes. I have been in the right place at the right time in my profession to watch the wildlife pendulum swing from the worst of times to the best of times; now it's heading back the other way, perhaps a little farther than we would like. The evolution of how we, as humans, think of and share our habitats with the great diversity of species on earth continues. We still do not fully comprehend the value of the irreplaceable wildlife treasures we hold in our stewardship. Increasing human populations, pollution, global poverty, and hunger leave less and less room for wild animals. Would the founding fathers of the New York Zoological Society have believed that the fight would still be continuing, more than one hundred years after they feared for the decimation of deer populations in the mountain wilderness of New York? Or after they halted the millinery trade in feathers that threatened migratory birds and saved the last remnants of American bison herds from extinction?

A box of correspondence that lay wasting on the second floor of the Reptile House had contained only a smattering of the thousands of letters written by Raymond L. Ditmars during his tenure as curator of reptiles. Yet I recall, having spent many a lunch hour reading them while sitting on the dusty concrete floor, how he expressed his concern for the future of wildlife. Ditmars was passionate about educating people about animals and the value of preserving reptiles and amphibians in their native habitats, studying their behavior in the collections of the zoo, and documenting their moods and characteristics on miles of film and in thousands of photographs, now stored in the society's archives.

As much as Ditmars's books and articles inspired me as a child, I was even more taken by the feeling of his past presence at the Reptile House. The old worn desk and leather-covered swivel chair had been there in the same office, as had the green built-in wooden cabinet with the four-paned glass doors, and the brass coat hooks. Then there was the black-topped meeting table. All these things were relics of the past. Kids still came to the keepers' door with copies of one of Ditmars's books clutched under one arm. Sometimes, as the keepers closed and locked the rear door at the end of the night, one would call out, "Good night, Ray. Have a good night," imagining his spirit once again walking the passageways and corridors, stopping at a cage to check the health of a lizard, or pausing to read the feeding records of a picky snake.

I hadn't exactly followed in Ditmars's footsteps, as I never became curator of reptiles. That position has been well filled for the past twenty-plus years by John Behler. I had passed over that position and gone beyond it. Ditmars's career at the Bronx Zoo spanned forty-three years; my working career with the New York Zoological Society spanned forty-four years. He began his career without a college degree and published scores of papers, books, and articles, only receiving an honorary doctorate many years later. I had a similar history, receiving my bachelor's and master's degrees later in life. I followed in his path and ideals, and more than a few of his accomplishments. I hope I took his initiatives and legacy a step further, helping make his lifelong hobby and interest, herpetology, a professional science and an adventure for the many young people to come.

So it was no wonder that when I retired, I should have a desire to find Ray, to pay my respects or at least to say, "Hi. I'm not quite finished. But you sure showed me a way to a great life." It wasn't difficult in these days of technological miracles to find copies of his obituary. But, I wondered, had he been buried or cremated? And if he had been buried, where? All I knew was that he had died in a New York hospital.

To my surprise, I found I could receive a copy of his death certificate for ten dollars; since he had been dead for more than fifty years, the information was public. A month after sending the state of New York my check, I held a copy of his death certificate in my hands and read that he had been born Raymond Lee Ditmars on June 22, 1876, in Newark, New Jersey. He had died at Saint Luke's Hospital in New York, after an illness of seventy-seven days, on May 12, 1942, at 7:57 P.M. He had been buried in a family plot in Ferncliff Cemetery, in Scarsdale, New York. I had the answer to a question that I had wondered about for years.

A few days later, as Joel Dobbin, an old colleague and friend, and I had breakfast at a local diner, I said, "Joel, how would you like to come with me and help me find the resting place of Raymond L. Ditmars?" That week, we drove to New York. Ferncliff is a large, old cemetery, bordering along what had once been a secluded country road. There was more traffic now, but the wooden rail fence still offered a feeling of country quiet.

We first stopped at the main office and were directed to a man who limped from a recent slip on the ice, and who was said to know how to locate every grave. He took us through a long building, a canyon of silent, subdued crypts in a marble mausoleum. Our footsteps squeaked as we walked across the polished stone floor. Once in a small anteroom, he soon had a ledger out on the table, and he carefully ran his finger down the elegantly handwritten column of entries, stopping at the name Ditmars. St. James was shown as the section, plots 98, 99, 100, and 101. "It's a family plot," he said. "I can't tell you which one is his from this book, but you can find it near the front, close to the road. It's one of the older plots," he added scribbling a note on a small piece of paper.

The man was right. It did not take us long to find the tall, over-grown evergreen hedges that formed a rectangle around a small cluster of headstones inscribed with the name Ditmars. His was an incon-spicuous stone, placed among those of his family members and set flat into the ground. We brushed away the covering of fresh snow to better see his name. We stayed for a while, conjuring up thoughts of his and our pasts, and the place where he and I had both spent the better parts of our careers. As we left, we could only say, "Thanks, Ray. Rest well." I think that after the thousands of letters Ray had answered from so many kids over his forty-three-year career, he wouldn't mind a visit or two.

Perhaps this book will be under the arm of some young person who shows up at the door of the Reptile House with a sparkle for ad-venture in their eyes, and the feeling that they're a little different.

RECOMMENDED READING

Austin, Jr., Oliver L. *Birds of the World: A Survey of the Twenty-seven Orders and One Hundred and Fifty-five Families.* New York: Golden Press, 1961.

Brazaitis, Peter, and Myrna E. Watanabe. *Snakes of the World.* New York: Crescent Books, 1992.

Brazaitis, Peter, and Myrna E. Watanabe, consulting eds. *The Fight for Survival: Animals in Nature.* New York: Michael Friedman Publishing Group, 1994.

Bridges, William. *Gathering of Animals: An Unconventional History of the New York Zoological Society.* New York: Harper & Row, 1974.

Goddard, Donald, ed. *Saving Wildlife: A Century of Conservation.* New York: Harry N. Abrams, 1995.

Gold, Don. *Zoo: A Behind-the-Scenes Look at the Animals and the People Who Care for Them.* Chicago: Contemporary Books, 1988.

Greene, Harry W. *Snakes: The Evolution of Mystery in Nature.* Berkeley: University of California Press, 1997.

Hahn, Emily. *Animal Gardens: or Zoos Around the World.* Annandale-on-Hudson: Begos & Rosenberg, 1967.

Nowak, Ronald M. *Walker's Mammals of the World,* 5th ed., vols. I and II. Baltimore: The Johns Hopkins University Press, 1991.

Ross, Charles A., consulting ed. *Crocodiles and Alligators.* Sydney: Weldon Owen Pty Limited, 1989.

Scott, Jack Denton. *City of Birds and Beasts: Behind the Scenes at the Bronx Zoo.* New York: G. P. Putnam's Sons, 1978.

Tobias, Michael. *Nature's Keepers: On the Front Lines of the Fight to Save Wildlife in America.* New York: John Wiley & Sons, 1998.

Wilson, Edward O. *Consilience: The Unity of Knowledge.* New York: Random House, 1998.

Zug, George R., Laurie J. Vitt, and Janalee P. Caldwell. *Herpetology: An Introductory Biology of Amphibians and Reptiles,* 2nd ed. San Diego: Academic Press, 2001.

INDEX

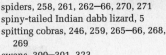